KT-416-173

HA1

A Year in the Life

A Year in the Life

ADVENTURES IN BRITISH SUBCULTURES

Lucy Leonelli

unbound

First published in 2022

Unbound
Level 1, Devonshire House, One Mayfair Place, London W1J 8AJ
www.unbound.com
All rights reserved

This book is a work of non-fiction based on the experiences and
recollections of the author. In some cases names of people, places,
dates or the detail of events have been changed solely to protect the
privacy of others. The author has stated to the publishers that, except
in such minor respects not affecting the substantial accuracy of the
work, the contents of this book are true.

Text design by PDQ Digital Media Solutions Ltd.

A CIP record for this book is available from the British Library

ISBN 978-1-80018-050-5 (paperback)
ISBN 978-1-80018-051-2 (ebook)

Printed in Great Britain by Clays Ltd, Elcograf S.p.A.

1 3 5 7 9 8 6 4 2

With special thanks to Mathieu Leonelli for his endless support.

Thank you to RSJ International for their generous support of this book.

RSJ International is a Global Logistics Company with offices in the South-West of England and South Wales. Clients include 3MUK, Geoquip Marine, Flood Control International and many others, all of whom depend on RSJ to reliably and efficiently export or import their products around the world.

Subculture (n): *Subdivision of a national culture or an enclave within it with a distinct integrated network of behaviour, beliefs and attitudes.*

This book depicts actual events as truthfully as possible. I've spent many an enjoyable hour cross-checking my story with the characters contained, and have been corrected mostly on chronology, the names of hills and whether or not a certain character does, indeed, have a baritone voice. Dialogue consistent with the character or nature of the person speaking has sometimes been abridged, and some names have been changed to respect the privacy of the individual/dog/celestial body in question.

Contents

It Starts

I think, at a child's birth, if a mother could ask a fairy
godmother to endow it with the most useful gift, that gift
should be curiosity.

Eleanor Roosevelt

Flames lick the base of my neck, knives prick the skin of my
lower back, and gravity tugs at the sockets of my aching knees.
The very thought of another hour sitting like this, cross-legged
on the floor with nothing but the sensations randomly occurring
on my upper lip to focus on, is sheer torture. I allow my mind
to wander, opening my right eye just a fraction to look around
me. The girl sitting in front of me has one arm up in the air at an
awkward gibbon-like angle, as if possessed. The lady to my right
is definitely asleep.

I am four days into my Vipassana course – a ten-day silent
meditation retreat in Hereford – and my commitment to
sitting for eleven hours a day with an empty mind is beginning
to waver. I fancied something different this year, you see – a
change from the usual summer beach holiday – a challenge
perhaps, like running a marathon or driving a tuk-tuk across
India or something. So my friend recommended this course on
the promise that it was the most challenging thing she had ever
done. And that was that. I signed up. No questions asked.

In the lead-up to the course, I pictured myself meditating
serenely for its entirety, the answers to life's questions flowing

through my mind like a gently ambling stream. Instead, I'm locked in a state of perpetual frustration, my comfort zone a mere speck on the horizon.

I take the opportunity to think about a question I probably should know the answer to by now: what the bloody hell do I want to do with my life? The problem is, I am not really *exceptional* at anything. There are lots of things that I am pretty good at – closing overstuffed suitcases, fixing things with unconventional tools, retaining obscure 1960s song lyrics – but none of these jump out as potential career options. So if I'm going to be mediocre at something, I may as well enjoy it, right? I switch to looking back over the last twelve months of my life, searching for the time I was at my happiest. My mind settles on a memory, a game my best friend Kate and I had been playing, arranging weekly outings with one another, each inspired by a different letter of the alphabet.

For 'A' I chose art. Specifically, a life-drawing class, using charcoal to recreate the exposed contours of a young, self-conscious model.

'B' was Kate's choice, and in response to her 'Can we come and ring with you?' email, the bell-ringers of St Dunstan's Church in Stepney invited us along to one of their rehearsals to teach us the ropes. Yup. I went there, and I'm not even sorry.

We met outside the church at 5.30 and followed the group as they snaked around the spiral staircase and up into the icy bell tower, where we were welcomed like old friends with steaming cups of tea. The ringers warmed up around us, a perfectly choreographed dance of rising and falling arms, before Kate and I were called up to have a go ourselves. Our first surprise was how heavy the ropes were, requiring the strength of our whole bodies to bring them down, and our second was the depth of concentration it took to time each exhausting pull in rhythm with the group, who seemed to operate as one holistic unit to create the beautifully timed peal, like the hand-cranked wheel of a music box. The chaos of not knowing what we were doing and the deafening sounds of our mistimed 'dongs' was kindly overlooked by our ever-patient hosts, complete strangers to us until a couple of hours before. After our lesson, we were invited to the local pub, the Prospect of Whitby, for a post-ringing pint, and were regaled with stories about the campanology community, populated by thousands of eager participants across the breadth of the country, many of whom had followed in the footsteps of the generations before them, as daughters, sons, grandchildren and great-great grandchildren in a long line of bell-ringers. From the London bankers who meet during their lunch breaks to ring in the old City churches, to the engineers who travel for work, wandering into local churches and volunteering their skills for the week they are due to be in town. It felt as if we had propped open the lid of a hidden subculture, a secret world, a buried treasure chest waiting to be discovered.

I remember walking home that night beaming from ear to ear, my entire body warm and vibrating as if I had electricity in my veins.

The memory sparks something in me, a sense of inexplicable euphoria. I don't believe in eureka moments, just as I don't believe in miracles, or love at first sight. But I can honestly say that, for the first time in my life, I was certain that this was my purpose. Not the bell-ringing – sadly you're not about to read an entire book about bell-ringing – my purpose was to discover and infiltrate the fascinating communities of Great Britain; to demystify its subcultures and lift the lid on its treasure troves, sharing its hidden gems with the rest of the world. I would chase this euphoric feeling and devote an entire year of my life to this project, working my way through an alphabetical romp of lifestyles and subcultures, investigating each community and immersing myself in their rituals and customs.

The idea comes to me in a whirlwind before I realise that I am still surrounded by 130 tie-dyed tops and enormous pairs of trousers. Fidgeting uncontrollably, I run through options for each of the letters in my head, desperate to get out of the room and release all of this dammed-up energy.

Three days later – or at least that's what twenty minutes felt like – I erupt through the doors of the meditation hall like a bargain hunter on Black Friday and head back to my room, scanning the surfaces for a pen or pencil to capture the ideas that are desperate to escape my head. No luck. One of the 'precepts' I had signed up to for the duration of this course was 'I will not read or write', so I had handed in all of this stuff, including my iPhone, during the gadget and pen amnesty at the start of the course. Shit.

I close my eyes. Think, Lucy, think. Perhaps I can find a pen just lying around within the boundaries of the course? The trouble with this option is that another precept for this course is 'I will not steal'.

Fuck it. I begin exploring the cupboards in the course buildings, which is no easy feat, I can tell you. Obviously, I can't let anybody see me doing this, because then they would discover my plan to break my precepts, so I wait for the cover of darkness to sneak around the buildings, pulse racing as I scan the shelves one by one, flicking my gaze back to the door at the slightest noise.

No luck.

Popping into the loo, where I do most of my good thinking, I am overjoyed to discover a small stash of blue paper towels behind the sinks. Something to write on! I take three and hastily shove them up the front of my jumper.

Now for the pen.

After another stealthy rummage in the cupboards, and close to giving up, I discover a sign-up sheet for chores just inside the meditation hall. Next to it, held by a long piece of string and circling the air like an exotic dancer, is a thick black marker pen.

I can't steal that, can I? No. I couldn't. Unless? Oh, sod it! I grab it, feed it up my sleeve and shimmy back out along the wall.

So this was how my adventure was born: an idea scrawled in the dead of night on blotting paper so thirsty it soaked up the black marker pen like a top-of-the-range Dyson. When the job was done, I opened a window to release the inky smells and avoid being discovered by my sleeping roommate. Thankful for the enormous pants my mum persists in buying me every Christmas, I used a pair to waft the final traces of inky rebellion through the open window.

I feel guilty, lulling you in with daring tales of delinquency at meditation camp. The truth is, by most measures, I am pretty damn normal. I enjoyed a happy upbringing in a family that deftly straddles the border between working and middle class. I did well at school, but was never the star pupil. I have only ever been in serious trouble once in my life (for throwing a Stephen Gately rubber at the teacher... for a dare), and within two weeks of graduating university, I began my first job in the company that still pays my wages. Not exactly the best platform for a story, is it?

But don't give up on me yet. I do have an odd habit. I like to collect things. Not stamps, not novelty erasers, not political teapots from the 1920s. No. I like to collect different versions of myself.

Overwhelmed by a sense of my own mortality – aren't we all? – and the limitations this puts on how many roles I will get to play in this life, I find myself unable to commit to being one version of myself for too long. As a result of this affliction, my life so far has been a collection of experiments to try and find an identity I am happy to settle into, resulting in a series of distinct chapters. The Wicca chapter – reciting spells through black-painted lips. The fantasy chapter – studying werewolves and collecting model dragons. The Kappa tracksuit chapter – single-handedly keeping the hairspray industry afloat. The cowboy chapter – mustering cattle and riding bulls in the Australian outback. The country-bumpkin chapter – in full Barbour-jacket stereotype. Right up to my current chapter – the bespoke-suited capitalist.

The philosophy geek in me would like to explain this as Carl Jung's concept of individuation, a process we all go through as we attempt to define our personalities against the concept of 'other', trying on various labels and archetypes and integrating them to form a 'self'. It could be this, yes, but it could also be something as simple as a serious case of FOMO (fear of missing out), characterised by an unwillingness to commit to one version of myself without first experiencing every possible option out there.

Take Glastonbury Festival. I went for the first time recently and it soon became clear that places like this aren't made for people like me, people with my level of FOMO. I wanted to see everything and spent most of the time thinking about the next thing I needed to see rather than enjoying where I was, worried that I was missing out on something in another tent… something over there. Should I be taking psychedelic drugs in Shangri-La? Watching the comedy in the arts tent? Listening to the bands? Learning circus skills? I found myself almost running from one place to another in an attempt to see absolutely everything on offer, abandoning my friends for the day and heading out alone so I could be more efficient with my time.

Glastonbury Festival is a microcosm of my life. I feel as if I need to experience everything and live every version of myself before my holiday in this world is over. And, although I have thoroughly enjoyed my chapter in the corporate world, I can't help but feel like I have lingered here too long, to the detriment of experiencing everything else the world has to offer. There is just so much more out there, a terrifying smorgasbord of bountiful opportunity, and the thought of missing out on all of this in exchange for another year of dinner parties, work drinks and skiing holidays scares the shit out of me. I just cannot bear another year of missing out.

And so, in a bid to slay the terror, I will indulge this overwhelming curiosity and live in twenty-six different worlds over the course of one year, experiencing different lifestyles and collecting as many versions of myself as possible. Casting off any narrow-mindedness and putting aside my prejudices, I will take the opportunity to discover which worlds I am happy to cross off my list until I can finally commit to one.

I will indulge my FOMO, and, in so doing, cure it.

Well, that's the plan anyway...

A is for... Aristocrats

You don't polish your apples?!

I grew up in a modest family where tea wasn't just a drink; it was a mealtime. Then at the age of fourteen, I was offered a place at a local grammar school, and in the time it took for my lovably distinct Bristolian accent to be replaced by a bland BBC English, I had betrayed my roots, and allowed 'tea' to become 'dinner'.

Then I turned twenty-one, got a corporate job in London and started to discover the world of the wealthy. I bought myself a posh suit from Hobbs, a pair of pearl earrings and started ordering my steak medium rare in an attempt to fit in. But through it all I have remained an outsider, a voyeur of the posh, who would much rather tuck into BBQ ribs at a Harvester than quaff three courses of foam at a Michelin-starred restaurant. So the ladder won't take me any higher, and the defining characteristic of a posh person will always be just out of my reach: 'dinner', I have to accept, will never become 'supper'.

I am convinced that this small nuance of my vocabulary is entirely to blame as I set myself on the first challenge for my FOMO and toil for weeks to infiltrate the aristocracy. Was I really missing out on something wonderful by not being a part of this old-money world? Was this a lifestyle I should aspire to, like a modern-day Cinderella? I vowed to find out.

And so it was that – after hundreds of unanswered emails, seventeen unacknowledged letters, God knows how many unreturned voicemails to the estates of various lords and ladies, multiple 'Does anyone know someone remotely connected to the aristocracy?' Facebook pleas, and even a returned letter from the Queen (who politely declined my request to spend a week in Buckingham Palace) – I was finally connected to my boss's wife's friend's aunt, who just so happens to be Auriol, Marchioness of Linlithgow.

Auriol's forefathers were highly respected Welsh landowners and knights, descended from Urien Rheged – a sixth-century king – and Thomas Wayte, a regicide who signed the death warrant for Charles I, an original copy of which hangs in her downstairs loo.

Shortly after a charming introductory phone call, I am kindly invited to spend a week with Auriol at her country estate in Wales. Her great-great-grandfather, Martin Williams, graduate of Eton and Oxford, bought Bryngwyn Hall in 1813. The 450-acre property includes extensive forestry, a farm, a series of outbuildings, a swimming pool, a tennis court, a croquet lawn and a lake.

Navigating the long, winding drive, I swerve manically to avoid kamikaze pheasants as the beauty of Bryngwyn Hall comes closer into view. Once at the top, I park next to a tractor with a huge rug draped over its elevated forks.

'Is Auriol around?' I ask a pretty and athletic-looking lady in soil-covered jeans as she vigorously beats the rug with what looks like a broom handle.

She stops and turns around. 'Ah, Lady L,' she says, smiling. 'Yes, I think she is in her office.'

I am sent into the enormous front hall, edged with floor-to-ceiling bookshelves that burst with ancient gold-leafed books and taxidermy birds. A giant fireplace holds centre stage in the room, above which hangs an eight-foot painting of Auriol's great-uncle, whom she later explains was killed by injuries sustained while lion hunting in Somaliland. Suddenly my mid-range bottle of Rioja and withering Co-op flowers seem rather underwhelming; embarrassing, even.

I am greeted by a kindly lady with a matriarchal air, cropped hair and a blue-and-white-striped apron around her middle. A pair of glasses hang from a chain around her neck.

'Hello, I'm Christine.' She wipes her hand on her apron and shakes my hand vigorously. 'Christine the cook.' Beginning her tenure as the nanny of Auriol's son, Christine explains that she has been a loyal employee of the family for thirty-two years.

A moment later Auriol breezes into the vast kitchen and accepts my bunch of flowers with an earnest smile. She squints over a pair of square glasses, her shoulder-length blonde hair framing a make-up-free face.

'The wine is to apologise for the flowers.' I offer a hopeful smile.

'Oh, they're beautiful,' she beams, before asking Lisa from the housekeeping team to show me to my room. 'Bedroom five and bathroom two.'

I walk up the elegant wraparound staircase that dominates the enormous hallway, passing horse statues and bronze busts on my way. My bedroom is large and full of what I can only assume is antique wooden furniture, with two beds, high ceilings and an open fireplace. I unpack my carefully researched wardrobe for the week (modelled mostly on my poshest friends from Exeter University), change into a cream shirt under a simple grey sweater, and head back down to the kitchen.

'You hev a b-yew-tiful home,' I say, sounding like a child doing an impression of the Queen, as we sit down to lunch. I decide to abandon my posh voice.

'I love it here. To me it's heaven.' Auriol smiles wistfully before giving a swift nod and switching to the unique no-nonsense timbre of rural Britain. 'But the house has to earn its keep,' she says. 'We all work terribly hard hosting weddings, garden tours and shooting parties. You always have to be thinking outside the box for ways the house and gardens can pay for themselves.'

The estate currently employs mainly part-time and seasonal staff, including a cook/housekeeper, cleaners, a head gardener, two groundsmen, a bookkeeper and a series of contractors.

'I have had all sorts of people work for me,' Auriol tells me. 'One couple arrived while I was having a dinner party. Christine walked into the dining room and said, "His hair's longer than yours, *and* they're vegetarian." They lasted two weeks.'

After lunch, Auriol takes me out for a tour of her land in a four-wheel drive. We head over to a large piece of forestry on the opposite side of the valley, grown for conservation purposes – 'because I love trees' – and eventually as a way of making money when the wood is ready for sale.

'How often are you able to get a crop?' I ask.

'Oh, they won't be ready for felling any time soon,' she says. 'My son will be lucky to get even a thin crop from them during his lifetime. It's more for the generations to come.'

I struggle to comprehend this sense of responsibility for future generations; of gratification delayed to the extent of not being around to see it. It's such an alien concept to me. I am too wrapped up in my own mortality, my own ego, to even consider creating a legacy for my children's children. I mean, I can't even bring myself to start a pension. But lineage and ancestry are still deeply important to people like Auriol. I suppose this must be the result of knowing so much about your ancestors, of seeing their pictures hanging in your house as a child and being able to trace back your bloodline all the way to the Tudors. I just can't imagine what that would be like.

We walk Auriol's black Labrador a little further along the side of a hill towards the woodland, the meandering path edged with occasional small black shards and discs that look like furniture castor cups. Auriol tuts when she sees them, explaining that they are the remnants of the last day's shooting on her land.

'Do you see inheriting this place as a burden or a blessing?' I ask, as she bends to pick up the pieces of broken clay.

She stands up straight, frowning slightly as she considers her answer. 'I think, quite honestly, it's a bit of a poisoned chalice', she says, eyebrows fixed. 'I mean, I love it, but it's a huge responsibility. I don't feel like I have ever owned it, not really. I feel like more of a custodian, a steward.'

'Would you ever sell?'

'No, never ever.' She shakes her head as if to clear the unwelcome image from her mind. 'My ancestors walked the boards of Bryngwyn. I am so happy here. It's my place of belonging.'

Within a few hours, we are back at the dinner table, where I am presented with a dinner of poached egg and ratatouille. I have been allergic to egg since I was a kid, but instead of confessing this, I cut it into small pieces, move it around my plate a bit and make 'mmm' sounds for ten minutes so as not to seem rude. What an idiot.

The discussion turns to coming-out ceremonies.

'My father didn't want me to go to university,' Auriol says, pouring a can of Strongbow into a glass and taking a long sip. 'He didn't believe that girls should be educated, because then they might argue back, so I was sent off to finishing school in Verbier for six months. We learned to sew, cook, ski and speak French. I think we were given the oldest, ugliest ski instructor going' – she looks at me, serious for a moment, before opening into a playful smile – 'but of course we all fell desperately in love with him.'

'I remember my sister being presented at court when she was eighteen,' she continues. 'My mother took a house in London for four months. We had to go to Buckingham Palace to sign a register to say that she was "in town". We called it "coming out". I was too young to be presented at court – that had all been done away with before I was eighteen – so I came out at the London Season.'

A custom since the late 1700s, the London Season attracted families from the upper echelons of British society, who would travel to London at the end of the hunting season for the purpose of introducing their teenage children into society with the hope of securing a match. The 'debutantes', aged seventeen or eighteen, would be given a formal introduction to the reigning monarch and a debut at a high-profile ball, followed by a season of extravagant parties and sporting events that would last for several months.

'It was a marriage fair, really,' she continues. I nod and fidget, desperately fighting the urge to rest my elbows on the table. 'Party after party for a whole year. All of the parents would throw events in big, grand houses, or at places like Claridge's, Ascot, and Goodwood. The pinnacle was the Queen Charlotte Ball, where all the young girls who were coming out that season had to curtsy to a big cake.' She takes a puff on her cigarette and looks confused. 'It's all a bit odd when you think about it.'

The following morning, I watch Auriol dart all over the place, running from one task to another – answering emails in her office, taking calls to arrange weddings, shoots and charity events, helping Andrea the gardener, running errands, visiting tenants, checking on the land and meeting with staff – working late into the night and seemingly never stopping to rest.

She is easily distracted, so our conversation flits from one subject to the next, like a bird flitting from branch to branch. When she becomes uncomfortable with my line of questioning, she asks me about my plans for the year to come, or about my philosophy degree. 'I think it's wonderfully ironic that you are calling the aristocracy a subculture' – she flashes me another of her playful smiles as we clear our plates away after breakfast – 'but you must tell me more about Nietzsche.'

As soon as I begin a story, she becomes distracted. 'Come and talk to me in the office,' she says to me mid-sentence, before dashing out of the room.

Once there, she promptly orders a book on Nietzsche from Amazon. 'I really should be showing you around the place, but I'm fascinated by this,' she says – scrolling down Wikipedia to read about various German philosophers, squinting at one through her glasses for a short while before losing interest and skipping to the next. 'I have a curious mind, you see.'

The telephone rings and Auriol receives a request from the local district nurses for a donation to the 'leg club' for the elderly. She offers a personal contribution and to host a charity dinner party. After the call she looks back over her shoulder at me. 'One of the things I feel passionately about is that old people don't get treated very well in our country, certainly not as well as people who have ten illegitimate children.'

I can't remember the last time I heard the word 'illegitimate'; I didn't even know that was still a thing.

'Now.' Auriol spins around on her chair and looks at me straight on.

'You should do goths for letter G, I think. What do you know about them?' She smiles again, a warm 'I am genuinely interested in what you have to say' smile.

'Well, I don't know yet really, but I guess a starting point would be heavy-metal music—'

'Ooo, I love heavy-metal music.'

I can't help but laugh. 'Really?'

'Oh yes, love it. I'm interested in everything, really. My mother had a broad canvas too. She recognised that times changed. My father was very straight down the line, though, terribly strict.'

'And P will be pagans?' she asks as we wander back into the kitchen.

'Yes, I'm going up to Stonehenge and—'

'Oh yes, they built it on ley lines, didn't they? I want to get someone in here to balance the ley lines of this house.'

Christine, who has been beavering around the Aga, looks up at us. 'She's a witch, you know.' She looks at Auriol and they share a smile. 'She has a dowsing pendulum and everything.'

Auriol grins and leans in, conspiratorially. 'I do,' she whispers.

Later that morning I head out to the gardens to help the head groundsman, who has worked for 'Lady L' for ten years. It takes us three hours to load up the pruned branches of one tree into a trailer, piling them on the other side of the land using a quad bike, a pick-up truck and a tractor. There are thousands upon thousands of trees here. I cannot even comprehend how difficult it must be to manage the upkeep of a place like this.

Tired, and smelling like someone who has been hauling branches for three hours, I walk back into the kitchen to the hustle of a Sainsbury's order being delivered. It seems strikingly anachronistic to see a Sainsbury's van parked on the driveway, and I pause for a moment to challenge my expectations here. I mean, what had I expected to happen? That the groceries would arrive by horse and cart in hessian sacks, delivered to the door by a Dickensian young boy with a face covered in flour? I realise that yes, this is exactly what I had been expecting, and deflate with disappointment.

I try to slip through the kitchen unnoticed, hoping for a reviving shower before lunch, but Christine beckons for me to sit at the kitchen table and puts me to work polishing the apples for the fruit bowl.

'How do you polish an apple?' I ask, the left side of my lip creeping up to meet my nose.

She returns my expression. 'You don't polish your apples?!'

'Erm... no.' I feel irrationally ashamed.

'Well. It's easy', she says, picking up a tea towel to demonstrate. 'You just rub them with a clean cloth until they shine.'

She hands me a tea towel and sits down next to me with a bowl of potatoes and a peeler.

'Houses like this one used to be almost entirely self-sufficient', she explains as we work together on our respective tasks. 'They would have a vegetable garden, wild game in the woods, a lake full of fish, and eggs from the chicken coop. Then anything that can't be eaten – like acorns from the trees – would be sold or traded.'

The philosophy is maintained to this day at Bryngwyn: orange peel goes into the Aga to be dried out and used as kindling; plate scraps go out to feed the chickens; bones go to the dogs; jam jars are washed and refilled; and old glass bottles are used to make sloe gin and elderflower cordial.

Foraging was also commonplace on a country estate and remains so for Auriol, who often gathers nettles and mushrooms from the garden to eat. She has recently installed a 'Poison Garden' feature in the grounds, containing plants like the castor-oil plant, wolfs bane and hemlock, unlocking the long-forgotten common knowledge of what is and isn't safe to eat.

Ten minutes of apple polishing later, I feel a sense of accomplishment as I arrange the gleaming spheres neatly in the fruit bowl, placing it in the centre of one of the huge dining-room tables. My reward is a bowl of Christine's famous 'fridge soup', containing all of the leftovers from the previous week's shooting party – spaghetti, fondant potatoes, cauliflower cheese, carrots, onion, cheese and a giant wedge of quiche – all mashed together, warmed in a big pot and served with a paving slab of fresh bread.

After lunch, and a much-needed shower, I waddle out of the kitchen to explore the rest of the house alone, expecting to find Narnia behind each door. The first gem I discover on my self-guided tour is an enormous billiard room with walls draped in war paraphernalia, antelope heads, Tibetan cymbals, an alligator head and the full skin of a Burmese python.

Everything is old here. The entire house is strewn with old books, paintings, china cabinets, tapestries, coats of arms, ceremonial swords, guns, statues, old jewellery, letters and photographs. I don't really understand antiques – it all just seems like old tat to me – but Auriol loves them. 'Oh, that's terribly important,' she'll say, finding an old piece of paper or a trinket in a drawer and searching to find a place for it on a surface or in a display cabinet.

As the sun dips lower in the sky on my second day at Bryngwyn, I become increasingly nervous about what is going to unfold. Everybody has to be terrible at something in life, and my something is tennis. I never seem to have remotely got the hang of it. On the rare occasion my racket actually makes contact with the ball, I get so overexcited I end up hitting it onto the bonnet of a car parked six streets away. So, you can imagine my dismay when I am invited to make up a four for a doubles tennis match with Auriol and her two friends.

My inability to say no holds fast, and after a short disclaimer about how excruciatingly terrible I am, Auriol lends me a racket and we walk down the garden to the tennis court.

The game begins, and the ladies career around the court shouting 'What fun!' each time they manage to hit the ball, and 'Bugger!' each time they don't. Yellow orbs whizz past my face as I try desperately to make contact with them – *thwack*. The ladies cheer each of my successful hits with equal vigour, despite more than half of them going over the fence behind us.

Enjoying my lack of hand–eye co-ordination, Faith the gun dog expertly fetches my numerous stray balls. Ducks fly over our heads and a gentle fog hangs over the green valley beside the court. Auriol spots me looking at the sky as a particularly noisy flock pass overhead. 'Achingly beautiful, isn't it?' she says, covered in smiles.

The next day, twelve men descend on Bryngwyn for a day's clay-pigeon shooting. I pull my curtains to see the driveway filled with half a dozen Land Rovers.

A typical bird day ('proper shooting') at a large corporate shoot will provide anywhere from 100 to 400 birds for a group of eight people, at the cost of around £42 per bird. On top of this, you pay for your cartridges, and £100 per day for somebody to stand next to you and load your gun. Needless to say, most shooters of this ilk tend to be successful businessmen, those of 'private wealth', and rich farmers.

Clay-pigeon shooting is much less of an assault on one's bank balance, at £250 per head, thus attracting a more eclectic crowd of property managers, dentists and accountants. The group today are part of a syndicate, all (male) friends and family members of the 'host' for the day, i.e. the splendid chap who is footing the bill.

Auriol often has big CEOs at her 'clay days', with some shooting up to seventy-five days a year. She tells me about one particular customer, who started off in business by picking up small pieces of coal on the ground and selling them door to door. Now he is a multimillionaire coal-mine owner, and one of her biggest customers.

'It took pure graft for him to get to where he is,' she says. 'I am in awe of people like him. I am humbled by them. I think they are an inspiration.'

'Are people ever rude or obnoxious?'

She thinks for a while before shaking her head. 'No, not really. The only thing I can't stand is when people are rude to my staff, because they can't answer back, and that's simply not fair.'

Having been invited to join the shooters for the day's session, I set about putting on my cobbled-together country clothes and follow the sound of chatter into the vast dining room. The men all look terribly important, and I feel wildly out of place, intimidated even. I turn back for the safety of the kitchen, hoping to eat breakfast with Christine and the staff, but Auriol walks over to stop me. 'Just plonk yourself down next to anyone,' she whispers, turning me around and gesturing towards the table.

'This is Lucy Feltham,' Auriol introduces me with my full (maiden) name as I take a seat at the table next to the youngest-looking man in the room. He smiles to welcome me.

'Hi,' I manage weakly.

'Hello, Lucy, I'm Dean Curran' – he turns to shake my hand – 'nice to meet you.'

'What brought you here today, Dean?' I ask, hoping to sound more confident than I feel.

'Well,' he begins, turning back to look at me, 'the son of today's host is a childhood friend of mine, but I'm a bit out of place here, really.' He smiles and lowers his voice to a near whisper, 'I don't shoot very often, and I'm not terribly good at it!'

I let out a breathy chuckle and feel my whole body begin to soften as I tuck my chair under the table and try not to look bemused by the array of cutlery before me. We continue to make pleasant small talk over a cooked breakfast, me carefully rearranging my egg into small pieces at the edge of my plate again, before we are all called outside for our safety briefing.

After a short 'don't shoot yourselves, or each other' talk in front of the house, we step into a convoy of Land Rovers and make for the day's first site. I can feel the orange juice and second helping of bacon swirling around my tummy with every bump in the road.

Once at the site, it takes no time at all for the men to expertly pull out their long guns and fire at the black clays hurled from a powerful machine at the top of the hill. After about forty-five minutes of shooting, we gather around a table for champagne, with a shot of damson gin in each glass. The drink is known as a damgasm, and it tastes just like its name. After two glasses I am feeling much more confident, and begin to enjoy networking among the men, sharing my story and listening to theirs in return. I am careful to ease my way in when giving examples of the subcultures I plan on exploring over the next year, deciding in this company to stick to fox hunting and pagans.

We move on to another round of shooting at a different location before it is time for 'elevenses at the lake': more damgasms, cauliflower-cheese soup, sausages, ginger cake... and even more damgasms. My tummy feels like a cement mixer.

Over elevenses I talk to Monty, who has been shooting for fifty-seven years. Monty wears a seemingly standard-issue flat cap, a blue shirt with a black gilet, and fawn corduroy trousers. He shoots around twenty days a year, mainly grouse, duck, partridge, pheasants, woodcock, pigeons and rabbits, but not hares, 'Because I like to preserve them.' I ask if I can load Monty's gun for him as we gather for the next round of shooting. The cartridges pop out and hit me in the face when he snaps the gun open after each round, filling my nostrils with the smell of burning metal.

When the round is finished, we are offered a gin and tonic and taken to a collection of three-sided wooden pens nestled into the countryside, known as the grouse butts, and it is here that I fire my first twelve-bore shotgun. The shot kicks back into my shoulder with such force it almost sends me over backwards. I feel the rest of the group's eyes on me and turn towards them sheepishly. They look at me for a second, reading my bemused expression before bursting out laughing.

'Holy shit!' I exclaim, enjoying my own naivety as I rub my shoulder and laugh along.

'Keep at it, girl!' Monty yells from his position on the far side, his eyes glued to the skyline.

After the grouse butts, we head back for lunch, a hot meal of beef and red wine stew, followed by freshly made blackberry cake and a cheese board, all washed down with lashings of wine. I have finally realised that 'shooting' is pretty much eating and drinking all day, with short intervals of standing in a field with a gun.

Feeling bloated and tipsy, I leave the party and heave my way up into Auriol's Land Rover, headed for a nearby road to help her clear some pieces of clay. We sit in the car as the shooters take aim over a ridge ahead of us, listening to Classic FM and talking about the effect of politics on the landowning class.

'It's amazing,' Auriol says. 'Apparently, if the independence of Scotland had gone through, Salmond said nobody should own more than five hundred acres. Imagine that.'

She winds down the window to see if the men have finished the round.

'What would happen?' I ask.

'It would be terrible for the economy. People have grouse moors, they have fishing, forestry and pheasant shoots. Then you have farmers, who have to buy equipment, and it's not worth doing it for five hundred acres; it's not viable.'

Auriol hops out of the car to pick up some loose clays. I follow her, hoping the fresh air will ease my creeping nausea of overindulgence. 'In Scotland you also have the "right to roam", she says, 'which you don't have here. Can you imagine if everybody could walk wherever they wanted? It would be a nightmare. They would litter, leave the gates open, the sheep would get out. Urban people make all the laws, but they don't understand the countryside.'

I draw out my lips and suppress a frown. Surely, this land ownership stuff is all just made up anyway. Who says you own thousands of acres of land just because your ancestors put a flag in it hundreds of years ago? Especially while others have so little. It just doesn't make any sense to me. This is what I should say, but I don't. I like Auriol, and I want her to be my friend, so I smile and nod, wagging my metaphorical tail. I wonder if my journalistic courage will develop over time, and if I will have the guts to push back on statements like this later in my journey. I hope so, but this is all so new and think I'm still in survival mode, so I will just have to forgive myself for the tail-wagging for now. It's hard being a stranger in somebody else's world.

The shoot continues after lunch, with another break for champagne, ending with tea and cake back at the house at around 5 p.m. Oh, and more gin.

'What tea would you like?' Auriol asks me after she has served the punters. 'India or China?'

'What's the difference?'

'India is builder's,' she says to me, picking up one of the pots as if to say, 'This is the one you'll want.'

'What is Chinese tea, then?' I ask.

One of the shooters looks at me from the sofa and raises an eyebrow. 'Earl Grey,' he says, 'which is from China. Black tea comes from India.'

'Quite,' Auriol says.

I shrug. We just have Tetley tea at home.

Later that evening, after the men have left, Auriol and I sit on the fire surround in the entrance hall. The embers glow next to us, warming our feet as Auriol sips at her Strongbow and I cradle a glass of red wine.

'Are places like this dying out?' I ask her.

'Well,' she looks up thoughtfully, 'the genuine aristocracy, the landed gentry I mean – and some of them have huge estates, including property in central London – they generate an enormous amount of income, so they are beyond the point of being a headache. But small estates like this are a struggle.' She strikes a match and lights another cigarette. 'They are bloody hard work.'

From my experience of living with Auriol this week, I can attest to the truth of this, in her case at least. I have never seen anyone work harder than Auriol, who operates as more of a live-in estate manager than the lady of leisure I had expected, always searching for new and creative ideas to bring enough revenue into the house to keep the estate above water.

I stand by my conviction that the aristocracy is a subculture, a non-mainstream community who tend to stick together, a value system rooted in history and tradition, with all the accordant nuances of wardrobe and diction. 'I think it's wonderfully ironic that you are calling the aristocracy a subculture,' Auriol had said to me earlier this week, and perhaps she was right. It *is* ironic that the once ruling class, who sat at the top of the mainstream pyramid, now seem to occupy their own unattainable bubble outside of it, continuing their traditional way of life tangentially to the fast-changing world around them.

The following morning, I switch my leather wellies for trainers, climb into my car and wind my way back up the long gravel drive. I think I expected to feel more alien here, in a world I can never truly be part of due to the circumstances of my birth – the ultimate FOMO – but I find myself sad to be waving goodbye to Auriol. She has been hospitable and kind, welcoming me into her home like an old friend without prejudice or judgement, which is more than I can say for myself.

Beaming from ear to ear, I pause for a moment to watch a couple of horses trot past the entrance to the estate. It *is* breathtakingly beautiful here, but this lifestyle just isn't right for a terrible tennis player who doesn't know one end of a shotgun from another, and for some reason this no longer sparks my FOMO. I am happy to know that this world exists, to have lifted the lid on it, but I'm also happy to finally cross something off my list.

Move aside, Fairy Godmother, Cinders is staying with her singing mice.

I open my phone and search for the nearest Harvester. If I hurry, I might just catch the Earlybird 2-for-1.

B is for... Battle Re-Enactors

We're just weird and nice, really

I bloody love dressing up – most of the best nights of my life have unfolded while dressed as something ridiculous, like Mr Potato Head, or an armadillo – so I was excited about this one, and spent hours poring over the websites of numerous re-enactment groups around the UK in search of friendly-looking faces, and, more importantly, awesome costumes. I settled on an English Civil War re-enactment society called the Sealed Knot, the largest and oldest re-enactment group in the UK, with a membership of several thousand. Signing up as a member of the Royalist army, I would be fighting with Sir Marmaduke Rawdon's Regiment of Foote (affectionately known as Rawdons) for a public re-enactment of the Battle of Cheriton at a multi-period event in Oxfordshire.

The weekend of the battle comes around quickly, and after the long drive I am met at the entrance to the camp by Chris, Rawdons' PR officer and an instantly amiable chap who looks every bit the Scout leader he is, with a handsome, weathered face.

'Hello,' he beams through my car window before I have had the chance to wind it down, 'you must be Lucy.' He steps back, waves me on and directs me through the campsite to park in 'Living History' – an area devoted in its authenticity to the seventeenth century – where I make a 304-point turn to squeeze into a parking spot between two trees.

'Lucy, this is Vic', Chris says as I sheepishly clamber out and shimmy around the trees.

Vic, in his fifties, with a sharp grey goatee and wide, friendly eyes, kisses me three times. 'That's Dutch', he says proudly, before pointing in the direction of a white canvas tent that is to be my home for the weekend.

'It's a replica of a seventeenth-century soldier's tent', Chris explains, proud to be sharing his world with somebody new. 'Vic makes them.'

I heave my camping gear into the tent and emerge to see Vic struggling past with a water barrel. 'Can I help?' I ask him. He grins and motions for me to join him, picking up an old-fashioned musket and passing it through the handle of the water barrel. He gives me one side of the gun and picks up the other.

'Made that', he says as we stagger through the campsite with the heavy load, proudly pointing out various tents, chairs and awnings along the way.

'Made that one too.'

When we return with a full and even heavier water barrel, we join four other members of Rawdons sitting on wooden chairs arranged around a fire grate. Chris hands me a silver tankard full to the brim with Old Speckled Hen while Vic drinks from a small, uneven-looking brown cup.

'What's your cup made of, Vic?'

He shuffles his head back on his shoulders. 'You've never seen a horn cup before?'

I shake my head.

'I can't believe it!' he says, his mouth like a fish gasping for air.

'They might not be as popular in London circles, Vic,' Chris says diplomatically.

Vic continues to shake his head in amazement, baffled at how somebody could breeze through one third of their life without seeing a cup made from a hollowed-out piece of horn.

Feeling increasingly conscious of my jeans and hoodie, I pop into my tent to try on the two spare costumes that Chris has brought for me to wear. First, the men's kit: a pair of brown leather boots, a large pair of grey woollen britches that tie at the knee with a thick ribbon, a cotton shirt with an open neck, a yellow woollen jacket and a black felt hat.

The three fighting units in Rawdons are Musket, Pike and Artillery, and I will be fighting with the musketeers tomorrow, so I am also handed a leather 'belt of twelve apostles' – wooden containers that each hold a measure of gunpowder tied to a leather strap – a leather bag housing spare 'match' (rope soaked in Vic's pee to make it more flammable when lighting the muskets) and a polished horn, which would be used as a funnel for the gunpowder.

Chris looks up as I emerge from the tent. 'You look like you've been doing this for years!' he says with a grin. Vic gives me an enthusiastic double thumbs-up.

My lady's kit is less successful: a long green cotton skirt, a head covering ('coif'), a white linen shift and a blue jacket. Chris had emailed me the week before saying: *I think it's only fair to tell you that the ladies usually go for a big-cleavage look when in women's kit, so you may want to pack accordingly... Not sure if you'll be able to borrow supportive corsetry, so I'll leave that one to you.*

I didn't manage to find any and have resorted to wearing two bras to try and give me a bit more hoist, but it hasn't worked at all. I just look fat.

Vic shakes his head when he sees me. 'Nah,' he says, 'you look better as a man.'

This 'muster' is a multi-period event, attracting over 1,000 re-enactors from the Napoleonic Wars, the English and American Civil Wars and World War II, the last of whom have built a system of trenches behind our campsite. They also have a small pub that they carry with them on the back of a trailer, decorated to look just like a 1940s boozer, complete with period songs blaring from an old-fashioned radio.

As well as the Living History area, there is another camp designated for modern tents and motorhomes, set back from public view in a big field. Known as 'Plastic', this is where the majority of people camp, and is also referred to by everyone in the authentic camp as 'the caravan club'.

'You have to meet the others,' Chris decides with sudden urgency, standing up to announce our departure. When we arrive at Plastic, I walk through forty other members of Rawdons Regiment – scattered around a circle on camp chairs – and take a seat next to Tweety, whose all-yellow outfit provides his nickname. Quietly self-assured, with long hair and a bushy red beard, Tweety was born into Rawdons Regiment, the third of now four generations to be members. His mum and dad met in Rawdons, his nan met her husband, and all of his sisters met their partners. He also has a goddaughter in the regiment, his godparents are in the regiment, and his sister's godparents are – you guessed it – also in the regiment.

'I'm trying to introduce a breeding programme,' he jokes, after a brief introduction. 'Every member of the regiment has to provide at least two kids, to keep the whole thing going.'

I am also introduced to Tosh, the commanding officer of Rawdons Regiment, so named because he joined with a chap called Mac many years ago. Tosh is a charismatic, good-looking chap in his early forties who has a high-ranking sales job in a large consumer-goods company. A natural leader who oozes confidence, he first joined Rawdons as a nineteen-year-old after witnessing re-enactors take over his local pub in Basingstoke.

'We get together for a re-enactment about eight times a year,' he explains.

'What keeps you coming back?'

'Well,' he says, leaning forward on his seat as if to prime himself for a speech, 'the thing I always say about re-enactment is that it's a great leveller. You rarely know what people do for a living outside of these weekends, and you don't want to. It's a chance to escape from that. There is one guy in our seventeenth-century regiment who is very senior in the twenty-first-century army during his day job, but when he comes here, he just gets to be a pleb. It's like a second life, another chance.'

It sounds like this could be the answer to all my problems.

I bury my hands deep into my woollen breeches. 'So, if battle re-enacting got outlawed tomorrow, would you all still...' – I search for the right phrase – 'errr... hang out?'

He looks at me in disbelief. There is a pause. 'God, yeah!' he manages. 'The battle side is a lot of fun, of course, but it's the social side that keeps people coming back. The battle just gives the weekend structure, really. You could take that away, but not the social side; it wouldn't survive.'

'I met my ex-wife here,' he continues, 'but this is such a passion for people that if one half of a couple isn't into it, it can really cause problems.'

The rain starts to descend, prompting Chris, Vic and me to head back to the quiet of the Living History area, where we sit under a canvas awning around a crackling fire, listening to the rain and telling our stories until the tiredness consumes us.

I wake up the following morning to the smell of sausages cooking in a pan over the fire. I take a seat in the sun and stare out at the rolling hills where the original Battle of Cheriton was fought, watching the shadows of the clouds streaming across the green fields. The birds sing cheerfully, their celebration breaking through the stillness of the morning. Vic produces thick slabs of brown bread and smothers them with butter, handing me a horn cup of water. There is something so romantic about living this way, re-enacting the past, as if trying to enchant it back to life. This must be why people do this, why people obsess over the past. The opportunity to recreate something, just the way you want it to have been. The escapism of immersing yourself in a forgotten time. I get it. I totally get it.

After breakfast, I am taken over to Plastic for a musket drill. Donning my full (male) gear, I hide my camera, phone and sunglasses in a canvas sack before heading off. Members of the public will flood the site for the next two days, and it is a strict rule not to be seen with any anachronisms. The drill involves marching, wheeling, filing and learning all of the commands for the musket unit, like how to load it – although I will be using a dummy, unlike the others, because I don't have a firearms licence – how to stand and how to lift it onto my shoulder in a three-part motion. It's all very complicated, and it takes me an embarrassingly long time to pick it up. The guns are real, as is the gunpowder, but they only fire harmless wadding, so it's all pretty safe, I am promised.

While we wait for the real battle, I sit watching Chris sew a red seam around the edge of his jacket. Behind us, the sound of the World War II demonstration cannons boom, shaking the ground and making me jump every single time. Vic and Chris don't flinch.

As Chris sews, Vic tells me his story.

Vic heard about the Sealed Knot at a beer festival nearly thirty years ago and, being a self-proclaimed history buff, he signed up then and there. He took to it like a young boy to war games, and it has since become his full-time job, his hobby and the place he met his ex-wife and current girlfriend.

'Do people ever get seriously injured?' I ask, as he picks up a shirt to begin some sewing of his own.

'What, fifty to a hundred strong pike blocks smashing into each other?' He raises an eyebrow. 'Course they do! In the seventies and eighties a few people did die. You can imagine a load of men in their late thirties: "Put this wool jacket on, wool socks, metal helmet, pick up this blooming great telegraph pole and off you go." They'd drink lots of beer, go out on the field and...' He makes a choking sound, drawing his finger across his throat.

'The last person to die on the battlefield was in our regiment. Darren. He was thirty-eight. Big lad. Road worker. Smoked like a chimney. Strong as an ox. He just keeled over on the battlefield. Second or third push he went down and they all shouted, "Man down!" They did CPR on the field, but he was gone. Artery burst open in his chest.'

Chris looks up from his sewing. 'Remember his funeral, Vic?'

Vic leans so far forward he nearly falls off his stool. 'It's always full drums and colours at funerals. We pull out all the stops,' he says, fidgeting from side to side. 'Hundreds of people went to Darren's funeral. Eight of us from the regiment carried him – pallbearers we were. He was such a big chap his coffin wouldn't fit in the lift, so we had to put him into the furnace ourselves. As soon as it opened, the coffin burst into flames and we just had to push him in – "Bye, Darren" – weeeee, and off he went.'

With that, he pulls a tarnished silver pocket watch on a chain from his pocket, 'Right-o,' he says, 'time for battle.'

We meet the rest of Rawdons Regiment dressed in our full gear, gather behind Tosh in formation and head down to the field below to meet the rest of the Royalist army, just in time for a medal presentation to a Sealed Knot veteran who has been a member for forty years. The crowd all yell, 'Hip-hip… huzzah!' at the end of the speech – thankfully loud enough to drown out my over enthusiastic 'Hooray!' – before gathering into a huge block to march down for battle.

'Shoulder your muskets,' Trefor – known in the regiment as 'Christmas' because he accidentally knocked a girl's front teeth out with his musket during his first battle – commands as we march in time with the tin whistles and pounding drums. I allow myself a little smile that flinches up and down as we march along, balancing conflicting emotions of embarrassed self-awareness and joy.

Rain begins to descend in thick sheets as we march for ten minutes up a steep country lane to the battlefield. By the time we arrive, most of the public are taking cover in the beer tent. The ground is sticky, and our woollen clothes soak up the water like a thirsty sponge. The grey vista gradually turns to a sea of red as the Parliamentarians flood in from the other side, holding pikes and muskets aloft. They line up in parallel to us – a battlefield of about five hundred soldiers, and eight mounted cavalry members stretching the length of a football pitch – faces scowling through the downpour.

The drumming units on both sides bring their patter to a crescendo as we are briefed by the head of the Royalist army, the lord general, who wears a hat with a big white feather that is bent double by the pounding rain. I can't hear a word he is saying, but the atmosphere becomes decidedly electric as he makes what I can only assume is a rousing speech.

A booming cannon, positioned just behind our unit, announces the start of the battle. My stomach starts its progression up into my mouth, and my hands begin to shake.

'Maaaaaake ready!' Trefor hollers, as those with licences load their weapons with gunpowder. 'Prepare to fire!' We lift our muskets onto our shoulders and take aim. 'Aaaaand fire!' The world flashes yellow and white as the deafening guns explode around me.

Matches keep going out, causing the guns to misfire as everything on the field becomes increasingly sodden. With the muskets failing us, Trefor calls for our unit to press forward into hand-to-hand combat. I turn my dummy weapon around in my hand, as I had been taught in drill this morning, and march forward, leading with the butt. The closer I get, the more it becomes apparent that my hand-to-hand combat partner is a tall man with a long grey beard. He looks mean, roaring and glaring at me as he breaks into a jog. Shit.

Caught up in the moment, I decide the only way to come out of this alive is to be meaner than him. I fix my face into a glare and charge at him with a guttural growl, surprised by the sounds coming from inside me. We are face to face within moments, grappling awkwardly with the butts of our guns and pushing with our shoulders. After a few seconds he winks at me, opens his face into a grimace, and shouts, 'Ah, you got me', collapsing onto the floor dramatically. I can't help but laugh as relief disarms me, and I finally remember this is all pretend.

As per the script – which is at a regimental rather than individual level and basically says which side will win and which will lose, in line with historical accuracy – after half an hour of shooting and grappling, we lose the battle and 'run away' back to the campsite.

Once there, we sit around a crackling fire and pass bottles of port around the circle. Soaked to the core and relieved it's all over, I lean back on my canvas chair and lift my sodden feet up to the fire.

'Do you think we're all a bit... strange?' I am asked by a woman with windswept grey hair, dressed in a much better version of my Civil War women's kit, who sits down next to me.

Strange is not a word I would use to describe this community – for some reason the word conjures negative connotations for me, and I love everything about this group of people. I love the geekiness of it all. I love the lack of judgement. I love the mix of old and young. I love all of the different characters and the way they banter together, bouncing off each other but always remaining patient and kind.

'Well, it depends what you mean by strange,' I answer. 'If you mean "not mainstream" then I guess you are.'

'All of my colleagues think I am strange,' she goes on. 'They say, "What are you doing this weekend?" And I say, "Being a lady of the Napoleonic Wars." They never know what to say then, so they just walk away. Conversation over. When I get back, they never ask me about it either. It's like they're afraid of it. Like it's so far outside of their comfort zone, they just want to shut it out and pretend it doesn't exist.'

'That's a shame.' We share a resigned nod.

I do a quick poll and discover I am surrounded by architects, actors, a brigadier general, consultants, salesmen, cleaners, dustmen, doctors, craftsmen, teachers, cowmen, military-aircraft fitters and horse-riding instructors.

'We're just weird and nice, really, aren't we?' Vic says, looking around at the group after everyone has finished introducing themselves. We laugh, and raise our tankards in a toast: 'To being weird and nice.'

Before long, an old accordion emerges, and the stories turn into folk songs about buxom wenches and eunuchs. The group teach me the words and we sing for hours before heading over to the beer tent, where Tweety hands me a pint of Skull Crusher and I dance with an old man who looks like he has stepped straight from the set of *Les Misérables*.

I stumble back to the camp with Chris at two in the morning – narrowly avoiding falling down a World War II trench in the process – and decide to treat the sleeping masses to a full-lunged rendition of 'Roll Out the Barrel' before collapsing into a dreamless sleep.

The following morning I wake up, wrestle down a stale piece of bread and a sip of water that does nothing to ease my parched throat, put my gear on and head over to Plastic for my pike drill. The rest of the pike unit crawl from their tents when I arrive, rubbing their heads as they stagger over to join me, most still dressed in their pyjamas.

While under the influence of Skull Crusher the previous evening, I had been convinced to give pike fighting a go, despite being warned against it by everybody who isn't in the unit. I am handed a six-metre-long weapon that looks like a sharpened telegraph pole. 'Shoulder your pikes,' Tweety shouts. I try and lift my pike off of the ground, shaking with the effort. It is heavy and unwieldy, and I wonder how the others make it look so easy. This is when I realise that I am the only girl in the unit and that most of the men here are at least twice my size.

The pike is used for charging and skewering the opposition to protect the musket unit from a distance. But that's not the hard part. Once you have missed each other, which happens every time, you launch yourself into the opposition, forming a tight unit like a scrum. In a moment of foolish bravado, I declare to the unit that I will be totally fine because I used to play women's rugby, so they promptly assign me to the place where you feel the most crush in the second row.

We rehearse the action. 'Close,' Tweety shouts as we squeeze in tightly together. 'Closer.' We squeeze even tighter, pushing with all our might. 'Advance.' We drive forward, bending our knees, keeping as low as possible while the front row sit back onto the rest of the scrum to keep it upright. I am exhausted already, an increasing dread for this afternoon's battle making my already pounding headache even worse.

Apparently, the push isn't historically accurate, because if the pike units were that close, they would have probably hacked at each other with swords rather than just push for ground. But we didn't have swords, and even if we did, hacking chunks out of each other just wouldn't be in the spirit of the weekend.

'Are you sure you want to do this in the battle?' Tweety asks me at the end of the drill.

'Sure. Why not?' I lie.

I am a stubborn idiot.

I'll tell you why not, I thought to myself back at Living History, because every single person I've told about this plan on the way over here has looked at me as if I'm completely mad.

'Oh, God,' Vic says when I return to camp, 'are you sure?!'

'Don't say I didn't warn you!' Chris says on the march

together down to the battlefield a couple of hours later, 'I think your regimental name should be "Have a go Rawdon".

I'll take it.

I comfort myself that if I do end up dying on the battlefield, at least I will have full drums and colours at my funeral, and this is probably my only opportunity to have an epic funeral like that. I hold on to this thought ten minutes later as I charge into my first contact, when all of the air is squeezed from my lungs, and I don't have space to fill them again. I try to focus my attention on pushing with all my might, simultaneously trying to hold on to my pike and stay on my feet to avoid the whole unit falling on top of me.

My chest is crushed between two sheets of metal armour, and I get hit so hard in the chin that my head snaps back and I think I am going to pass out. The studs on the shoes of the row in front of me drag down my shins as we are pushed backwards. I scream and grunt, trying to sound brave when really, I'm terrified that any moment now I am going to get something sliced off, or my teeth knocked out by flying pieces of metal.

I have to force myself to keep trudging on as I get pushed and pulled closer and closer into the front section of the unit. I just don't care whether we win or not; all I care about is coming out alive. I would make a terrible soldier.

Every time we come out of a push, I get that euphoric feeling you get when you step off a roller coaster and realise you are still alive. But within seconds we are being screamed at to 're-form', and the whole thing starts all over again. It's relentless.

After another forty minutes of continuous 'pushing' in thick woollen clothes and a metal helmet, soaked with sweat in the baking sun and panting like an overworked sheepdog, all I can think is, when will this torture end?

It ends rather abruptly, minutes later, when my thumb gets caught between a piece of armour and my pike. I hear a crunch, and a stabbing pain shoots through my hand and up my arm. Unable to hold my pike any longer, I sit out for the final five minutes and nurse my broken thumb.

C is for... Circus

*Waking up early, driving to work
and sitting at a desk for eight hours...
that scares the shit out of me*

My senses are overwhelmed by the nostalgic, sickly-sweet smell of mulched grass and the sound of eerie tinkling circus music that I can't help but associate with Tim Curry in a retro clown suit.

In the depths of a particularly cold winter I have been invited to spend a week with the circus. Having spent some time researching the history of the circus and its place in the modern world, I toyed with the various options that might be open to me – from the modern spectacle of Cirque du Soleil to the retro-vintage charm of Giffords Circus – and made the decision to approach only the older, more traditional circuses such as Zippos, Circus Fantasia and Billy Smart's. I wanted to re-experience the nostalgic circuses of my childhood – the classic circus music, the clowns, the flying trapeze and the big top tents – and to understand their evolving place in today's world.

Dating back to 1934, this particular circus, once famous for its travelling elephants, now relies solely on human performers to entertain the crowds. Although the reason for this shift was never officially confirmed, the removal of the lion tamers and tigers leaping through flames was undoubtedly a reaction to the changing public sensibilities and an increased concern for animal welfare, especially the aversion to wild animals being kept in cages and used to entertain.

The big top is alive with kids running and screaming, waving flashing lightsabers and tugging on the sleeves of their wearied parents. To my left is a long 'Burger and Tea' bar, manned by two young girls with heavily made-up faces.

As promised in an email exchange with the circus manager, a striking denim-eyed man waits to greet me next to the popcorn vendor. Seemingly aggrieved at having to entertain me, he nods wordlessly and beckons for me to follow him, leading me straight past the audience to introduce me to the performers backstage. We pull the curtain back, and I bump straight into a wall of rock-hard flesh with white teeth, silver sparkly shorts and a black mohawk.

'Hi, I'm Alex,' the grinning young man says, extending a hand illuminated by the blue lighting that floods the backstage area. Wow. I look around me to discover three more equally chiselled torsos waiting backstage, stretching, jumping and shaking out their bodies.

'These are the Flying Aces,' my guide announces, introducing me to the trapeze act as they gather around me to shake my hand.

'Are you pumped about going on?' I ask them, immediately regretting my choice of word.

Alex jumps in: 'Shit, yeah. I love the trapeze.' He smiles with an enthusiasm that consumes him, like a Border collie puppy. 'This morning we had a disastrous fall during rehearsal, but I couldn't wait to get back up there! I love falling, I love catching, I love all of it!' His eyes sparkle as he talks and I can't help but grin, enchanted by his zest for life.

After a few more minutes of soaking up the electric energy backstage, I am led to a seat in the front row as the bell sounds to summon the beginning of the show. It opens with a parade of all of the performers, juggling, jumping over giant skipping ropes and clapping along to live music. The clown buffoons around at the front of the ring, making the kids scream with laughter and the adults smile reluctantly.

A solo trapeze artist takes to the ring for the first act, performed on a giant swing hanging thirty feet in the air. Her face is fixed with an unrelenting smile, her eyes reflect the different coloured lights and her painted-on eyebrows give an impression of permanent surprise. Her act is polished and meticulously delivered, culminating in an extravagant spin down to the ground, supported only by a rope at the nape of her neck. The first half continues with a juggling act, a full set from the clown and an acrobatic act by a man dressed as a fireman, who clambers over spinning ladders.

After a break for a cup of tea and some candyfloss, the second half welcomes the Flying Aces, soaring through the air, tucking into triple somersaults before being caught by their feet and launched back up into the altitude. The tent is filled with an aura of power and strength, and the boys look like they are having the time of their lives. After each swing they shout, 'Aaaayyyy!' at the top of their voices and beam down at the audience.

After the Flying Aces there is another short act from the clown, a young hand-balancer who shoots a bow and arrow into a balloon with her feet, and a final display by an acrobatic troupe: big, burly, dark-haired men who catapult tiny women into soaring somersaults using teeterboards before stacking themselves onto each other's shoulders like human Jenga. I find myself holding my breath until each woman lands safely. After each successful catch they all shout, 'Hey!' and throw their hands up into a V shape to encourage applause. For some reason it makes me laugh every time.

I am so impressed by the energy, discipline and strength it must take to pull this off, and find myself cheering along enthusiastically with the crowd as each of the acts parades back into the ring to take a bow.

The audience leave, smiling and talking excitedly about their favourite acts. I leave with them, weaving my way through the caravan site, jogging to keep up with my guide, who shows me to my home for the coming week. He points at what can only be described as a long, terraced caravan with six entrance doors and says, 'You'll be staying here, in the bunk wagon.'

'Thank you,' I say, searching my memory for the name of this man, who has pointed me wordlessly around the site like the ghost of Christmas yet to come. I turn around to ask him, but he is already halfway on his walk towards the caravans on the other side of the big top. How does this man walk so fast? I begin to wonder if I'm in some kind of creepy dream.

I open the middle door of the bunk wagon and I can't help but hope that this *is* all a dream as I take in the six-by-four-foot room, containing a metal and foam bed crammed next to a small cupboard with a sink built into it. The room is like a giant freezer, with no heater in sight and a small window at the back that appears to be jammed open.

I drop my bag of clothes for the week onto the floor, unpack my sleeping bag and pyjamas onto the bed and prop my toothbrush against a bottle of water that I place into the sink. I sit on the bed, shivering, and take in the fibreglass box that surrounds me.

This place feels more alien than anything I have done so far, and perhaps more so because I don't feel as if I have much of a role here, so all I can do is observe. I haven't had time to learn any circus skills – well, I did have one flying-trapeze lesson in Hyde Park a couple of weeks ago, but I'm not exactly feeling... er... performance-ready – so I can't join in the way I was able to with the apple polishing and the Battle of Cheriton. I suddenly feel very alone. Perhaps I've gone a little bit too far out of my comfort zone this time, I think to myself, hoping I can at least last the week.

Looking at my watch I see that it's only half nine, so I drag myself back outside again to explore, resisting the urge to curl up in my sleeping bag and have a little cry.

Emerging from the door of the bunk wagon, I walk back towards the big top and bump into a young member of the Flying Aces, who had shaken my hand earlier.

'Hi, I'm Lucy,' I say with forced confidence. 'I'm the one hanging out with you guys for a week to learn about the circus. Can we have a chat?'

'Sure.' He smiles shyly and beckons for me to follow him.

He introduces himself as Tim, a twenty-two-year-old originally from Liverpool. Tim seems very young to me and a little fragile. Handsome, with dark hair, brown eyes and sharp features, he invites me into his van, where we sit in the front cab to escape from the biting cold outside.

'I'm feeling a bit overwhelmed by everything,' I confess to him. 'I guess it's just because I don't really know anyone yet, though.' I shrug, and gesture back towards my new home, 'I'm staying in the bunk wagon over there. Do you know if anyone else lives in there?'

'Oh yeah,' he says. 'It's where most of the ring boys live. They do a lot of the repairs and maintenance around the site. The room on the far left is where the cook lives.' He points back at the edge of the bunk wagon. 'He makes Polish food for the ring boys and they sort of keep themselves to themselves, really.'

'Where do the performers live, then?' I ask.

'Oh, they're all in their own trailers' – he waves his hands in the air – 'scattered all around the site. They're all pretty well equipped, linked up to water and electricity and stuff. Some of them have dogs too.'

'Do you remember how *you* felt when you first arrived here?' I ask him, desperately seeking a kindred spirit, or trying to excuse my own sense of feeling so out of place here. Probably both.

'Well, most circuses are very family-orientated,' he explains, looking at the floor and kicking at invisible stones with the black shoes he wears for the opening of the show, one of which has a band of masking tape covering up a hole. 'Everyone knows each other. They all rock up in their massive trailers as a statement of who is making the most money. Everyone is competing and worried about whether or not they are going to get another season. So I turned up as an outsider and wasn't allowed to stay in a trailer with everyone else. I ended up sleeping in the back of my van on a mattress. If you aren't from a circus background, the circus families don't accept you. They call you a "private" – that means anyone who isn't "from circus". As far as they are concerned, you are coming from the outside and taking their money.'

Tim goes on to explain that school was tough for him; he had a problem with anger and was regularly expelled for fighting. He didn't finish school and decided to move to America when he was sixteen years old, finding work in a bar at a resort, appropriately called Club Getaway. After a stint learning and teaching wakeboarding, it was the trapeze that was to be his saviour, the only thing that could keep his focus and make him want to achieve something. Now he has built a career for himself, and his family has become closer as a result. They are proud of him.

He talks about why it is difficult for him to date other circus performers, explaining that it's important for the children of circus families to be in a position to look after their older members when their bodies can no longer keep up and they are forced into retirement with no work-related pension or social security 'So the last thing they want is for their daughters to end up with a ring boy without a home of his own, or a private like me who might persuade them to leave the circus.'

Feeling a lot better after my conversation with Tim, I invite myself to the local pub with some performers from the Netherlands National Circus, who gather noisily outside the big top. I introduce myself to a lofty Dutch clown, a Mexican dancer who gets swung around in circles by her hair, and a Moroccan acrobat who swings under the belly of galloping horses. They explain that they have come for the weekend to watch the show and visit the various performers, or artists as they call them, that they have crossed paths and made friends with over the years.

When we make it to the bar, I order a pint and plonk myself in the middle of the rowdy group at a long table. I feel as if I am on a night out with a bunch of celebrities and tell every bartender and passer-by who will listen that these are *real* circus performers, looking on proudly as the boys juggle with limes they have stolen from a display on the bar.

Towards the end of the night I win a 'down-in-one' pint-drinking competition with Eddie the Polish electrician. He beams at me, as if this is the most impressive thing he has ever seen, yelling incomprehensible words at me and clapping his hands. I swell with pride, decide that this may just be the most impressive thing I have ever done, and promptly do it again. Eddie buys me a quadruple vodka shot in appreciation, reassuring me that 'it's normal' and pointing at his own glass to prove it.

'What's your problem then?' the lofty Dutch clown asks me, interrupting a sudden wave of nausea.

'What do you mean, problem?' I stammer, affronted.

'Well, why else would you have come to live with the circus?'

When I wake up the next morning – with my shoes still safely on my feet where I left them – I decide to spend the day exploring the giant clown's question: why do people join the circus?

I spy Alex and Craig from the Flying Aces returning from their practice in the big top and invite them to join me for lunch to continue my investigation. I have to stop myself telling the waitress that these guys are *real* circus performers as she serves us our burgers. I still find them so exciting. Be cool, Lucy, be cool.

'How do people react when you tell them you are in the circus?' I begin, looking up from my burger at Alex.

He thinks for a while, circling his finger around the rim of his Diet Coke. 'It varies,' he decides. 'If I tell people I am in the circus, they think that's awesome. But the general perception is that the circus is full of freaks. If they know me first, they are OK with it, but they would still judge all of the performers they haven't met.'

Craig nods in agreement. The manager of the Flying Aces, Craig is thirty-one years old and originally from Brisbane. His blond hair hangs in tight curls around his face, framing intense light blue eyes and an angular nose. He describes his upbringing as 'relatively normal'; his mother was a teacher and his father worked in property. At school he enjoyed maths and went on to read business studies at university with the aim of getting into a 'Big Four' accountancy firm after graduation. Although he didn't succeed in this straight away, after two years in a second-tier firm he was offered a job by Ernst & Young, the third largest professional services firm in the world.

While working for EY, Craig found a contemporary circus across the road and started going along to the odd training session. From there he began having trapeze lessons and instantly fell in love. He trained every free hour he could, and within the year he had handed in his notice to EY to take a shot at going professional.

'I had just missed out on being resourced onto an interesting fraud project and got put on a dull audit instead,' he tells me. 'That was the straw that broke me, really. I wanted to live to work, not work to live. If I would have been put on the fraud project, I might still be an accountant.'

Craig's experience feels understandable to me, a relatable white-collar access point into this alien world. I admire his bravery at leaving behind the life that was expected of him and diving headfirst into the prejudice-ridden life of a circus performer; from sitting in an office every day, in a safe and secure job with 'prospects', to becoming a trapeze artist, experiencing the world through the window of a tiny caravan.

My research continues over the course of the day, via continued interviews with other artists and ring boys as they drift in and out of the big top for practices and rigging adjustments, and I begin to pull together an idea of what it is like to have a career in the circus. Each artist is employed on a freelance, seasonal basis, as opposed to what I had previously assumed was more of a family affair of continuous employment. The average wage for an artist who is just starting out is around £300 per week, plus a contribution towards petrol, and free electricity and water. The ring boys earn £225 per week to work from 9 a.m. until 10 p.m. six days a week, as well as food courtesy of the in-house cook, utilities and accommodation in the bunk wagon.

There are two shows every day, and three on a Saturday. Most of the artists also train for up to three hours every day to maintain fitness and strength. This means that days off are rare, if ever, and the schedule is gruelling. It can also be difficult for artists to find jobs, and worry about where the next job might come from is never far from their minds. A season with this circus can last for nine months, but others are far shorter, and the timing is often difficult to manage, leaving long periods with no salary coming in. Employment from season to season is never guaranteed, and many artists will hop from circus to circus as an opportunity presents itself in relation to their personal brand and networking ability.

After the final show of the day, the artists practise religiously for an hour, along with all of the children who were born into the circus. Most of the people here are very young, and I learn that 'real life' starts much earlier in the circus, as people are often professionals before they are eighteen. This is entirely alien to me, being from a generation that rarely graduates before the age of twenty-two, taking gap years and staying on to complete master's degrees to delay the onslaught of the real world for as long as possible. It feels old-fashioned, nostalgic perhaps, but I am curiously envious of it; of knowing who you are and what you will do from such a young age; of feeling like you belong somewhere.

So why do it? For the flying-trapeze troupe, I get it. The thrill of performing death-defying acts every day, the adrenaline.

It's enough to make you put up with the mud, the politics and perhaps even the uncertainty. Others choose this career for the freedom offered by life in the circus: the freedom from bureaucracy and taxation; the freedom from the monotony of 'regular' life; perhaps even the freedom from the paralysis of choice. And some are born into this life, growing up in its cocoon as the only way of being they have ever known, so the question for these people is, why stay?

For the next couple of evenings, I decide to spend the second half of the performance backstage, and notice a stark difference between the young trapeze artists, who diligently warm up before each show, and the Romanian acrobat troupe, who sit around smoking backstage right up to their cue. They are old hands. After their stint here, they will go to Portugal for a Christmas show, where they will be part of a 6,000-person circus performing up to six shows a day.

There are currently three children travelling with this circus: the two-year-old daughter of two acrobats, who practises the hula-hoop and already speaks three languages; and two more who practise clowning, hand-balancing and foot-juggling every night. During the day they go to school via an online portal.

'What if they decide they don't want to be in the circus?' I ask the clown as we sit and watch his children practise after the show, rubbing our hands to keep warm in the chill of the evening. He fixes his gaze straight ahead. 'That's OK,' he says. 'It won't upset me. I just want to give them the options my parents gave me. It's good for their bodies to practise, and it teaches them self-discipline.'

As I emerge from the big top at around ten thirty, I notice Ivan the acrobat sitting under the awning outside his caravan, watching the rain. He invites me into his cosy caravan for a whisky while we listen to the birds tap-dancing on the roof. I am pleased to be somewhere warm; having been flitting between the big top and my freezing-cold room for the past five days, I didn't think my bones would ever thaw and was beginning to develop a nasty cold.

Having grown up in Eastern Europe, Ivan has a compact, muscular physique with an energetic glow. As we discuss his life story he seamlessly moves through a spectrum of emotions, from nostalgia, through ecstasy and anger.

'I loved my childhood,' he says. 'Times were hard, and food was rationed, but it taught me so much about family, community and value.' He smiles and shakes his head, his eyes lighting up as if about to burst with joy.

'Ha! Value. Value. Value. My father wanted me to play football and make money. But I loved horses. So my mum brought me to a riding school where I learned to ride, and we would make gymnastics on the horses... The first time I walked into a circus it was the most incredible thing.' His eyes widen, and his face opens into an enormous grin. 'The smell of the elephants and horses – it was there, in the walls. I was fourteen, and I fell in love with the circus.

'I got invited to join a troupe as a Cossack rider. I got given a huge black horse. I would practise with my horse all day, every day.' He sits up in his chair, positioned to rein back a galloping horse. 'He would go faster and faster, and my hands would bleed. He was so strong.

'I worked with horses for nine years, then we took the show on tour. From Romania to Rio de Janeiro – whoa! I went with my girlfriend from back home, but we broke up. Of course, we broke up. You go from Bulgaria to Brazil, and you see all those bouncing asses!'

He laughs.

'But I have lost a bit the passion for circus,' he says, his voice soft and his body deflating to a smaller size. 'I am at the end, but it's hard to let go. It feels safe, and I am afraid to go out of it, but it doesn't fit me any more. I am terrified by the idea of normal life. Waking up early, driving to work and sitting at a desk for eight hours. Doing something I don't want to do for eight hours a day! That scares the shit out of me. The thought of it chokes me. So, I don't know what will come next.'

Ivan pours us both another whisky and sits back on the floor, announcing that now it is time to meditate together. This doesn't come as a huge surprise to me: his caravan smells of incense, and every surface is covered in spiritual paraphernalia.

After twenty minutes of awkward silence, me trying not to sniff too loudly as we both sit cross-legged on the floor, Ivan stands up to announce the end of our ritual and returns to sipping from his clay mug as the rain continues to hammer on the roof.

'Man. Living in a caravan connects you to the earth,' Ivan muses. 'I know where my water comes from, where my electricity comes from, where my waste goes. It's a more natural way of living.'

This resonates with me. I often think about how alienated most of society is from the source of what we consume. I have no idea how water gets to my tap; I just expect it to be there. My waste goes either in the bin or down the toilet, and electricity comes from the plug socket. Beyond that, I really have no idea what the chain looks like.

'I remember when I saw a caravan for the first time,' he goes on, 'it was bigger than this, but I remember thinking, "How the hell can people live here? It's so small. You've gotta be kidding me."

So I can understand what private people think when they look at us now, but I love it here. It's nothing, but it's everything. You can have a massive bedroom but, fuck it, you just go there to sleep.'

On my final morning with the circus, I take my usual seat in the big top to watch the performers practise. The circus is calm and quiet during the day. The artists keep themselves to themselves as the ring boys mill around fixing things, and the big top keeps to a strict schedule of practice times. This morning it is the turn of the Flying Aces, and I sit watching them rehearse, singing and trading banter across the top of the tent, just as I would have done across the desks with my colleagues in the City.

I am still enjoying their slick and professional performance, despite having already seen the show more than ten times. Sometimes things go a bit wrong – a trapeze flyer falls into the net or the hand-balancer misses the target with her bow and arrow – which is enough to keep it real and remind the audience of how challenging these feats really are.

The circus is much quieter for this afternoon's performance. There are fewer than a hundred people in the audience, and the clown is trying desperately hard to get them to interact. I look across at him trying to sell some spinning lights during the interval with no one around to buy them, circus music relentlessly tinkling in the background. It feels a bit like a last-ditch attempt to keep beating the heart of a tradition that could have died years ago.

'Twenty years ago the circus coming to town would have been one of the most exciting events of the year; everybody would come,' the clown tells me as we watch his kids practise after the final show that evening. 'In Portugal all of the small circuses like this one are finished now. Only the big names are left.'

The consensus here seems to be that this country has lost its appetite for this old-style traditional circus, a trend mirrored in most developed countries, where there is now a myriad of other entertainment to choose from.

Craig believes that the Flying Aces have an increasingly difficult time impressing the kids who come to see the show because they are so desensitised by a culture of CGI and special effects.

'I once heard a kid shout, "Spider-Man does that all the time," after Alex had executed a perfect triple spin,' he tells me. 'So now we're competing with Spider-Man!'

Television, gaming and streaming on the internet all offer the public the means to entertain themselves in their own homes. So perhaps we are all a bit less willing to put in the effort to venture out and see a circus. It feels a bit sad, the decline of this type of circus in the face of modern technology; that years of tradition can be replaced by a five-second YouTube clip. But there will always be people out there who are nostalgic, and hungry for the more traditional things in life, and it is here I believe that the circus will always have a place. Perhaps this is behind the surge in popularity of purposefully vintage circuses like Giffords, whose shows have repeatedly been selling out since its inception in the year 2000. I have no doubt that circus will survive, in one form or the other, but most of the artists here agree that to do so, it needs to modernise and adapt to the changes in wider society rather than rail against them.

'Circus families cause a lot of problems,' Ivan had said to me the previous night. 'They are too rigid and want to keep things the way they have always been. So maybe, in this way, circus deserves his fall.'

The place still feels alien to me, even after six days, but the people here have been nothing but kind and welcoming. It is clear that circus is another world, with rich histories and customs, seemingly frozen in time, and my mind has been blown by the all-consuming dedication the performers put into their art.

The circus packs up to move to its next location as I find myself unexpectedly and slightly humiliatingly sobbing into my soggy sleeve on my drive back to London the following morning. I am sad to be leaving new friends behind, but mainly I'm feeling sorry for myself because I have a bad cold and am exhausted to my core at having to make so much effort every day to connect with people who have such very different lives from me and who, quite understandably, have no real reason to welcome me into their world. I am realising that simply inserting myself into a community doesn't automatically mean that they will accept or welcome my interest, and I wonder at my naivety that this has come as a surprise. This is harder than I thought it would be, and I don't really know what I'm doing most of the time. I have learned so much about this distinct and complex world, but I am a 'private' and can never be otherwise, so it's not the world for me. I don't have the talent, for a start!

D is for... Dog Showing

*That must be the most peed-
on lamp post in the country*

The best dog in the world was a small brown mongrel called Dotty. She was my bodyguard on the first day I was allowed to walk to the shops alone, my comfort when I broke up with my first boyfriend, and my first-ever passenger on the day I passed my driving test. That dog put up with a lot. A friend and I used to take her to the local village show and enter her into the only class that was accepting of her dubious pedigree: the dog with the waggiest tail. After that we would drag her unwillingly around the agility course, having trained her for months beforehand over jumps made from bamboo sticks and upturned plant pots in our back garden. Poor Dotty.

Given this formative exposure to the world of dog showing, I presumed I knew a thing or two about it.

I didn't.

On a bright, crisp morning, I made for the City to meet Jane Cooper. A gentle lady wearing a green coat and bright-coloured scarf, Jane has qualified her golden retriever, William, for Crufts this year. There are a number of ways to qualify a dog for Crufts, such as being named Best in Show, Reserve or Best Puppy of a local Kennel Club-affiliated show, or being placed in the top three of a Championship Show, but what each of these routes share in common is how difficult they are to accomplish. Needless to say, Jane is suitably thrilled and it's all very exciting.

William is, first and foremost, a pet. He lives in the house and is treated like a normal dog. But Jane explains that there are a lot of people out there who take dog showing far more seriously than her, housing their prized champions in detached kennel blocks where they are waited on hand and paw by professional kennel maids.

The British dog-showing scene is mostly female. 'I would say women between sixty and seventy make up the vast majority,' Jane says, and the community was mostly daunting and unfriendly to her when she first started to get involved a few years ago. 'Some people can be quite bossy and territorial, and they don't have a lot of time for newbies.'

Three weeks later, Jane calls me up to ask if I want to be her assistant for an open show she is stewarding for in Didcot. When we arrive at the venue, the rain is relentlessly hammering down, and the car park is frantic with people ferrying dogs back and forward, many tucked under arms to avoid wetting perfectly manicured paws. One woman holds an umbrella over her Rhodesian ridgeback while she walks along next to it, water dripping from her nose.

As I walk through the door, I am overwhelmed by the sound of yapping and the smell of wet dog. Jane leads me past stalls selling brushes, diamond-encrusted leads and gourmet venison dog sausages. By the time we arrive at our ring, there is already a line of dogs waiting for the first class: American cockers. I mean, I love dogs and all, but these really are ugly little grumpy things that perpetually look like they are having the worst day of their lives. I introduce myself to the judge, who has driven down from Liverpool this morning, getting up at 4 a.m. to be here on time. Nobody is getting paid.

As stewards, we are in charge of keeping things running smoothly in the ring, making announcements, keeping all of the paperwork up to date and presenting prizes. I am given the honour of presenting the rosettes and announcing the winning dogs to those surrounding the ring, none of whom are listening. Every time I come back, Jane gives me some feedback on how to improve my performance next time. 'That one was really good,' she beams, 'just try it a bit louder next time.'

When they are not being fluffed up, the smaller dogs are either kept in crates or tied to an overhead contraption that forces them to stand up with their necks at an awkward swan-like angle. On the table in front of me is a copy of *Dog World* magazine. A hypnotherapist offers her services to nervous showers on the front cover: 'Don't let your dog down, banish your nerves and show him to his full potential.'

One of the ladies in the Weimaraner class we are stewarding threatens to pull her dog out if we do not lengthen the ring. 'How can you possibly be expected to judge his gait in a ring this small?' she scoffs. We don't adjust the ring – there is no room to – so she continues to stomp and huff her way around the ring before being awarded second prize. When I present her with the rosette, she wrinkles her nose as if I've just handed her a used tissue.

The following weekend I walk into the Birmingham National Exhibition Centre as part of a canine cavalcade for Crufts, the self-proclaimed 'greatest dog show in the world'.

'That must be the most peed-on lamp post in the country,' says the lady in front of me, as her friend's spaniel cocks his leg to add to the growing wet patch. Her Weimaraner is wearing a cow-print onesie, which does not seem to allow for the fact that dogs need to pee. It cocks its leg and looks surprised when nothing comes out. After a few seconds, something trickles out the bottom of its left trouser leg and I have to cross the road to laugh as the woman angrily wrestles the dog out of its costume.

At the tail end of a bout of gastric flu and blemished with chapped lips, a red nose and a cold sore, I'm not looking forward to approaching strangers to engage them in conversation. That is until I am handed a badge that inexplicably identifies me as a 'Reporter' at the entrance, having been granted a free pass and press accreditation by the organisers in exchange for an email declaring my intention to 'write about it'. Things are looking up.

The show covers over 2 million square feet of shining floors and bright lights, split into five halls, each packed with arenas, stalls, show rings, dog benches and displays. As I walk around, it's impossible not to notice the huge signs bearing the phrase 'Celebrating healthy, happy dogs', undoubtedly the result of a documentary called *Pedigree Dogs Exposed* that aired in 2008, a watershed moment in the dog-showing world. I came across the controversial documentary on one of my many YouTube rabbit-hole days.

The documentary exposed the numerous health problems experienced by certain dog breeds due to being selectively bred (and interbred) to produce qualities that are deemed 'desirable' by the Kennel Club. Examples include pugs, whose faces are now so flat they struggle to breathe and cool themselves, Cavalier King Charles spaniels, whose brains sometimes outgrow their skulls, leading to terrible neurological problems, and bulldogs, whose heads have become so huge that most can no longer give birth naturally and require caesarean sections. The airing resulted in Crufts losing multiple sponsorship contracts as well as its BBC coverage. It also triggered the Kennel Club to introduce a ban on father-daughter mating, to open a DNA research and health-testing centre, and to make some revisions to its breed standards, such as changing the official size of the bulldog's head from 'massive' to 'large'.

Despite the impact of the documentary, Crufts remains a popular event, with 22,000 dogs taking part this year across a range of showing, agility, flyball (a team racing, tennis-ball-catching extravaganza) and obedience competitions, as well as multiple demonstrations.

Everywhere I look people are grooming, nail clipping, curling, walk practising (yup, a thing), fluffing or backcombing the hair of their resigned companions. The basset hounds wear shower caps to protect their ears, and the Afghans have clips holding the hair around their undercarriage away from their crotch, presumably so they don't pee on their perfectly coiffed coats.

'How long does it take to get her looking like that?' I ask Michael, the owner of a striking Afghan hound called Runa.

'Well,' he says, 'we arrived at eight this morning, having already bathed and dried her, and I finished getting her ready about ten minutes ago.' I look at my watch. It is 2 p.m.

I have no idea how the judges choose between these beautiful and glamorous dogs. They all look the same to me. I decide to stick around and watch Runa in her class as I scribble notes about the contents of her grooming kit. She gets 'thrown out' (doesn't make the final shortlist). Michael walks back over and starts to pack up his six different brushes, bag full of hair clips, tangle teaser, oil coat spray, conditioning coat spray, de-tangling coat spray, baby powder, large comb and a pair of GHD hair straighteners.

I ask him how he feels. He shrugs his shoulders. 'Well, we all think we are taking the best dog home, whatever happens.' He rubs his ever-patient dog on the head. 'Isn't that right, Runa?'

The dogs seem to do an awful lot of waiting around, and then when they finally do get to the competition ring, they are repeatedly fiddled with by the owners and judges: leg placing, head lifting, tail straightening. The handlers all make this weird motion with their hand to make the dog look up, sweeping their hand round elaborately and gathering it up into an upside-down claw. Then the whole process is topped off with a good cupping as the judges check they have two testicles. The dogs just stand there, putting up with it. Stupid humans, they must be thinking. I wonder if dogs can roll their eyes.

'How important is it that a dog has two testicles?' I ask a short, stout lady who breeds West Highland whites.

'Very,' she says, straight-faced. 'If they do not have two fully descended testicles, they will be either listed as having a "severe fault" or outright disqualified.'

If this happens, the missing testicles are usually in there somewhere but haven't yet dropped down. In the rare case that they cannot be found at all, owners will sometimes pay for them to have prosthetics implanted, which are difficult to detect, although this is officially cheating.

I read an article earlier that morning, in a well-thumbed copy of *Dog World* I found on a table in the press area, that explained how owners of neutered dogs in America are increasingly using this service because they believe it makes their dogs 'feel better about themselves.' The most popular brand on the market at the moment is Neuticles, selling for around $500 a pair, with nearly a million already implanted into pets around the world.

'There was this breeder in America,' the stout lady continues, already giggling, 'who had a dog that was a unilateral cryptorchid' – she notices my glazed expression – 'oh, he only had one ball. Anyway, the breeder took him to a plastic surgeon and got a prosthetic so he could compete. Then as the dog was flying across the country to his first show, the high pressure in the cabin caused his other ball to drop.' She stops and bites her lip to compose herself. 'The owner hadn't realised and took him to the show...' She stops again, shoulders shaking as she snorts in a deep breath. 'And the judge had to disqualify him for having three balls!'

I can't help but laugh with her, scanning the crowd gathering around us who lean in eagerly to try and catch the punchline.

She goes on to tell me, after catching her breath, that pet plastic surgery is a growing business, with owners inflicting tummy tucks and facelifts on their dogs, as well as Botox injections to correct wrinkles and make their ears 'fall better'.

I can't quite bring myself to believe this and decide to google 'pet plastic surgery' on my phone over lunch. 'Why not be beautiful?' one of the world's leading dog plastic surgeons says in an interview with Bloomberg. 'It's very important. If the pet is beautiful, the owner is happy and wants to show their pet to their friends.' I finish my jacket potato feeling utterly depressed.

The big competitions and displays take place in the main arena, where I spend my first evening watching the agility. The dogs race around an obstacle course of jumps, seesaws, tunnels and weaving posts. Before each competition starts, the handlers 'walk the course' without their dogs, simulating how they will guide them around and gesticulating as they run past each obstacle. They do this repeatedly for ten minutes, wearing professional running tracksuits with the names of their dogs emblazoned on the back.

In contrast to the showing ring, the dogs seem to really be enjoying themselves in this environment, barking and wagging their tails furiously as they hare around the course. The spotlights and dramatic music give the event a real sense of glamour and the audience 'awwww' as each dog walks into the ring.

In between runs, I speak with a young couple sitting just in front of me in the stalls. They introduce themselves as Sarah, Duncan and Kevin the Lakeland terrier. They explain to me the three different breeds of dog showers: fun amateurs, genuine professionals and old dog ladies. 'The one similarity is that they all want to win!' Duncan says. 'Some do it for the money they can make from breeding, but for most people, it's a passion. The Lakeland terrier who won best of breed last year was flown in by private jet from the USA, along with his full-time groom and professional handler. Now that's money.'

'Do people ever get spiteful about it?' I ask.

'Well,' Sarah joins in, 'when Kevin won his first class, one woman stormed out because a "pet" won.' She shrugs. 'Fair enough, I suppose. If you do it for a living, it must feel unfair when someone swans in from the outside and takes a prize away from a dog you've worked so hard to breed.' I think Sarah is being very nice. That woman sounds like a complete knob to me.

The following day I spend a couple of hours with the Yorkshire terriers, who have to be shown with red bows on top of their heads and presented on little stools with red cushions, which looks as creepy as it sounds. They require an enormous amount of grooming and hair straightening, standing patiently between classes with their faces covered in tissue wrapped up with tape to stop them getting eye and nose secretions on their pristine faces.

One woman's dog doesn't make the cut and is thrown out

of its class. As they walk out of the ring, the woman points at another lady and shouts to her friend, 'Look at the state of that second one. How on earth did that make the shortlist? The whole thing is rigged!' She slumps into her seat and crosses her arms, yanking her dog towards her on its lead.

Later that afternoon my request to the press office to 'have a go' at the agility is granted and I am told that someone is willing to lend me their dog. I head over to the display arena for 1 p.m. and am greeted by the compere for the day's proceedings.

'You must be Lucy, the reporter.'

'Er... yup. That's me!' I reply, hoping she isn't going to ask me who I report for.

I am whisked across and introduced to Jed, a small black crossbreed who looks up at me, tail wagging expectantly. I bend down to make a fuss of him and introduce myself, but he is fixated on the squeaky toy being handed to me by his owner and tries to wrestle it from my hand.

'Just take him around the jumps and through the tunnel,' his owner tells me. 'He will follow that toy wherever it goes.'

I wait my turn, giving Jed a pep talk about how we are going to nail this, and show all the other dogs up. When it is our turn, an announcement goes around the arena. 'Lucy is a famous reporter and wants to try her hand at agility. She will be running Jed. Please give Lucy a round of applause.'

I blush. Am I a fraud? Yes, of course I am.

I walk out, Jed yapping at my heels, and do an awkward spin around to wave at the audience. I stumble over Jed and rescue myself just as I am about to face dive, provoking a mass 'Ooooo' from the stands.

I blush even more. 'I'm OK!' I squeak, trying to concentrate on the task at hand. I lead Jed up to the first jump and ask him to sit. He sort of obliges, but he is so excited he can't quite bring himself to commit, so he squats awkwardly and hovers. I panic that this position means he is probably going to do a poo in front of all these people and decide to set off immediately.

'Come on, Jed!' I run around, pointing at all of the jumps like the professionals do, shouting 'tunnel' as we approach it. He flies around like a pro, the audience cheering as we clear the final jump.

I wait for my time, but it never comes. It turns out they didn't time me as it was 'just a bit of fun'. What?! I leave the ring waving and smiling like the fake celebrity I am, belying my inner devastation.

The show ring next to the agility course is playing host to the Irish setters. Tall and smartly dressed, Jon has been showing and breeding these elegant dogs for the last forty years, with two 'dog rooms' assigned to the ten dogs who share his home.

'I'm getting a bit old and cynical now,' he tells me. 'It's a political and bitchy world. A lot of people give up because they can't hack it – you need to have very thick skin.'

'What keeps you coming back?' I ask him.

'I still get a buzz from winning,' he says, shrugging his shoulders. 'It's like a drug.'

'You just pray you have a good judge,' he continues, pulling at a tiny knot on a shining red ear. 'One who judges your dog on the day. Some judges only look at pedigree and lineage. They all like different things, so you try and be clever about it – match the right dog to the right judge – but it doesn't always work. Most judges are afraid to pick a dog that isn't expected to win.'

There is a pause while we listen to the results from the last class.

'I went over to Westminster Dog Show,' he continues, 'the

American equivalent of Crufts, and it's different over there. People celebrate success. Here people are just jealous, and they can't wait for you to fail. And even if you win, people just want to point fingers and pick holes.'

The Afghan that won Best in Breed came here from America, flown over along with its professional handler and groom, having already won at Westminster within the last month.

'Everyone knew it was going to win,' Jon says. 'It wasn't the best bitch here, but it was presented perfectly. It showed its socks off.'

I love the idea of a dog 'showing its socks off', picturing it flouncing up and down a catwalk, its hair pinned back by a giant fan.

He introduces me to two of his dogs, Pop Tart and Jigs. 'You can tell when you get them out of the car whether or not they are going to show,' he says, stroking Jigs with the back of his hand. 'Sometimes they look as miserable as sin and you just think, I may as well turn around and go home.'

'What do you do if a dog never shows?' I ask him, proud to be picking up the lingo.

'Sometimes you have to find it a pet home, but this gets tricky once they get past six months because you get attached to them. Unfortunately, some people give their dogs away once they are made up to champions.' He looks defeated. 'The competition is over, and they just aren't interested in them any more.'

My four days at Crufts are brought to a close with the crowning event, Best in Show. I am lucky enough to be given front-row tickets, right behind Clare Balding presenting live on Channel 4. I don't really know how this happened; I would just advise anyone coming to an event like this to write beforehand and claim to be writing a book.

The winners of each group category are displayed before the audience, while the lady on the tannoy reads a summary of the breed characteristics. 'The Irish terrier is an honest companion. Stout-hearted, with a lot of spunk, he is independent, smart and strong-willed. He makes a wonderful pet, loved for his curious and plucky nature and his excellent sense of humour.'

I had been told from my first day at Crufts that there could only be one winner of Best in Show: Ricky the standard poodle, who had swept the board this year, winning competitions all over the world. And lo, it was. Did this mean that the whole thing was a fix? I didn't think so, but who knows. What I do now know for sure, however, is what it means for a dog to show its socks off. What a diva!

I leave the event with mixed emotions. I'm not sure the showing world is always that kind to dogs, but I guess putting up with a few days a year of floofing and waiting around isn't a big price to pay for an adoring home, so long as it is that way. I preferred the classes where dogs are allowed to have fun, like the working classes, the dancing dogs, the agility and the flyball. The dogs in these competitions were so full of energy and enthusiasm, their little tails wagging their whole bodies from side to side, all chasing the ultimate high of being declared a 'good boy'. Thank goodness none of these dogs made it into mine and Dotty's 'dog with the waggiest tail' classes all those years ago, now that would have been some serious competition.

E is for... Essex

*I ain't never had four girls show
me their vajazzles before*

Driving an hour from my east London home, I arrive in
Brentwood, Essex, to a high street littered with 'boutiques'
selling row after row of tight dresses. Capitalising on an upsurge
of tourism created by the reality TV show *The Only Way is Essex*
(*TOWIE*), the shops, owned by the cast members themselves,
wouldn't look out of place in a nostalgic seaside town. The signs
are brightly coloured square logos on white backgrounds, made
all the more garish by their contrast to the mass of grey concrete
that makes up the rest of the high street.

I suppose I ought to issue a disclaimer here: by 'Essex', I
am referring to the small part of the large and beautiful county
represented by *TOWIE*. I am acutely aware that the culture of this
community of young revellers is by no means exclusive to this part
of the world – it can be found in most big towns around the country;
in fact, it is relatively mainstream. Nor is the contained culture of
this specific group of people living in Brentwood indicative of the
entire county. Far from it; Essex is a rich and diverse county, within
which the *TOWIE* gang represent a tiny population. Regardless,
when I refer to this subculture as Essex, you know what I mean.

The *TOWIE* (henceforth referred to as Essex) subculture is associated with extreme consumption and celebrity aspiration, where investment in personal appearance is directly correlated with social and professional success, and access to the trappings of wealth and tabloid fame – expensive cars, champagne, glamorous VIP nightclubs and huge houses – are available to all. The hyperbole around the community created by the *TOWIE* phenomenon was calling to me, and I wanted to see how close to reality this reality TV show really was.

Frantically sending pictures of myself from the dressing room to my friends – 'Is this tight enough?', 'Bright enough?', 'Revealing enough?' – my Essex experience begins with an early-morning quest to prepare my wardrobe for the weekend. I settle on a figure-hugging blue number, complete with diamanté clusters across the straps, and an outrageous pair of white skyscraper heels that I will have no chance of being able to walk in.

Feeling pleased with my ensemble, I head to a beauty salon for my first experience of fake tanning. My nose tingles with the smell of warm hair and chemicals as I descend the staircase for the tanning studio in the bowels of the building. The beautician pulls on a pair of rubber gloves, her drawn-on eyebrows making her look like an evil air hostess.

'Hello,' I say.

Shooting me a rather unfriendly look, she nods in acknowledgement. 'How dark do you want to go, then?'

'As dark as possible,' I reply confidently.

She looks taken aback. 'I have never been asked for that before.' She pauses to think. 'Like dark-dark?'

'Er... yes... I think so... dark-dark,' I reply, a little less confidently.

'I'll have to do three separate coats then,' she says with a resigned sigh. 'If you strip down and put those paper pants on, I'll come back in a couple of minutes.'

I begin disrobing, a little uncomfortable at the indignity of the paper pants, before the beautician re-enters and sets about positioning me like a plasticine Morph figure. I end up in the shape of a goalkeeper, my hands and arms away from my body in an awkward squat position while she sprays a fine mist of icy liquid all over my body. The cold takes my breath away.

Twenty minutes and three coats later, and my arms are aching. 'OK, you're done,' she says finally. I breathe a sigh of relief and lower my arms, excited by the prospect of warm clothes. 'Oh no,' she says, positioning a large fan to blow straight onto my body, 'you have to stay in that position for another ten minutes while you dry.'

For fuck's sake.

Still shivering and wondering if it's possible to get frostbite on my nipples, I distract myself by calling a salon owned by Amy Childs, one of the major characters in *TOWIE*, to make another appointment.

'Can you fit in four vajazzles tomorrow morning?' I try to keep my voice low as I walk down the street.

'Yep, that's fine,' says the receptionist. 'You're all booked in for eleven a.m.'

When I finally get back to my hotel, I put on the lightest clothes I can find to avoid rubbing all my fake tan off before it has the chance to develop, and spend the next few hours with the heating up on full whack, watching back-to-back episodes of *TOWIE* on my laptop.

Nestled in the twilight zone between the real and not real, the conversations don't seem too scripted but the situations the cast find themselves in do stretch the concept of 'reality' a little further than my usual interactions with friends. Or perhaps my group of girls are just a bit boring and could do with more drama in our lives. The vast majority of the episodes focus on the dizzyingly complex relationships between the cast members, the gossip surrounding those, and a LOT of preening and partying.

I rack up five hours of research before pouring a warm bath. Easing myself into the water, I make the sound of an old man getting up from a chair and sit there for twenty minutes, the bath water turning a disturbing shade of brown around me. When I finally emerge from what any onlooker would presume to be a tub of Bisto, the mirror above the sink confirms that I still belong in the company of Willy Wonka. I pour myself a big glass of wine.

An hour later Moira, Sian and Jo – my best friends and allies for the weekend – make their entrance, interrupting yet another episode of *TOWIE*, and spend about ten minutes laughing hysterically at my face. By now it is 5 p.m. and time for us to begin our evening preparations for a night on the town. I start by attempting to attach a handful of cheap hair extensions I had ordered from the internet onto my head. Sian lets me spend a while becoming hopelessly entangled in the nylon hair before deciding to rescue me. She clips each clump of hair underneath my real hair in layers, and it becomes increasingly evident that my real hair is about forty-seven shades lighter than the extensions I had bought.

We stare at each other for a moment. 'Maybe they'll look a bit better if you cut them?' she says, unconvincingly.

'What kind of scissors do you want?' the receptionist asks me after an embarrassing lift ride with two businessmen.

I point at my blatantly ridiculous hair, 'Errr...'

She nods sympathetically, handing me the only pair she has in her drawer.

Unsurprisingly, even after a brutal attack with the scissors, I still look ludicrous and decide to abort the mission, unclipping the tatty party-shop pieces of hair one by one, wishing I had pushed the boat out a bit here and gone more upmarket with my choice of extensions.

I decide to move on to make-up, something I'm a little more comfortable with, applying layers of foundation, bronzer and blusher. Already looking like I've been lost at sea for a month, I turn to Moira. 'More blusher?'

'Definitely,' she says. 'More is more!'

I apply another layer to my face, which seems to have gained half an inch of protrusion.

Next the eyelashes.

'Er... which way round do they go?' I ask Sian, shaking a finger they appear to be already stuck to.

Sian loses her patience. 'I think you presume we've all read a book about this stuff,' she says, 'but it's just common sense!'

Is it? Should I have been born with an innate knowledge of how to attach different types of artificial hair to myself? I don't know how to put fake eyelashes on, I don't know how to put hair extensions in, I am crap at doing make-up, crap at doing my hair and I can't walk in high heels. I wonder why my friends seem to be so much better at these things than me, why it comes so naturally to them.

I go back to the eyelashes and pick up the box, discovering the very clear instructions printed on the back for how to attach them. What an idiot. Of course, I could have just looked at the box, why didn't I think of that? Perhaps I am somehow proud that I don't know these things, placing personal value on a more natural look and therefore thinking badly of anyone who doesn't. I cringe at the thought. Could my whining and moaning to Sian just be an attempt at drawing attention to the fact that I consider myself to be above this level of preening, like some kind of judgy badge of honour? Or is this reaction a manifestation of my always feeling like an outsider in these moments of girly camaraderie? I was often called a 'tomboy' growing up – choosing to wear combat trousers over dresses and never releasing my hair from its pulled-back ponytail – so I guess it might just be both.

To add to my shaky sense of femininity, I am informed that I am not allowed to wear the blue dress I bought earlier that day. 'It's more Southend-on-Sea than *TOWIE*,' Sian explains. 'People will think you're taking the piss.'

I am a bit upset by this, I think because I wanted to look silly, and probably was just seeing this all as a big joke. But if I am going to really experience this world, I need to keep these feelings in check, and stop being such a twat. I resign myself to yanking my body into a red figure-hugging dress of Sian's, which actually looks quite nice.

We hail a taxi to Sugar Hut, a popular nightclub owned and frequented by *TOWIE* cast members, teeter past the bouncers in our skyscraper heels and have our photo taken by the official photographer, doing the standard hand-on-hip-and-looking-back-over-the-shoulder pose.

I look around at my fellow revellers – nearly every other girl here is wearing fake eyelashes, fake tan, fake hair, skyscraper heels and a body-con dress, some so tight you can see when they last had a wax – and I start to feel a bit angry, as if this might be a feminist issue. Why should we women have to go to all of this effort? Spending three hours adjusting our appearances so we can all look as close as possible to a carbon copy of Cheryl

Cole? Rubbing out our imperfections, rubbing out our identity, so we all look the same: the same big, curly, thick hair, the same spray tans, the same smoky eyes, the same dramatic eyelashes. Then I take another look around the room and realise that a lot of the men in here have done exactly the same – most have plucked, waxed or threaded their eyebrows, have clearly done as many coats of fake tan as I have, and wear tight, low-cut t-shirts revealing painstakingly toned bodies. It makes me feel a bit better.

One guy pushes in next to me at the bar. He is wearing a crisp grey suit, a white shirt with a thin black tie and a V-neck peach cashmere jumper. He looks immaculate, like a 'Ken does preppy' doll. 'Ahhhh, you look so sweet,' the words fall out of my patronising mouth before I engage my brain. I grimace, waiting for the tirade of abuse I deserve in return.

'Thanks, hon. You look really nice too,' he says, revealing a genuine smile that floods me with guilt.

He is no exception; everybody we meet here seems to be exceedingly friendly. The atmosphere is welcoming, and my discomfort eases with every accepting smile. Suddenly, the bartender jumps up onto the bar and leans towards me.

'Babe – am I coming detached at the edge?' she asks.

'Er... what?' I have absolutely no idea what she is talking about.

She points to the edge of her eye. 'My eyelash, is it coming off?'

'Oh, no, you're fine,' I say, feeling a glowing pride that she trusted me with this girly question. Maybe this feeling of belonging is what I have been missing all along. Maybe I haven't felt like I belong in this world because I have been fighting my transformation to enter it on its own terms.

We somehow manage to blag our way into the VIP section, where I have a stunted but relatively polite conversation with one of the *TOWIE* cast – I'm not sure if she is being purposefully nonchalant or just struggling to move her face due to overenthusiastic use of Botox – before joining another reality TV celebrity for a dance on the sofas. I decide to sneak a glass of Grey Goose vodka from one of their tables and the rest of the night disappears into a black hole. At this rate, I may have to save chapter R for Rehab.

The next morning, wearing dark glasses and clutching a bottle of water, I join the girls for the painfully long two-day (ten-minute) schlep to Amy Childs' beauty salon. Our bubbly beautician welcomes us with an enthusiasm that creates a small volcano in my head.

'Is Amy here?' I ask her, through a mouth drier than the Simpson Desert.

'No,' she says, smoothing down her bright pink apron. 'She's in her shop today, but you gotta go see her after. She'll love you girls coz you're pretty!'

She realises what she has just said. '... Not that she only likes pretty girls.'

'She just likes them more?' Sian offers.

She laughs. 'Exactly!'

With that, she leans over Moira, who is lying horizontally on a treatment table, looking as if she is about to undergo a serious operation. She is. Moira is about to be vajazzled.

A type of body jewellery made famous by *TOWIE*, a vajazzle involves attaching small stick-on diamanté crystals around your pubic region, typically around and under the bikini line, to bedazzle the area up.

We had been given two vajazzle options: the initials 'A. C.' (Amy Childs), and the one we all ended up choosing, 'Well Jel'. One of the *TOWIE* catchphrases, 'Well Jel' means 'well jealous', and is used to express an aspiration, to convey envy and also as a kind of compliment in response to an achievement. We each take turns lying on the beautician's bench while she applies the £20 transfer. Although the options are limited, and extremely tame when compared to the elaborate vajazzles Google had promised us, we all decide that having another girl's initials on our vajayjays would be a bit *too* weird.

The remainder of our day is spent trying to replicate a day in the life of an Essex girl, indulging in an extended getting-ready routine for another night out in Sugar Hut. It starts with a blow-dry at a hair salon. 'Big is best' in Essex, and apparently, we all want our hair to be in thick, cascading curls. I feel like I am back at Crufts as my hairdresser backcombs and plumps up my hair for over an hour. I take the opportunity to quiz her about what it means to be an Essex girl.

Up until now, I haven't had to prepare questions when I am interviewing people for this book; I am so interested in their lives that they just spill out of me, resulting in some unplanned interviews lasting for hours. But today I find myself wishing I had done a little more preparation as I struggle to find an access point.

'What do you like about living in Essex?' I try.

'People are very friendly, like one big family, and everyone looks nice here. Everyone makes an effort.'

'Some come in here to get their hair done every weekend,' she continues, 'or they just come in for a blow-dry when they've got a night out. For some of them, I think it's just an excuse to sit down and have a bit of a gossip.'

I reflect on this. I have never liked chatting at the hairdresser's. I always sit there feeling self-conscious and worrying that I am not saying the right thing or behaving in the right way, that I somehow don't belong. My obsession with fitting in and being liked seems to be at its most challenged here, and I wonder what this says about me. I can see how the hairdresser's chair might be a safe space for a lot of women, a place to discuss things that they wouldn't usually open up about, an excuse to have a gossip and a giggle in a world that is usually so damn heavy. I wonder again if this just means I am an awful snob who considers herself above gossip, or if it's actually another case of feeling like I am not part of this club, of not feeling like I belong in this particular version of life as a woman.

After another hour of chatting and coiffing, we leave the salon looking like dolls with oversized heads, and wander over to visit Amy Childs, who is holding court in her boutique across the high street.

We find her in the corner of her white-walled high-street palace, on a silver and purple throne befitting the undisputed Queen of Brentwood.

'All right girls!' she says to us as we walk over.

'We thought we would come over and show you our vajazzles,' I say to her, pulling down the front of my trousers to reveal the top line of the gems. Sian, Moira and Jo do the same, and we all giggle like schoolgirls.

Amy looks impressed. 'I ain't never had four girls show me their vajazzles before!' she says, pulling out her smartphone. 'I'm gonna tweet about this later.'

You know that feeling when you walk along the road, shoulders back, boobs out, acutely aware of how incredible you look?

Well, I feel absolutely nothing like that when, after another three-hour preening session, we head back to Sugar Hut later that evening. Instead I feel self-conscious and depressingly sober. But I know that so many of the girls around me *do* feel incredible walking into Sugar Hut, that this is the raison d'être of all that preening, and I desperately want to feel part of this. I think I know where to find it and head straight for the club bathroom to be greeted by a sea of girls applying make-up and reattaching eyelashes.

'Do you wanna borrow some blusher, babe?' the girl next to me at the mirror asks. I take that as a hint that I am looking a bit pale and trowel on another layer. My face is now so far beyond its usual prominence, I calculate that there would be a thirteen-second delay between being punched in the face and feeling the physical impact.

I look around me at the girls helping each other to get ready, chatting in the stalls as they take it in turns to use the loo, laughing and sharing tips with each other, and I think I am finally starting to get it. The energy in here is so positive.

Back at the bar I talk to Barry, a self-proclaimed Essex lad born in Brentwood.

'Do you prefer the girls when they're glammed up?' I ask him, marvelling at his meticulously groomed appearance.

'Not really. I prefer them more natural-looking,' he says. 'But I don't think any of it is for the guys. All of the glam is for the other girls, a competitive thing between each other. That's the only way I can explain it, because most guys prefer them to look more natural.'

I reflect on this and wonder if there is any truth in the statement that this level of preening is a competitive thing. Are people here putting in all of this effort to look nice or are they doing it to fit in because the bar of what is acceptable has been raised? As soon as one girl puts fake eyelashes on, the rest of the girls in the room look like they have short and underwhelming eyelashes, so they all need to wear them to reset the playing field. It's like an arms race. If one girl gets fake boobs, the other girls have to get them to stay competitive. If one older woman defies wrinkles with a Botox injection, other wrinkly women of that age are at a disadvantage. And where does it all end?

By the end of the night, I am fed up and ready to go home. I can't walk in my shoes, my feet are in agony, and I want to tear my eyelashes off. I am still struggling to work out why I am so annoyed by all of this preening. I do enjoy looking pretty, but right now I just don't feel pretty at all. For me, the joy of make-up is to make it seem as if you naturally look that way. The joy is the lie – I have no blemishes, and my eyes are naturally this defined, honestly – but there is no lying with this amount of make-up; it's blatantly obvious how much of an effort I have put in to look like this.

But I have to remember that this is just the way *I* view make-up, when the joy for many is not the lie; the joy is in the glamour, and the amazing transformation that make-up and fake eyelashes can facilitate, and who the hell am I to pass judgement if this is your thing? Why do I embrace the absurdity of grown men dressing up in woollen britches and firing fake guns at each other, but rile against people who love to get glammed up? Especially because the transformation here is, in a way, accessing a fantasy world every bit as complete as the battle re-enactors. These girls are not just competitive: they are absolutely living their dreams of *being* Cheryl Cole, or any celebrity. They are dressing up, living their best lives and loving it. I also have to give them credit for being able to walk in these beautiful torture shoes and being nails enough to not even complain about how bloody painful they are. I yank the enormous heels from my feet as we climb into the taxi, wince at the pain of my weeping blisters and massage my aching heels. I will just never cut it as an Essex girl.

F is for... Fox Hunters

Horse & Hound magazine call me hunting's most eligible bachelor

I thought the flat cap I bought for a farmer-themed rugby social at university was resigned to wallowing at the bottom of my dressing-up box for the rest of its sorry existence. Not so. On a freezing-cold Tuesday morning, I drag myself out of bed at 6 a.m., don a pair of leather wellies, a borrowed tweed jacket and give the little fellow the outing he deserves.

A tough pick for me, given how divisive the issue continues to be, I chose to spend time with this community because of its roots in the British countryside. I have always loved and been fascinated by the idea of rural life and the people who live it. Having grown up and always lived in cities, the country life is a huge source of FOMO for me, to the point that I used to close my eyes tight when I blew out the birthday candles as a kid, and wish year after year that I could live in the depths of the countryside, alone and naked but for a pet horse and some friendly woodland creatures. God, I was a weird kid.

My destination is Leicestershire, where I have been invited by George Halsworth for a day's 'foot following' with a local hunt.

'I have been reliably informed that you are the best man to

show me the world of hunting.' I adopt a bit of shameless flattery during our introductory phone call.

'I should think so,' he replies. '*Horse & Hound* magazine call me hunting's most eligible bachelor.'

I am nervous on my drive to meet George. Am I going to enjoy spending time with this community? Being an avid animal-welfare advocate and having written my undergrad philosophy dissertation on animal rights and the moral question of fox hunting, I was dubious. Memories from my childhood play on loop in my mind, of sitting cross-legged in front of *The Animals of Farthing Wood*, rooting for Vixen as the hunt closes in on her trembling frame. I wonder if I can ever justify being on the other side of this chase, but vow to keep an open mind and reserve my judgement. For now.

I find George in the garage of a local farm, where the hunt is due to meet, wearing white britches, brown leather tan-top boots and the obligatory flat cap.

'You must be Lucy.' He strides over to shake my hand before introducing me to the surrounding company in his outside voice. 'Everybody, this is Lucy,' he hollers. 'She is writing a book about us mad lot.'

Feeling a bit out of place, I decide to throw myself into what seems to be the task at hand: moving shortbread, chipolatas, cake, cheese biscuits and home-made sausage rolls from Tupperware boxes onto foil platters. Once finished, I help George pour generous measures of port into white plastic cups.

A short while later the surrounding walls ring with the sound of scraping hooves as the driveway suddenly fills with men and women on horseback turned out impeccably in hunting jackets, their white 'stocks' (cotton neckerchiefs) folded tightly and held in place with shiny pins. The smell of leather soap mingles with the overpowering smell of clean horse as the enormous beasts, with plaited manes and buffed, shining coats, fidget excitedly.

'They have to wait for the hunt servants to turn up before they are allowed to enter the field,' George's mum tells me.

'The hunt has servants?'

She laughs. 'No, no. That's just what we call the people who work for the hunt, dear, the staff.'

Within a few minutes the yapping and howling of hounds can be heard – I have already been told off for calling them dogs – and I can see a cluster of red coats approaching the yard. A chorus of 'good mornings' reverberates around the yard as the servants parade through and head straight for the adjoining field.

I help the team on foot by offering around the food and drink, while the 'mounted field' (people on horses) shake hands and make their introductions. The horses stand politely still while their well-spoken riders introduce themselves, using their full names as they had at Auriol's shoot, and giving context in a manner that I had presumed exclusive to Tolkien novels.

'Katherine Wrington of Pembleton Farm.'

'Martin Giles, son of Robert Giles at Fouracres.'

Everybody is almost comically polite to me, smiling and thanking me profusely as I pass them cake. It's hard for them to balance their port, cake and reins in just two hands, so they fumble around, repeatedly apologising for their lack of co-ordination: 'Gosh, I am frightfully sorry!'

The men doff their caps at me as I walk past.

There are twenty-five hounds out today, or twelve and a half 'couples'. 'They are always hunted in odd numbers,' I am told by Jim, a regular foot follower who wears a leather baseball cap and a pair of binoculars around his neck. 'You would never talk about a single hound if you ever had to; they would be referred to as "half a couple".

Now a fencing contractor, Jim used to work in hunting and knows everything about the sport and the surrounding country. He explains that during the meet the hounds are supposed to be in a tight pack behind the huntsman, but a few of the naughty ones wander off, following their noses to the honey and mustard chipolatas, and licking the faces of anyone leaning down to pet them.

After half an hour or so, the huntsman, sitting astride a huge white horse, hushes the crowd. He makes a short speech, thanking the landowners and the hosts for the food and drink. 'It's been a splendid meet', he says, 'and as you will see, we are hunting our bird of prey today' – he points to a chap who looks like a Dickensian villain, holding up an eagle owl with a leather mask over its eyes – 'so we are acting within the law'.

Hunting foxes with hounds was banned under UK law in 2004, but hunting packs continue to operate around the country, sidestepping the law by utilising its loopholes. Some have converted to drag hunting, which involves trailing an artificially scented cloth around a predetermined course that the hounds are trained to follow. This is generally regarded as the most humane option because there is minimal risk of the hounds picking up the track of a fox accidentally and killing it. This hunt uses a combination of trail laying and the falconry exemption, which states that hunting is permitted for the purpose of enabling a bird of prey to hunt the wild mammal.

The huntsman sounds his horn, sending the hounds into a barking frenzy, and the field follow them through the gate, up the road and out of sight.

I tag along with Jim and his group of regular foot followers, who spend the day sharing their knowledge with me. They explain that a hunt begins with the 'casting of the hounds' – sending them across the field, like casting a net – until they pick up the trail (the 'line'). As soon as they have picked up a scent they will 'speak', and the huntsman will sound his horn to alert the field that they will soon be off following the trail.

I am invited into Jim's off-roader, to save my urban car's paintwork. As we drive, the conversation turns to the problems that the hunt has had with anti-hunt campaigners, known in this world as 'antis'.

He shares that antis have been known to send out death threats and plant car bombs. In the year 2000, two members of a hunt in Kent were warned by the Hunt Retribution Squad that if hunting was not stopped immediately, 'non-compliance will result in every member and supporter of the hunt becoming a legitimate target'. One morning shortly afterwards, one of the hunt servants heard an explosion and ran outside to find his van in flames. Five hours later a similar device had to be removed by bomb-disposal experts from underneath the vehicle of a female hunt member.

'A lot of them come down from the universities,' Jim says. 'They all get paid twenty-five pounds and a free packed lunch if they come out for the day and cause trouble.'

I am unconvinced, and a later Google investigation for evidence of Jim's claim falls flat.

'We had terrible trouble with them about fifteen years ago,' another follower joins in from the back seat. 'They put a big motorbike chain around the hounds and boxed them in, kicking and beating them. One of our guys was cracked over the head with a coffee flask. Blood everywhere.'

We arrive at a good spot to watch over the proceedings and I join the group of four regulars sitting on the bonnet of Jim's car. A tall man in a waxed jacket sits next to me. 'Most of us foot followers were brought up in the countryside, so hunting has always been a part of our lives.' He stares straight ahead as he talks to me. 'We come out to follow the pack and catch up on all the local chit-chat.'

Our collective eyes scan the rolling hills as the hounds stream across them, noses glued to the ground, a collage of white, brown and red rocking hypnotically behind them.

'Working hounds is an art form,' Jim whispers, listening intently for the sound of them speaking. 'I'm not really interested in watching the horses, nor the fate of the fox, if there is even a fox around. For me, it's all about the test for the hounds.'

Over the next couple of hours, I am amazed by how much the group know about the land: where the fox might be, what line it might take, where it is likely to take cover and which direction the scent might come from. Knowledge passed down through the ages from our hunter-gatherer days – of how our quarry will behave and how best to outwit them – that is fast disappearing from our collective consciousness, replaced by knowledge of where to buy neatly packaged, faceless meat from a supermarket shelf.

After spending a morning hurtling around the countryside, the horses begin to tire and the field stop to 'second horse' at 2 p.m., forcing those without a second horse into an early retirement.

At the beginning of this project I had committed to participate wherever possible to give me the best chance of understanding each world. And so, given that I have been obsessed with horses since I could crawl, and thanks to nearly three decades spent progressing from mucking out stables to teaching at local riding schools, I had no excuse but to try and understand this world from a higher vantage point; it was time to progress from foot following from afar to joining the field on horseback.

Months earlier, I had set to work trying to find a hunt that would allow me to join the field. I thought this would be easy – I have decent connections in the horsey world, and friends who grew up on farms – but it was bafflingly difficult. Fox hunting is now such a controversial subject in this country that the community seems to have put up high walls of protection around themselves, so perhaps it is unsurprising that they are suspicious of an outsider who plans on writing about them. I imagine them passing around my emails like a grenade.

In the end I am saved by Leah, a lady master of a West Country hunt, who invites me to join them for the day. Leah is from America, marrying into a British hunting family in which her husband is also a master. Her forefathers first came into contact with this hunt during World War II, when it became frowned upon to keep animals that weren't edible. Hounds are incredibly valuable – it is possible to trace their lineage back for hundreds of years, successfully breeding in certain traits that make them great at their job – so, for the hunt to have to destroy all of their hounds and start again after the war was unthinkable. To get around this, the hounds were packed into containers and shipped over to the USA, where they lived out the war in safety, before being returned after VE Day. Leah's family had been the hounds' stewards.

First on my list was to find myself a trusty steed for the day, so Leah refers me to a lady who regularly rents her horses for hunting. I speak to her, ask for a 'nice, safe horse', and enquire about the cost.

'Two hundred and twenty-five pounds for half a day,' she replies casually. I gulp, stopping myself just in time from shrieking "ow much?!", and instead adopt a bumbling British burble about how reasonable this all is, and find myself agreeing to part with this monstrous sum of money next week.

Still reeling from the impending assault on my bank balance, I call Leah back to inform her that I now have a horse and will be joining the hunt next Wednesday.

'Great,' she says, referring me to the etiquette section of the hunt's website in preparation, which says, *The first thing to do is telephone the Hunt Secretary and ask if you may join the hunt for the day and check with him/her the amount (cap) you will be required to pay.*

I call the secretary to let her know I will be joining. 'Where is the meet?' I ask her.

'We'll tell you nearer the time,' she reassures me. 'Oh, and the cap for a day's mid-week hunting is seventy pounds.' On top of the £225 I am spending to rent the horse. This is turning out to be a very extravagant way to spend four hours.

I call again the day before to double check all is well but am still not told the location of the meet. 'We will tell you tomorrow,' she fobs me off, clearly still suspicious. At the last minute, and after reminding her I can't pay her unless I know where we are meeting, I manage to wrangle it out of the lady renting me a horse.

Black or navy-blue coats should be worn with three black buttons. Ladies should wear buff breeches with plain black butcher boots. Hair should always be tied up and held in a suitable hairnet. A hunting tie should be worn with the pin placed horizontally for safety. Earrings and other piercings, let's just not go there!

I spend the days leading up to the hunt pulling together everything I need, investing in a posh velvet hat, a hairnet and some leather gloves. I borrow a hunting jacket, stock and tiepin from a friend. I don't really understand the 'earrings, let's just not go there' statement; perhaps it's like when Maggie Thatcher allegedly turned up to go deer-stalking with the Queen in her urban shoes and bright blue suit. It just isn't done.

Etiquette demands that you should say good morning to the Joint Masters. The correct greeting being 'Good morning, Master' (even if you know them personally).

On the morning of the hunt, I drive to meet Smarty, my trusty steed for the day. He is huge, standing at around 17 hands, with a white-flecked coat and a vast head, lined with small, rolled plaits.

'Is there anything I should know about him?' I ask as I am heaved up onto his back.

'No, nothing,' she says. 'He's a gentleman.'

I hand her the money, shaking with nerves at the thought of taking part in an incredibly dangerous sport on a giant creature with its own mind, and spin around to trot up the road.

Once there, I squeeze past a group of mud-splattered Land Rovers filled with old women wearing headscarves, to be greeted by a beautiful lady sitting astride an equally beautiful bay horse.

'You must be Lucy,' she beams. 'I'm Leah.'

'How did you know it was me?' I ask her, disappointed that I must look a bit amateur.

'I can spot the rental horses a mile off,' she says, pointing at Smarty.

One of the secretaries rides over to introduce herself. She is young and impeccably turned out, with dark hair swept immaculately into a hairnet, a flawless complexion and perfectly straight pearlescent teeth.

'Welcome,' she says. 'Is that a rental horse?' Before I can answer, she wrinkles her nose and tips her head to the side, 'I can spot them a mile off.'

I want to put my hands over Smarty's ears so he can't hear. 'It's OK, boy – they're only saying that because you're so handsome,' I whisper to him after she leaves, rubbing his thick, muscular neck.

I decide to ride around and talk to a few more people, picking up a plastic cup filled with warm mulled wine from a floating tray en route. 'Good morning!' 'Good morning!' 'Good morning!' The men tap their caps and elaborately introduce themselves. 'Ah, splendid,' the hunt master brays when I reveal this is my first hunt. 'You have picked a glorious day.'

I *have* picked a glorious day. The sun is shining, and the air is still. It is the first drizzle-free day we've had in months.

At all times ride behind the field master. Do not attempt to jump if there is a hound anywhere near a jump.

When the mulled wine supply starts to dry up, the huntsman sounds his horn – 'badooo badooo' – and we are off, cantering across the countryside en masse.

Within the first few minutes we are faced with an enormous hedge, and I watch the field of forty-odd horses leaping over it with dread. Looking around for a gate, I realise with a pounding heart that the jump is the only way out. I haven't jumped anything that big for a very, very long time, but there is nothing for it. I point Smarty at the hedge and ask him to canter towards it with all the confidence I can muster.

The hedge seems to grow bigger and bigger as we approach it, and within seconds it is towering over us, our view obscured by a sea of flying hooves and muscular backsides. I squeeze with my legs and hold my breath as Smarty leaps into the air. We hang, suspended in the air for what feels like minutes, before landing unscathed on the other side. The exhilaration of realising I am still alive floods my veins with adrenaline.

We travel almost entirely on farmland for the next four hours, passing over rolling hills in every shade of green, through endless miles of country without a road in sight. Cantering in a line, we jump a rail and post to enter a big sloping field. The sunlight streams on to one side of the valley, leaving the other side in shade as the hounds spread out, flecks of brown against the iridescent grass. I feel a sense of awe at the tremendous beauty of nature in the absence of anything man-made.

It is your responsibility to shut gates or call back 'gate please.' In the event that riders behind are out of earshot, a raised whip or hand is the method of communication.

'Gate, please!' We pass through dozens of livestock holding gates over the course of the morning. In between I quietly practise this phrase over and over again in my posh accent, hoping not to get found out when it's my turn to shout.

As the hounds are cast into a nearby copse, I use the opportunity to speak with Anne, who hunts her ex-racehorse twice a week when she isn't treating her physio clients.

'The weekday meets are the best to come along to,' she tells me. 'At the weekend you get all the dribs and drabs, the London lot who rent horses and don't have any idea what they are doing. They're all over the place and can be a real pain.'

I had come from London, rented a horse and didn't know what I was doing. I look at her. 'Erm. Isn't that me?'

She smiles. 'No, of course not. You're... you're fine.'

We both know it is me.

At the end of a meet, it is customary to say, 'Good night.'

Regardless of the time of day! 'Good night,' I dutifully say to everyone I walk past as I head back to the horsebox at 2 p.m. I didn't have a second horse – I hadn't had time to list all my earthly possessions on eBay – so it was time for me to retire.

The day had been an intense experience from beginning to end. I didn't have much idea what was going on, didn't even glimpse a fox (thankfully) and spent the whole time enjoying the beautiful horse I was riding and the views across the countryside.

'I am on the fence about fox hunting,' Anne had told me earlier that day, as we were lining up to jump a hedge, 'but hunting is the only way you can guarantee a beautiful, fast ride without too much time on the roads.'

This may seem like an odd statement to make while out fox hunting, sure, but I think I get it. You are almost always restricted to roads and bridle paths when riding horses in this country, so to be allowed to hare across the countryside jumping everything in sight is a rare treat, and I'm sure the reason a lot of people do this. But is all that worth killing a fox over?

'I am a vegetarian,' Anne had continued, 'and I really care about animal welfare. But for me, hunting with hounds occasionally is much more humane than eating bacon. I prefer to participate in nature rather than sterilise it. But aside from all that, I come hunting for the riding, not the hounds.'

I had felt like an impostor for most of the day, felt somehow different from those around me, but this was a familiar feeling for me now. I was alone, tagging along and constantly badgering people with questions. I guess this naturally makes you feel like an outsider, and however welcoming people are initially, you will inevitably get on their nerves after a while.

The only person who put me entirely at ease that day was Sam, an effervescent, open-faced pleasure of a man I met on my way back to return my four-footed Ferrari. The gay partner of a local farmer, Sam manages a chain of hairdressing salons. He lives in North London during the week and keeps his horse with his partner, saving up all of his days off so the couple can hunt together.

'It's a great life,' he tells me in a melodic voice. 'I am very lucky. You get to meet all kinds of people down here.' He leans over and touches my arm. 'I'm sure you didn't expect to meet someone like me though, did you, darling?'

He throws his head back and laughs.

So what was the conclusion to my dissertation on the ethics of fox hunting? Well, just like any good piece of academia, the answer was somewhere in the middle. I didn't condemn the practice in its entirety, but I didn't approve of it either. For my part, I was relieved not to have witnessed the death of a fox over the last week, and if my FOMO kicked in again on this one, I know I would favour going drag hunting, but to choose to focus my judgement only here, while I continue to eat burgers, trap rats, poison entire armies of ants and consume materials that destroy habitats, merely to keep my life abundant and convenient, is probably a bit hypocritical. I think there are far bigger battles than fox hunting when it comes to animal welfare.

So I'm in the middle. I'm in the grey. It's a strange place to be, and an uncomfortable one in today's climate of binary politics, but having now spent time with this community, I feel more than ever that it's a mistake to pass judgement on a whole group of people – be they capitalists or socialists, vegans or meat eaters, pros or antis – where part of the job description of belonging to each group is to hate everything about the other side, robbing each individual of their humanity.

And although the middle is grey, it's still full of colourful characters.

Unless you are a goth, that is.

G is for... Goths

*Goths never fight - they might
smudge their eyeliner*

Whitby Goth Weekend began with an ad hoc get together of some dark-clad friends in a central Whitby pub. Fast-forward a year and, unable to keep up with the swelling crowds, the Elsinore pub was literally drunk dry over the course of the weekend, giving birth to the first official Whitby Goth Weekend (WGW).

Today, over twenty years later, the festival has become a major event in the goth calendar, drawing thousands of revellers from across the world to the blustery coastal town.

It was 31 October, and, like the famous slayer Eric Brooks (otherwise known as Blade), I had originally decided to begin researching my 'V is for...' chapter by making for WGW in search of vampires. I had hoped that Whitby, where Bram Stoker's Dracula first set foot in England, would be a beacon for them over the Halloween weekend. Due to some poor preparation on my part, all of the hotels had already been booked up, so a friend's aunt and uncle (whom I had never met) were putting me up at the last minute.

Wishing I had access to the wardrobe of my fourteen-year-old self during my three-month goth phase, I crammed every dark piece of clothing I owned into my car and hit the road. Within an hour of arriving, I found myself sipping wine in the living room of my hosts, them dressed exactly as a wholesome middle-aged couple should be, slippers and all; me dressed entirely in black lace, with fake blood running from the edges of my white-contact-lensed vampire eyes. We talked about the rain and the traffic on the M1. I bloody love this country.

The first stop on my vampire hunt is RAW, a nightclub in Whitby town centre. Crippled by a familiar, anxious nausea that grips me the first time I walk into one of these new worlds, I enter the club and take in the sea of black souls heaving around me. My pathetic attempt at goth attire makes me feel like a fraud and my ears pound with the sound of death metal. Self-consciously picking my way through the alarming crowd, I make for the bar to order a stiff drink.

I take a stool next to a guy wearing a leather corset, black eyeliner and leather trousers. He looks me up and down and locks his eyes on mine, his face void of expression. I give him one of my 'I'm being polite, but I'm actually terrified of you' smiles. I didn't even know I had one of those.

'Have you ever been to a fet night?' he asks me, without a word of greeting, pouting his lips and flicking long greasy hair away from his austere face.

'I... erm... I don't know what that is,' I confess, desperately regretting my choice of seat.

'Fetish, my love,' he says, over-pronouncing each word and leaning in closer, as if trying to sniff my neck. I back away and shudder.

Oh God. Had I made a mistake in coming here? Gone too far outside my comfort zone this time? I stand up and turn to leave, bumping straight into a very tall, three-piece suit with an elaborately styled moustache.

'Lee!' I squeal, hurling myself at him and engulfing him in a desperate hug. I had only met Lee once before, at a vampire boat party where I had been doing some initial 'V is for...' research a month earlier (more about that later), so my greeting was a tad overfamiliar.

'What on earth are you doing here?' He looks dumbfounded.

I feel a strange combination of relief and vulnerability; glad to see a familiar face, but dejected to have been exposed so early into the weekend by the only man in Whitby who knows I'm not a real goth. I decide to come clean.

'Trying to find some vampires, of course,' I say casually.

'Well, I am sorry to disappoint you,' he says, 'but you won't find many vampires here.'

'Why not?'

'They fell out with the Goth Weekend years ago,' he says. 'They don't come here for Halloween any more. I think they have their own thing.'

I picture a Crips and Bloods-style showdown between the goths and the vampires in a graveyard, an organ playing the Death March as mist surrounds their platform boots.

'But what you should *really* be doing this weekend,' he continues, 'is exploring the goth community, like I told you. Now *that's* a subculture!'

Lee had tried to sell me on this the last time we met, but I wasn't convinced. Are goths an interesting enough subculture to warrant a whole chapter? I take another sweep of the scene around me, of the shadowed forms pulsating against the wall of sound, and give an inward nod. Yup.

We head back to the bar, where a giant poster informs me that this evening's event is a S.O.P.H.I.E. fundraiser, a charity very close to the heart of the goth community. I read the poster. Sophie Lancaster, a twenty-year-old goth, was brutally beaten by a group of youths when walking through a park in 2007. They called her a 'mosher' and left her to die in a pool of her own blood. My throat tightens.

I suddenly feel much more comfortable here, perhaps spurred by my guilt at being so dismissive, at thinking I am so different from these people, at making assumptions based on their fashion choices. But seeing this poster has told me which side I want to be on, and I decide at that moment to be less afraid.

Pushing into the throng surrounding the stage, where a painfully awful band are screaming and abusing their guitars, I decide to try and join in the swaying dance moves. I sway a bit too enthusiastically and bump into a guy wearing a long black jacket held together by three sets of handcuffs. His black lipstick and eye make-up are immaculate. He actually looks kind of hot.

'God, sorry!' I bumble.

'What is that?!' he says in horror, eyeballing the dress I'd bought in a rush the day before, hoping that it looked goth enough for me to blend in. 'It looks like it's from New Look!'

I laugh and motion for him to look at the label towards the back of my neck. He finds it, and steps back, his eyes wide with horror. 'Oh God, I'm sooo sorry' – his face gapes further – 'I didn't think it actually was!'

I wake up the next morning with the familiar dry mouth that seems to follow my first night in every new subculture. After throwing myself around the dance floor in RAW for what felt like minutes, but was actually hours, I had finally rolled home at 3 a.m. I recount the details of the previous evening to my hosts over breakfast, both of whom seem remarkably unfazed by my descriptions of the elaborate scenes, presumably desensitised by the goths' returning presence in Whitby for the last two decades.

Not long after breakfast I dress in black riveted jeans (eBay), army boots (eBay) and a flimsy leather jacket (New Look, again), and brave the long, icy walk back into town. My destination is the Bizarre Bazaar, an alternative market so big it sprawls across three different venues. Thirty minutes later I arrive, frozen to my core, and enter a room that could easily be mistaken for Diagon Alley, the experience heightened by a musty smell of old clothes, books and incense.

I peruse the various stalls offering an arbitrary collection of treasures: old pocket watches, opera glasses, skulls, brass goggles, canes, horns, pendants, leather-bound journals, corsets, wigs and PVC fetware. See, I know what that is now.

Creative energy oozes from the costumes that surround me, resulting in an ethereal atmosphere that amplifies the visual effect of the stalls and their rambling array of wares. I watch a woman attempting to try on a pair of boots. She leans down to pick them up before realising, halfway down, that she can't get anywhere near her feet because her leather corset is far too tight. She calls her friend over to help. He tries to kneel down in front of her, but he can't get low enough because he has a huge gas cylinder on his back to power the propeller above his head as part of his steampunk costume. The two of them give up and collapse in giggles onto a nearby bench.

If you're wondering what a steampunk costume is, wonder no more. A quick Google search as I walk around the room, studying the various costumes, helps me to identify the multiple genres within the wider goth community.

- Steampunk goths – think *Around the World in Eighty Days*
- Cybergoths – *We Will Rock You* the musical

- Lolita or 'J' goths – cutesy Japanese goth
- Trad goths – traditional Gothic period dress, often Victorian
- Fetish goth – PVC, whips and chains
- Corporate goths – three-piece pinstripe suits
- Hippie goths – tie-dye, tassels and piercings

Long-haired and dressed in a three-piece suit, American Tom has already published two books on steampunk, the predominant genre at this event. He has a stall in the bazaar, selling top hats adorned with driving goggles, pocket watches, taxidermy animals, leather cuffs, items of brass machinery, and even books on how to make your own steampunk gadgets.

'Steampunk is a bit like science fiction,' he explains to me, 'but it's an adventure in a speculative past rather than a speculative future. The most important thing for a steampunk costume is that it tells a story. You can get away with almost anything, but it needs to have a scientific explanation. For example' – he points at a costume on the cover of one of his books that looks a bit like an imperial safari outfit, complete with a brass propeller and goggles – 'you might say, "This is my Lord Featherstone Dinosaur-hunting outfit for an expedition to Venus." Old pocket watches might be time-travel devices – hence the dinosaurs – and other old collected items can all be explained away as important props for the journey.'

'Why is steampunk so popular all of a sudden?' I ask, surprised by the number of top hats and backpacks with propellers I have seen gracing the corridors of the bazaar today.

He shrugs. 'Well, goth did what it could do,' he says. 'There is only so much black you can wear. So a lot of goths jumped over to steampunk because it allowed for more creativity. You dress goth, but with steampunk, you actually become your character.'

I continue my circuit of the bazaar and linger by the stall of Doctor Geof, artist and author of *Fetishman*, a comic-book series with a healthy following. Through a cheeky face with mad hair and bushy sideburns, he spends ten minutes trying to convince me to devote a chapter to the fet scene.

'There are different types of fet parties,' he explains. 'The more experienced among us will walk through the door knowing that they are here to participate in any number of... *activities*,' he raises his eyebrows theatrically. 'But there are also parties aimed just at those who are interested in the idea and want to see what it's all about in a safe environment.'

He pauses, enjoying my innocence.

'You are from London, no?' he says. 'So you must have heard of Torture Garden?'

There I was, thinking I was worldly and unshakeable, but this place makes me feel like I have grown up in a convent. I shake my head and lengthen my lips apologetically.

'Oh, Lucy, really?' Doctor Geof says, shaking his head, a grin progressing across his face. At that moment, a man with a very official-looking event-organiser badge steps in to join our conversation. All smiles, he wears thick-rimmed glasses and radiates warmth.

'Hi, I'm Matt,' the smiley man says, extending a hand. 'You look new around here.'

'Is it that obvious?' I say, tugging at the sleeves of my 'teenage fashion'-section leather jacket.

'I'm writing a book and want to talk a bit about what it means to be a goth,' I say, trying to steer the conversation back to my journalistic comfort zone.

'Good question.' He looks serious. 'Well, goth is all about

accepting people for who they are and not passing judgement,' he says. 'And this event is a celebration of non-conformity, diversity and freedom of expression.' He looks pleased with his well-rehearsed answer.

Doctor Geof drags his eye from his drawings and looks up at Matt. 'Where's your girlfriend?'

'She couldn't make it this time,' he replies chirpily, 'it's her five-year anniversary with her other boyfriend.'

'Oh?' I presume I've misheard.

'My girlfriend is polyamorous,' he says, as if telling me she has brown eyes.

'Poly-what?' I ask.

'Polyamory?' he says again, as if it might twig something for me. I look blank. 'It's the preference for multiple intimate relationships. Like polygamy but without the whole marriage thing. It's pretty widely recognised.' He smiles sweetly, trying very hard not to sound patronising. I like Matt.

'Oh, OK,' I say, trying to act cool. 'How many of you are there in your relationship?'

'Just three,' he says. 'I am good friends with the other boyfriend. She was with him already when we got together. Then when she decided that she wanted to bring me in, we all sat down together and discussed it. Worked out a rota system and everything. It was all very grown-up.' He cocks his head. 'It might seem a bit odd to other people, but it works for us.'

I take a few seconds to process this, wondering what being in a polyamorous relationship might be like. I could definitely see the pros, but what about the cons?

'Do you ever feel insecure?' I ask. 'You know... like you are being compared to her other boyfriend?'

'I would be lying if I said never.' He looks as if his smile is painted on. 'But it really isn't a big issue for me. She and I are thinking of bringing another girl in for a threesome soon, but before we do, we'll sit down and talk about it. It would have to work for everybody.'

My hangover is really starting to take hold, so I thank the two men and head up to Whitby Abbey for some fresh air. Today the abbey is playing host to a steampunk wedding, and the entrance is crowded with middle-aged men from the local camera clubs, lying in wait to get snaps of the extraordinary costumes against the dramatic ruins. I talk to one of the photographers, who shares his business card, and discover that it's a tradition for some of the more extroverted goths to come up to the abbey at midday to parade before the photographers, who travel for hundreds of miles to take advantage of the spectacle. It is an unwritten rule that photographers first ask the goths if they mind having their picture taken, before passing them a card with a link for them to view the photos online.

Three old women sit on a park bench nearby eating sandwiches from a Tupperware box. They wear ankle-length dresses, sensible shoes and knitted cardigans under long cotton coats. I ask them what they think of 'all of this', waving loosely in the direction of the goths.

One of the ladies, who must have applied her bright blue eyeliner in an earthquake, looks up at me and smiles. 'We think it's wonderful,' she says, offering me a plastic cup of grey tea from a thermos flask. I accept it gratefully, blowing the steam as we take in our surroundings.

We sit together for a while in silence.

'We come out to look at the goths every year,' another of the ladies explains after about ten minutes. 'There is always so much to look at. You never know what you are going to see.'

I look at the women huddled together, eyes wide, and realise

I'm surprised at how happy the local community seems to be about the twice-yearly influx of goths. I am sure the positive commercial impact they have on an otherwise sleepy winter town has something to do with it – perhaps my corporate self is creeping back in here – but it's more than that. I think it's the exhibition of it all, and the celebration of creativity and diversity. At the very least it's a break from Sunday afternoon reruns of *Keeping Up Appearances*.

I pose the question of why the goths are liked by the locals to Lee when I meet up with him for a walk around the town later that afternoon.

'Because we are all here to enjoy ourselves, and we never cause any trouble,' he says. 'Goths never fight – they might smudge their eyeliner.'

Although there was trouble once, he confesses, about ten years ago, when the residents found some graffiti on a church door. Even though the goths didn't believe it was done by a member of their community – because the 'tag' was shoddy, and goths take pride in their artistry – they immediately took to the streets with buckets and raised four times the amount to pay for a new door within the first hour.

We stop for an ice cream. 'I have a theory,' Lee says, 'that every goth has been bullied at some point in their lives. Either because they have been different, or they felt different.' He takes a lick of his 99. 'I was bullied as a child,' he goes on. 'Sent to a strict boarding school. It made me shy, and I developed a problem with anger.' I find it hard to imagine Lee ever being angry.

'Then when I went to university, I joined the Rock Society, and they invited me to the first WGW. It was a pivotal point in my life, and everything seemed to get better from then on. My personality just seemed to fit. I finally felt accepted among a group of people who were all looking for the same thing: acceptance.'

As we walk down the street together, I see him physically swell with pride at every greeting, his confidence and sense of belonging growing with every acknowledgement. He is a social butterfly among the goth community, and I hadn't yet met anybody who didn't at least know of him.

Lee's look seems to be a big part of his identity, especially his meticulously curled-up moustache, rendering him instantly recognisable. So far, most of the goths I have met have been quite introverted by nature, and I know it's a rather obvious interpretation, but I wonder if the costumes might be like some kind of second identity and way of generating confidence, a mask perhaps.

As I spend another hour reapplying my exaggerated dark make-up later that evening, I reflect on how unnatural and self-conscious I still feel in my goth gear. Perhaps it is the lack of authenticity that is affecting my self-assurance. I am an outsider pretending to fit in, and so my appearance is a disguise, rather than an outward expression of myself. In some ways, this is similar to my experiences in Essex, although with comfy boots instead of heels, light face powder instead of blusher, and lace hats with real animal skulls sewn into them instead of hair extensions. But I am drawn to the goth aesthetic more than I was drawn to the *TOWIE* look; I value the creativity more and find the community much more interesting, perhaps because it is less mainstream. I was neither popular nor unpopular at school, but I have always been more on the alternative side of things, so perhaps I feel less threatened by a group of self-professed underdogs than I did when hanging out with the 'cool kids' in *TOWIE*. I'm sure a psychiatrist would have a field day with all of this.

My mood is lifted when I swing by the Little Angel pub en route to the formal event. I arrive knowing nobody, as usual, and manage to make a whole new group of friends within about five minutes. Goths are such friendly and approachable people, belying their often unnerving appearance, and it still surprises me every time someone who looks half dead smiles at me and offers a warm 'hello'.

As well as the strange dichotomy of being both scary-looking and friendly, another important factor that binds the goth community together is music, and WGW is host to a series of live music events over the course of the weekend. Bands such as Diary of Dreams ('dark wave' – I have no idea what that means), Bella Morte ('metal/death rock') and Method Cell ('dark synth-pop' – again, no idea whatsoever) attract the crowds and justify the entrance fees.

Once inside the formal event space, next to where I'd been verbally deflowered at the Bizarre Bazaar, I found myself enthralled by the way the goths dance. The moves are free-flowing and expressive; hands wave as if casting spells and heads circle slowly on shoulders as if trying to avoid angry bees. When the guitars kick in, the spells and the bees dissipate, and everyone jumps. A lot.

The gathering in the foyer outside the live music room is as big as the crowd inside, demonstrating that music isn't the only reason people come here. I run this observation past Crimson, a professional fire-eater and WGW regular, who nods his head vigorously, throwing his red fedora into a frenzy.

'Coming to Whitby twice a year is like going to a family reunion,' he tells me. 'I always feel so loved and accepted here.'

Wearing a red three-piece suit, with long hair plaited at the nape of his neck, Crimson tells me about the various traditions that run from Thursday to Monday over every WGW.

Maffball, he explains, is played on the Sunday evening, the night of the goth beach party, which involves stripping down to your pants, lighting a paraffin-soaked toilet roll and hurling it at members of the opposing team, like an extreme version of dodgeball.

Although the goth beach party is technically illegal, police patrol the surrounding area every hour to ensure there is no trouble. Crimson explains that this is the result of some trouble a few years back when a couple of local yobs came down to the beach and threatened to kill the goths. The police came to the beach and told the goths that because they come here twice a year, cause no trouble and leave the beach cleaner than they find it, they will make sure this doesn't happen again. Given how polite and friendly I have found this community to be so far, I can quite believe it.

Before the beach party, there is always a football match in the local stadium: Whitby Gazette FC versus Goth FC. The goths have only won once in the history of the tradition, but it is always played in high spirits, complete with heckling and printed supporters' scarves.

Crimson tells me about a friend of his, Endel Öpik (aka Tal Stoneheart), who tragically died after catching pneumonia following one of the goth weekends. He was six foot eight with long blond hair, giving him the look of a Viking. The goth community was so saddened by the death of their dear friend that they decided to give him the first Viking funeral in the UK for 800 years. Having built a replica Viking longboat, they placed Tal's ashes into the middle before sending it out into the ocean and igniting it with flaming arrows. The funeral was orchestrated to live music, and the party continued long into the night, just as Tal would have wanted.

His brother, Lembit Öpik, a Liberal Democrat MP, was quoted in a local paper saying that Endel's wishes were for a traditional Viking funeral, adding, 'He really felt a sense of belonging in Whitby at the goth festival.'

Still enjoying the imagery of Crimson's stories, I thank him and head for the bar (as always), sliding my way to the front beside a strikingly beautiful woman.

I ask her name.

'Zarah,' she tells me.

Carrying herself in a modest and understated manner, Zarah has long dark silky hair that reaches her waist, flawless skin and a slight, feminine frame. To Zarah, I learn as we drink, the world through the lens of this current zeitgeist is a little disappointing. She would rather live in the world of film and literature, a fantasy world perhaps, in which society could have taken a different path, had we not become so closely wedded to science; a path in which fairies and corsets are as accepted a part of our society as maths and tracksuits.

I am beginning to understand why people like Zarah might feel a little alien in the mundane world (mundane being a word goths use to describe all that isn't goth) and why they might instead choose to absorb themselves into a society that accepts their desire to express themselves differently. She too believes that most goths have felt in some way different or alone in their lives, which is why they seek solace in a community where they are free to be different, where creativity in their appearance is lauded and where they don't have to look a certain way to be popular.

Having said that, despite claiming to be different and individual, I can't help but notice that a lot of the goths I have met this weekend look *very* similar and tend to like *very* similar music. So perhaps the goth look is fundamentally a rejection of the most widely accepted aesthetic, marking them out as recognisable to one another, the rebellion taking the form of a community uniform that makes them feel safe and offers an unconditional sense of belonging.

The following morning I wake up, pack away my things and head for the road, feeling more than a little relieved. I love the people, the spectacle, the creativity, but after only three days I am already over wearing black and committing to the hour-long ritual of piling on eyeliner and trying to do something interesting and goth-like with my hair. I'm just so crap at it. I even tried buying a mini purple pirate hat with a veil at the bazaar to jazz up my look, but I couldn't get the angle right and ended up looking like a complete twat. I've had a lot of fun here, but I have to face facts: I would make a pretty pathetic goth.

H is for... Hill Baggers

Hill bagging has nothing to do with sex

In 1980s Britain, according to film director Danny Boyle, the concept of a 'trainspotter' began to mean 'anybody who is obsessive about something trivial'. 'It's a very male thing,' he claims. 'The more chaotic the world becomes and the less we understand how it works, the more we want to conquer a territory.' Hold that thought.

Those who partake in hill bagging, a quintessentially British hobby, have a burning desire to 'collect' – reach the summit of – all of the hills on a given list, of which there are many. Most lists of hills have a name, like the 'Munros' of Scotland – with summits of at least 3,000 feet – or the 214 'Wainwrights' of the Lake District, with summits of at least 1,000 feet.

So how do you define a hill? This is a surprisingly controversial subject and one addressed in the book *The Relative Hills of Britain* by Alan Dawson (otherwise known as the Hill Baggers' bible). For Alan, the definition of a hill shouldn't just be about its height, because it may be on high ground – climbing 1.1 miles high in Denver is easier than doing the same in Norfolk – it should be relative to its surroundings, i.e. how it drops on all sides. This is often described as a hill's prominence or 're-ascent'.

Based on this definition, Alan identified 1,556 British hills that have at least 150 metres of prominence. Rather than name them after himself, he decided to call them Marilyns. I'll leave you to work that one out.

Apprehensive at the prospect of a weekend climbing hills with a nasty head cold, I booked a plane to Northumberland. 'Oh come on!' my friend had said to me the night before. 'Going walking with a bunch of middle-aged men – how hard can it be?' This made me feel marginally better. Maybe he was right. Maybe they would all be puffed-out geriatrics meeting up for a gentle stroll.

On the way to the airport, I get a text message from my mum.

'I'm worried about you going out on the hills with your cold. BE CAREFUL and don't take too many risks!'

Risks?! What on earth did she think I was going to be doing?

I take up residence in the Gatwick Airport Starbucks and navigate onto the *Relative Hills of Britain* forum, opening an article on a recent ascent of an offshore Marilyn. Home to around 14,000 breeding pairs of gannets, Stac Lee is 172 metres high, and 81 miles west of the Scottish mainland, so it can only be reached at certain times of the year by a chartered boat. The accompanying pictures show the team leaping from the boat onto barnacle-covered rocks lapped by crashing waves, laden with crampons, climbing ropes, harnesses and helmets. Oh shit.

Despite this, it isn't until I turn up to meet the group of twenty-two baggers the following morning, me dressed in Cotton Traders canvas boots and a white cagoule, that I realise the full extent of my mistake. Contrastingly clad in expert walking gear, complete with poles and rucksacks, the crowd before me is like a weird marriage of Bear Grylls and *Last of the Summer Wine*.

'Erm, do you have any gaiters?' my contact, Rick, asks me.

'Uh... no,' I say, 'but I have wellies?' I pull my bright red Hunters out of my boot.

The men laugh.

I turn the colour of my boots.

I am assigned for a day's 'tump' bagging (thirty-metre prominence hills) with Rob, an outdoorsy-looking chap with windswept unruly hair and a wise face. Last month Rob became the first man to complete the entire set of Marilyns, a feat worthy of the national news. He is also the top of the list for 'tumps' and 'trig points' (triangulation pillars), the latter of which are four-foot concrete pillars erected by Ordnance Survey to measure the exact layout and height of the country. Bagging trig points is also a highly competitive endeavour, with 2,600 contributors currently logging their bags on TrigpointingUK. Around 6,200 remain in the British countryside, of which Rob has bagged 6,140.

'What is the highest number of hills you've bagged in a day?' I ask him as we pull away in his blue Skoda.

'Well, the Paddy Buckley Round has forty-seven fells,' he says, 'including Snowdon, so I guess that's the most. It's a sixty-mile run over twenty-four hours.'

My mouth falls and my eyebrows soar. 'You ran sixty miles over mountains?'

'Yeah,' he shrugs. 'There are three challenges like that in the UK. I've completed all of them.'

Rob also travels all around the world climbing 'ultras', the most prominent hills in the world (e.g. Mount Kilimanjaro), of which there are 1,526. He holds second position to a chap who has bagged two more than him, but a lot of them are in antisocial parts of Afghanistan and war-torn regions of Africa, so he doubts he will ever complete the list.

Now feeling more than a little nervous about having to spend the day climbing hills with this Superman, you can imagine my joy when I discover that our first hill of the day is a 'drive-up' – driving as near to the top as possible and walking the short way to the summit. After locating the summit with the help of a map and Rob's trusty GPS device, and taking a photo of the bleak view of nothing, we head back in the car for our next bag. Struggling to grasp the point of all this, I pull out my phone and do some important Facebook browsing while we drive to the next tump.

'I love a well-hung gate,' Rob says, deadpan, as he holds one open for me on the way up our second hill. He runs his hand along the metal, appreciating the craftsmanship. I don't think there is any innuendo whatsoever in this statement. I think Rob loves a well-hung gate.

The top of the hill is declared with a ceremonious four-foot concrete pillar. Rob offers to take a photo of me standing next to the trig point so I can register my first bag. Lost for inspiration when it comes to incorporating a concrete block into a hilarious pose, I settle on the absolute classic of just standing next to it and pulling a grumpy British face. One for the grandkids.

Over the course of the day we summit Ridlees Cairn, Calf Lee, Dumbhope Law, Crigdon and Highspoon, all as equally arduous and purposeless as the next, but we do it with 25 per cent gusto and 75 per cent trudge, happy to be getting the hills in our figurative bags.

The final hill of the day involves crossing a stream and picking our way through waist-high heather for about twenty minutes, uphill. If you took the heather away, we would look like two escapees from the Ministry of Silly Walks. I didn't even know my legs could get up that high. Feeling utterly exhausted,

I make regular stop-offs to 'take photographs', my wheezes and pants easily mistakable for labour pains.

'I'll catch you up,' I lie. 'Just taking a picture of this interesting-looking log.'

When we finally make it to the top, Rob isn't sure where the summit is, so we have to traverse back down the hill and wrestle our way through the heather to climb yet another peak. Six days later, or so it felt, we make it to the summit of the second peak, where I promptly collapse into a heap of horrendously sharp heather and stay there for a few minutes, pretending I am pleased with my decision. Rob stares intently at his GPS, waiting for it to register. A smile creeps across his face, the kind of 'oh aren't I silly' smile someone might make when they put their shoes on the wrong feet.

'Oh no, my mistake,' he says casually, 'the first hill was the summit.'

I could have killed him.

Marilyn baggers have a 'hall of fame' that you can enter once you reach 600 summits. There are currently 260 members, some of whom gather every few weeks to celebrate various milestones, and this weekend will celebrate Rick and Jen's final English Marilyn.

One of the four women in the group looks up at me when Rob and I arrive back at the holiday cottages. Not a bagger herself, Moira occasionally accompanies her husband Iain on his bagging trips.

'Who are you, then?'

'I'm Lucy,' I say, feeling like I have to explain myself. 'I'm here to research hill bagging for a chapter in a book I'm writing.'

She looks satisfied. 'Well, you know that the only reason

these men do this sort of thing is to get out of doing jobs around the house, don't you?'

I laugh.

'I'm deadly serious.' She flashes Iain a knowing look.

As we sit around introducing ourselves, the group ask me to tell them about my other letters.

'A lot of them are linked to sex, aren't they?' Moira muses as I explain what it means to be polyamorous.

'Erm, I guess some of them are a bit, yes.'

'Well, don't worry,' she says. 'Hill bagging has nothing to do with sex.'

A timely cup of tea emerges from the kitchen. I get up to accept it and settle back down next to Lionel, a twitcher (birdwatcher) as well as a bagger. He tells me about a play he went to see – *Dead Funny* – in which a group of men get together and re-enact the skits of dead comedians.

'I thought it was brilliant,' he said to me, offering me a tot of whisky for my tea. 'Then my wife said to me – "You know it's about people like you, don't you?"' He laughs. 'It was a parody about people who become obsessive about arbitrary things.' He pauses to think, shrugs his shoulders and says, 'I still think it was brilliant.'

With seven tumps now ticked off my list, we all meet in a local pub later that evening for dinner and a debriefing session. I talk to Martin by the bar, a retired bagger who spends almost every day travelling from hill to hill in his motorhome.

'Communities like this can only exist thanks to the internet,' he says. 'We come together from all over the country – from Croydon up to the northernmost tip of Scotland. Communities are rarely built with your neighbours these days; they're based on shared interest.'

'My parents do a bit of rambling...' I say, hoping to find some common ground.

'Whatever you do, don't ever call a hill bagger a rambler,' he interrupts me, looking stern. 'We hate it. Some people look down on trig baggers too. Well, we need to have someone to make us feel better, don't we?' He gives me a half-smile. 'Then you have island baggers, country baggers, lighthouse baggers. You can find people who bag pretty much anything.'

'What is more important,' I ask him, 'enjoying the walk or bagging the hill?'

'Well, both really.' He shrugs. 'We all love walking, but the bagging gives you a purpose, something to aim for.' He takes a sip of his beer.

'It's hard to explain it to an outsider.' He thinks for a moment, remembering something. 'OK, for example, I met a couple walking in Austria. I was on my way up a hill, and they were on the way down it, and when I asked them what the top was like, they said, "We didn't go to the top. We got close, but we'd planned to head home at lunchtime, so we turned around"' – his mouth drops – 'I just couldn't believe it. They were that close to the summit and they didn't visit it? That sort of thing is just so hard for a hill bagger to swallow.'

He is deadly serious, but I get the sense he knows it's a bit ridiculous. And therein is the joy. To me, the arbitrariness of it all is what makes this hobby so damn wonderful. Yes, it's pointless. But isn't kicking a leather ball between two posts pointless? Isn't toiling over a jigsaw puzzle only to dismantle it pointless? Isn't life itself pointless? At least hill bagging doesn't pretend to be anything else. It is a celebration of purposelessness.

In a publication of the *Marilyn Hall of Fame News* (I think we can all wonder at how we've survived this long without this publication in our lives), Alan Dawson writes about the seven stages of hill bagging:

Stage 1: Ignorance. You are blissfully unaware that there is such a thing as bagging, enjoying the hills for their own sake rather than reducing them to ticks on a list.

Stage 2: Disdain. You find out that lists of hills exist, and you think the people that do this sort of thing are odd; 'a form of pond life, in the same genus as nerds and trainspotters'.

Stage 3: Denial. Slow changes occur as you continue to enjoy hill walking. You might start to keep a log of them and develop a preference for climbing new hills rather than repeating old ones. But you are definitely not a bagger, or so you tell yourself.

Stage 4: Acceptance. You meet a group of baggers and discover they are pretty normal people who seem to be having a good time, calling into question your pond-life assumptions. It takes time, but eventually you give in, and realise that you are one of them.

Stage 5: Devotion. By now it is all out in the open. You are a bagger. Your holidays are devoted to bagging. You buy specialist equipment, and ticking off the hills as quickly as possible becomes more important than an enjoyable walk. You enjoy the sense of purpose; 'like the heady days of a passionate love affair'.

Stage 6: Ambivalence. The passion starts to fade, and you start to choose a party or a football match over climbing an underwhelming hill. You still enjoy bagging, and your list continues to grow, but you start to weigh up the pros and cons of each hill and will consider other factors, such as the cost of petrol or the weather, when planning your trips.

Stage 7: Defection. Some may choose to shift their focus from bagging onto other things like families or careers. Others might defect to another form of bagging, like trigs or country summits. This stage isn't inevitable, but many reach it.

Although still going out with friends for hill-bagging activities, Alan admits to reaching the 'defection' stage himself. He has chosen to survey the height of hills as an alternative passion, lugging the expensive equipment to the top of hills and staying at the summit for up to an hour, sometimes more, to ensure an accurate reading.

After dinner, we head back en masse to the cottages for a nightcap. Bottles of expensive whisky are passed around as Alan plugs his laptop into the huge flat-screen TV for the traditional baggers' singing session. A karaoke version of 'Daydream Believer' can be heard, and a photo of Stac Lee appears in the background behind cascading lyrics. The words have been changed to pay homage to those who made the climb earlier this year.

Climbing up Stac Lee, would not frighten me.
I'm a daydream believer in a summiting team.

So follows a similar rendition of 'Unchained Melody' and 'Fairytale of New York': 'Your whinging and nagging is spoiling the bagging.'

This has to be one of the most eccentric and endearing hobbies imaginable.

The following morning is the big one: a climb up Peel Fell, where Rick and Jen will be ticking off their final English Marilyn. Six of us head off at 8.30 for the drive to the England–Scotland border.

I muscle my way into the car with Alan and Martin and quiz them during the hour-long drive. 'Most baggers start out collecting something,' Alan explains in his considered and articulate baritone. 'Stamps, bus tickets, car numbers, trains. You have to have the "ticking-off" gene to get into bagging.'

Alan's book contains details of each hill, along with a box to tick when it's been bagged, but no information on where to park, the best routes to take, warnings about unfriendly landowners, etc. You had to work out such things for yourselves until websites started popping up all over the place to share this advice. He has sold around 3,500 copies over 22 years.

'Have you ever collected anything?' Alan asks me.

'I collected stamps and cuddly foxes as a kid,' I tell him. 'And I keep a note of all the countries I've visited.'

'Oh, OK, so you have a bit of the instinct,' Alan says. 'You get it.'

'Yeah, I think so,' I nod. 'I guess you can just look at what I am doing now to see that. I like to tick things off.'

'That's good.' Alan seems genuinely pleased that I understand. 'When I saw your project, I thought, "Ah, that makes sense – yes – the alphabet." I got it, totally.'

'Some hill baggers worry that what we do is a bit sad,' Alan continues. 'But I ask them, "What's the alternative? Going to the pub every night? Shopping? Watching reality TV?" I think that's sadder.'

Alan got into bagging when he was looking for a purpose in

his life. 'I think everyone is looking for that,' he says, 'especially young men. It's a real problem.' He has never had a career as such, but has done lots of different jobs, from teaching to working with computers, so he needed something else to focus on. He settled on hill walking, which quickly turned into bagging.

'Is it ever dangerous?' I ask them.

'Oh yes,' Alan says. Martin nods in agreement. 'One of the group died out on a hill. She was out bagging alone when she went missing. She was found eventually, four years later by some canoeists down by the shoreline. It could have been anything – hypothermia, I would think – but we don't know.'

'There was someone else who died this year as well,' Martin says. 'A keen bagger, but not known to us. He died on Lewis. I think he may have been blown off the top.'

I blow my lips out. 'Wow. It's so much more dangerous than I realised.'

'Well, you have to put it all in perspective,' Alan says. 'A lot of us have lost loved ones to cancer, that's much more common. We're a responsible bunch, but occasionally anyone can get caught off-guard. One of the women at dinner last night lost her husband on a hill. She was with him when he died. That has to be about as bad as it gets really; I can't imagine what that was like.'

It's not only the hills that are a danger to baggers. In 1993 Fiona Torbet (née Graham) was staying at a B & B in the Western Highlands to do some solo bagging when her husband alerted the authorities that she had failed to return home. It was presumed that she had run into trouble on the hills, and it wasn't until a year later (when Fiona's bag was found in a ditch near the B & B) that a local police search was prompted. Her body was eventually found in the grounds of the B & B, where she had been murdered by the owner's son.

Before her untimely death, she and Alan were working on a similar list of 2,000–2,500-foot summits. Alan has since completed them and christened the summits 'Grahams' in memory of Fiona.

Much like the other communities, talk about what people do in their outside lives is rare. 'The question isn't what do you do for a living, it's what hill did you last climb?' says Martin. 'When I die, I want my ashes scattered on a hill I haven't done yet, so I can get my last bag in!'

With that, we pull over, tighten our rucksacks and begin the trek up Peel Fell. The ascent starts on a nice gentle path, but it isn't long before we go off-piste to find a more direct way to the top, thrashing our way through a forest and crawling on all fours to avoid the more inhospitable branches.

'Put your hood up, Lucy, and watch out for your eyes,' Rick warns me.

After a bog crossing and a leap over a ditch, the real climbing starts. Every time we get over a ledge that I think is the summit, another appears in the distance, seemingly stretching on forever.

To distract myself from the exhaustion, I talk Alan through my other letters.

'I'm starting to learn that a lot of what we think makes us different is just completely made up,' I self-righteously proclaim as we near the end of my story so far.

Alan jumps on my point. 'I like that. Everything is made up, isn't it? Apart from the hills – they're not made up – I think that's what I like about them.'

Some of the summits of Marilyns, 'humps' (hills of at least one hundred-metre prominence) and 'tumps' are on private land, so the group often run into what they call GOMLs ('Get off my land' types). Sometimes they avoid this by climbing the hills in the dark, or whenever they think it's unlikely that the landowner will be out and about on the land. Some even view bagging as a political act, stemming from the right of the working-class man to get out of the city and walk in the wild.

'But some of the landowners didn't like that,' Martin says, giving me a much-needed opportunity to catch my breath. 'A lot of privately owned land is badly managed; kept a certain way to be a playground for the rich, so they can come out and shoot their grouse without being disturbed by commoners. As long as we keep walking, we keep exercising our rights.'

I think of Auriol and tell him about her concern that people will drop litter and leave gates open if given the right to roam. Alan looks confused. 'I don't know any baggers who do either of those things,' he says. 'Most of them have a real appreciation of the countryside and want to preserve it.'

Martin nods in agreement. 'Yeah, I always pick up any rubbish I see when I'm out for a walk.'

'You get some grumpy landowners who resent that there is a right of way across their land,' Alan says. 'But most landowners are nice people; as long as you're polite, you rarely get any trouble.'

'It's worse in Ireland,' Martin says, 'because the access laws don't really exist, so it's ambiguous where you can and can't walk. You might be chased by a farmer with a pitchfork or invited into his house for a cup of tea. It's a bit of a lottery.'

When we finally make it to the summit, the feeling is euphoric. The trees on the horizon look like a herd of elephants walking trunk to tail. Jen and Rick ceremonially hold hands and ascend the highest point together to exuberant cheers from the group. This is Rick's 1,200th 'hump' so he is now entitled to enter the 'hump hall of fame'. To initiate him the group breaks into a chant.

'Hump hall of fame, hump hall of fame. All in all, glad we came. Peel Fell – hooray!'

Cake, whisky and plastic cups appear from a backpack to mark the occasion, and we manage to drink an entire bottle between six of us, keeping us warm on the blustery top as the rain starts to descend.

Once his surveying is complete, Alan rushes over to the group.

'We forgot a very important toast!' he says in a mild panic. 'Everyone, get your cups back out.' He pulls another bottle of whisky from his backpack and fills us all up. 'Here's to Lucy completing another chapter of her book!'

I is for... Intentional Communities

Folding sheets is an art form, you know ... It's absolutely delightful

In the early days, the Findhorn Foundation was known locally as 'that mad bunch of hippies on the hill' and allegedly referred to by the Home Office as Harmless Eccentrics, or simply 'HE' in their official files. But a lot has changed over the last decade. Recently dubbed 'ahead of its time' by the *Guardian*, the world-renowned intentional community near Inverness in Scotland is now widely accepted as a pioneering community in permaculture, sustainable-energy production and the cultivation of mindfulness.

The three 'founders', Eileen Caddy, Peter Caddy and Dorothy Maclean, had fallen on hard times, or so the story goes, and were forced to live in caravans on the outskirts of a village called Findhorn. Through following their 'inner guidance' and listening to the 'intelligence of nature', they managed to grow a bountiful garden of miraculous proportion. Tales of the 40 lb cabbages and roses that bloomed in the snow travelled for thousands of miles, and listeners flocked from as far as Australia and California to join the community that now boasts 250 permanent members.

I was pointed in the direction of the Findhorn Foundation (hereafter, simply Findhorn) by a friend, on the promise that I should 'expect a miracle' as per their slogan, but with little else by way of explanation. Excited by the prospect of my first jaunt into the New Age spiritual world, I picked up the phone and booked myself in for an experience week.

Travelling an hour north of Inverness, I pass endless fields of vivid green, old Presbyterian churches and small isolated villages made of crudely cut stone. As the train sways from side to side, I speculate about the people I will meet, the smell of incense and damp wool conjuring its way into my nostrils, accompanied by images of long beards and rainbow dresses.

After a short taxi ride from Forres railway station, I arrive at Cluny – an imposing grey-stone building that houses forty members of the Findhorn community – and am shown to my shared room on the first floor. There is no lock on the door, but the room is comfortable enough, and I am pleasantly surprised to find running water and central heating.

Before I even have time to don leather sandals and make a burdock-root tea, I am summoned to the Beech Tree Room to meet my fellow course attendees.

Huge south-facing bay windows flood the room with light as we arrange ourselves on mustard chairs around a forest of white candles. A hodgepodge of age, gender and nationality, the group are dressed in everything from fleeces and jeans to brightly coloured cotton dresses and woolly tights. Closer to stereotype, in a flannel shirt and corduroy trousers, a gentle middle-aged man with a bushy white beard stands up.

'Hello, everybody,' he says in a soft Yorkshire accent. 'I am Paul, and this is Gabriella,' he points to a petite, elven-looking lady wearing a billowy dress and wooden jewellery. 'We will be your focalisers for the week.'

He continues, 'Now, as is customary here, we will "tune in" to each other.' He puts his hands out in front of him in prayer position. 'I want you to place your palms together, put your thumbs to the right, then reach out to both sides and hold hands with your neighbours.'

Shit. I don't know why this was so unexpected; of course hippies hold hands. I take a deep breath and reach out for the hands either side of me. To my right is a middle-aged, tall man in a loose cotton shirt. His hands are large and cool. To my left is a younger man, perhaps in his early twenties with spiky ash-blond hair. His hand is warm and a little damp. He gives me a nervous smile.

'Now,' Paul continues, 'I want you to work on bringing yourselves to the present and feeling for the energy of the group; try to connect to it. Once you feel fully connected, pass a squeeze around the group to indicate that we are all here.'

Feel the energy? Hmmm. The only thing I feel right now is incredibly self-conscious. I close my eyes and try to lose myself in the sensation of my hands, feeling for the alleged energy. It doesn't work, and before long, my hand is squeezed by the tall man to my right. I pass the pressure along like a fraud and am relieved when we get to break the circle.

Gabriella stands up. 'Now you are all invited to share with the group,' she says in a hushed American lilt, pausing for a drawn-out, enlightened smile. 'Sharing means to speak openly about your feelings, and it's a big part of life here at Findhorn. You each have about five minutes to talk, introduce yourself and tell us what brought you here.'

Jumping in early, keen to get this over and done with, I explain that I am here to learn what life is like in an intentional community and tell the group about my decision to write this book, to remove my blinkers and open my mind. I tell them that I have always been interested in a more community-focused way of living, but that my corporate life seems to have taken me down a different path, to the point that I haven't met a single neighbour in my London apartment building. I wonder out loud if this way of living has also washed away some of what made me unique in my earlier life: the creativity I had as a child, the zest for life and the oneness I had always felt with nature, having grown up surrounded by animals. Out of nowhere, my voice starts to shake, and I have an overwhelming urge to cry. I realise that I have never spoken so openly to a group of complete strangers before and breathe a sigh of relief when my time is over, feeling exposed and vulnerable.

The sharing of the group is tinged with tragedy. A few members have recently lost a loved one, or been sick themselves, and hope that coming here will inspire life in them again. Most have known about Findhorn since the seventies and had felt a 'calling' to come here ever since. I am impressed with how emotionally articulate everyone is, seemingly far more comfortable in this exposing environment than I am.

The young man to my left reveals himself as Max, who has travelled here from Germany, and the tall gent to my right introduces himself as Sten from Denmark. His voice is deep and calm, as if harbouring all the wise secrets of the earth. I like him a lot. The more everybody talks, the more I like them too. Maybe they aren't so strange after all.

At the end of our session, Paul points at the flickering candle. 'Now we will all tune out,' he says, reaching his hands out to the group as we re-form the circle. 'And we will all blow the candle out together. Who shall we send its light to?' he asks.

I have no idea what he is talking about. One of the group steps forward. 'Can we send it to a dear friend I recently lost, please?' Paul smiles and closes his eyes, gesturing for us all to blow together.

After a lunch of salad, pulses and rice cakes, we are given a tour of The Park, home to around a hundred community members. I feel as if I have somehow wandered onto the set of *The Hobbit* as we walk past homes made from whisky barrels, eco-houses with grass roofs, log piles, compost mounds, shrines, wood carvings, wicker arches, overflowing brightly coloured flower borders and magnificent sprawling trees. Birds chirp, and the air is thick with wood smoke. As we walk, I am flooded with a strange sense of nostalgia, as if I have stepped into my own imagined memory of a simpler time. It feels romantic, and I feel a pang of belonging, as if I have somehow come home. I've probably just read too much Tolkien.

The community strives to be entirely self-sustaining, we are told, as we are shown around the printing press, pottery shop, weaving studio and candlestick workshop. The group smile serenely as we walk, sharing observations of our new surroundings. One of the women stops to smell a beautiful purple flower, closing her eyes for longer than I would ever find comfortable.

As we walk, our tour guide explains how the community functions.

Each foundation member is expected to work thirty-five hours a week in a service department – gardening, kitchen, maintenance, etc. – and in exchange is provided with all of their basic living needs, plus £50 a week. I think about how much of my pay cheque goes on rent, bills and food living in London and decide that £50 of expendable income each week doesn't actually sound that bad.

The main sources of income for the community are the workshops, experience weeks and other spiritual courses that run for fifty weeks of the year. Vegetarian meals are grown and prepared on-site, and eaten together in the community centre, and there are daily meditations and spiritual chanting as well. Waste is managed by tanks of living organisms (apparently snails eat poo – who knew?), and three huge wind turbines take care of the community's energy needs.

At the end of our tour, we stop off to visit the nature sanctuary, a meditation dome built from dry stone covered in heather. We are here to pick our Angels to guide us on our path over the next week. Of course we are.

'The Angel cards represent qualities we all have,' Paul explains as we all settle onto small cushions scattered around the floor. 'The Angel you choose will tell you what you need to focus on this week.'

Paul instructs us to wait until we feel a calling to a particular card and then reach forward and pick it up. On the flip side of that card is the name of our Angel.

The first person to pick is a dry-witted Australian who has already proved to be a bountiful source of laughs and entertainment for the group. She leans forward and picks a card on the opposite side from where she is sitting. Flipping it over, she reveals the Angel of Humour. The group share knowing looks as the atmosphere becomes noticeably more intense. I remind myself not to get sucked in, recalling my distrust of horoscopes. I cannot make these cards relevant just because I want them to be.

Next up is an endlessly smiling lady who has just been through a 'rebirthing' process, which she had meticulously explained to us over lunch. She picks the Angel of Birth.

Next, a concert pianist who has journeyed to Findhorn to kick-start a new life after a difficult divorce, picks the Angel of Awakening.

The more people make their selections, the more I find myself being drawn in. I just can't help it.

Then it comes to me. I am not sure if I feel drawn or just that I should go sooner rather than later. I lean forward, pick up a card and flip it over. Staring back at me is the Angel of Understanding. What better Angel to guide me through a year of exploring the different paths people have chosen than the Angel of Understanding? This can't be a coincidence, surely? She is perfect, I think, completely ignoring my own advice about getting drawn in. I look closer at the picture of her and... holy shit... she is reading a book!

I guess I am becoming quite accustomed to the hand-holding thing, because when we all pile into the Old Ballroom to close our first day with a session of 'sacred dancing', I surprise myself by finding it both fun and relaxing. At first, we all smile like idiots to hide our embarrassment as we shuffle around in circles holding hands, our bodies moving from side to side together as if one organism, but after the first few songs the awkwardness wears off, and by the end of the two-hour lesson my cheeks ache from smiling.

Even after one day here I feel like a part of myself I didn't know existed has been ignited: the part of me that feels instead of thinks. I watch this group of adults skipping around in a circle, swaying and looking into each other's eyes to the dulcet tones of Enya, and impulsively decide to try and incorporate the hand-holding and circle-dancing thing with my friends next time I see them. Perhaps in a fancy restaurant or bar during a night out. I have such lucky friends.

*

An incense stick burns in the corner as I walk into the 8 a.m. meditation in The Park the following morning. The group are positioned around a candle in the dimly lit Sanctuary. Smoke rises from the centre and spirals around the room. I take my seat just in time for the sound of the gong, signifying the start of a meditation.

The room falls quiet for thirty minutes, aside from the sound of gentle breathing and the odd muffled snore. This time last year I would have been completely out of my comfort zone in a situation like this, but after struggling my way through the meditation retreat and omming with Ivan the acrobat, I am now quite accustomed to (although still not good at) the practice of meditation.

My mind drifts to yesterday evening when we were instructed to 'attune' to our service departments to perform our daily 'love in action' (otherwise known as work). Posters had been pinned to three corners of the room, reading 'Homecare', 'Kitchen' and 'Gardening'.

'It's important that you tune in and listen to your intuition to tell you where you should be, rather than just walking to where you feel you want to be,' Paul had said.

The meditation gong drags me from my memory, and I leave the Sanctuary in a dream-like state to walk to the homecare 'nest', a cosy, Enid Blyton-esque room with two sofas and a number of misshapen wooden chairs. The walls are covered in posters, paintings and pinned messages describing the difference between fairies, gnomes and sprites.

'Hello there.' A gentle voice warms me as I take a seat. The voice belongs to Rory, the focaliser of the homecare department, who wears a baseball cap over his long white hair. American and a self-professed hippie, Rory arrived here in the seventies after a stint in Esalen, a famous commune in California. I try and fail to picture him in a suit, walking out of Bank station at 7 a.m. clutching a Starbucks and a copy of the *FT*.

Rory leads us in a fifteen-minute 'sharing' session, during which people say mundane things like 'I am feeling good today' and 'I had a nice breakfast' before tuning in, deciding on our jobs for the day and sending the light from our candle to Syria. Just two days in and that sentence doesn't even seem odd to me now.

I am to spend the morning cleaning and restocking the guest apartments. 'Take your time!' Rory shouts after me. 'Don't kill the job.'

After a day spent cleaning places that were already clean and stopping every hour for a cup of tea, the day finishes back in our group, where we meet for 'games'.

Now familiar with making tits of ourselves, our group embrace the ridiculous games with gay abandon. 'I am going to walk around and whisper an animal in your ear,' says Sarah, our young games instructor, who was born and raised at Findhorn, 'then I want you to drop to all fours, close your eyes and crawl around the room making the noise of that animal.' We all laugh at the idea, practising generic animal noises under our breath.

'The aim of the game is to find someone else making the same noise as you. Then when you have found everyone in your family, and you are all in one big group, you can open your eyes.'

Sarah walks around the room. 'Dog,' she whispers in my ear. I am elated. I am great at dog impressions.

We spend the next fifteen minutes meowing, barking, mooing and oinking our way around the room before we find ourselves in four groups.

The point of this exercise was very unclear, but it was a lot of fun and I am embracing this holiday from my ego, a challenge to my British reserve, where I can do silly things and just enjoy them for the sake of it. It is a new concept to me, as is this bond I have built so quickly with a group of strangers who wear their emotions on their sleeve, encouraging you to do the same and making you feel safe. There is a closeness in vulnerability, and I don't know why it has taken me so long to learn this lesson.

During my lunch break on day three, I interview Yvonne, who runs a programme to encourage better links with the corporate world and spread the Findhorn philosophy. Yvonne is a professional, no-nonsense character, wearing a smart office-like dress over a petite frame, finishing her look with bright pink lipstick.

'I never in a million years thought I would end up in a place like this,' she begins. 'I came in through the "life in crisis" door. I had been living a luxurious expat life in a seven-bedroom house with my ex-husband; financially rich, but emotionally poor. I was an English literature teacher and very closed down to anything that smelled of religion. I came here to find an answer to a particular question, and my voice just told me to stay here. So, after many tears, that's what I did.'

She continues, 'I helped to create the Building Bridges team because I found Findhorn too inward-looking and not spreading the word enough about what they do. I wanted to get out there, be relevant and make an impact, not just live in a little bubble. I thought every CEO and politician out there should do an experience week, so we should go out and meet people where they are, not just wait for them to come to us.'

'Do you ever find it frustrating here?' I ask her, revealing my impatience with the constant tea breaks and achingly slow pace of life.

'Sometimes,' she says, looking strained. 'My job can be especially frustrating because money is a highly contentious issue here. We claim there is no separation and that everybody is all part of the same thing, but with the corporate world there can be a real "them and us" mindset.'

She takes a sip of herbal tea and waves at a young girl balancing on a rock in the communal garden. 'Our aims are bringing love into the world and shifting consciousness, and many think that is at complete odds with making money, but I disagree with this. I think we could do wonderful things if we had more money.' Her eyes brighten. 'We are all interested in non-monetary abundance – life here is very, very rich – but we do need money because we still have to make our budget sheet balance every year.'

The sun rises on day four at Findhorn, and I make my way to the homecare nest for our tuning in. After a second cup of tea and a round of sharing about how good a night's sleep we all got, Rory sends me to restock an apartment half a mile down the road. I arrive fifteen minutes later, discover the job has already been done, turn around and walk back in a huff.

'Oh, I must have already done it,' Rory says when I return, without a hint of apology. 'But you were obviously supposed to take that walk.' He smiles and winks, looking pleased that he has apparently solved the mystery of his mistake.

'Why don't you come and help me in the laundry?' he suggests. 'Folding sheets is an art form, you know.' Unconvinced, I follow him into a big warm room, draped with sheets and smelling strongly of lemons. He teaches me his method of folding the sheets and ironing them with his hands until they are perfect squares. With each new sheet, a look of sheer joy lights up his face, as if this is the best thing he could possibly be doing. 'It's absolutely delightful.' He looks up at me, life bursting from his eyes.

His level of contentment for doing such menial work sparks a pang of envy. Why can't I find joy in such simple tasks? I rush through all of my jobs, always thinking about what's next rather than absorbing myself into what I am doing and enjoying the moment. Perhaps because I would lose at least three decades from my life if I took this long over such simple tasks, and that's a lot of social-media scrolling and Netflix binging I would be missing out on.

As we walk back to the homecare nest to tune out before lunch, Rory tells me that he was rejected for a job in Tesco a few years ago. I wonder what they would have made of him taking three hours to stack a shelf (and finding the process delightful). As I reach out to open the door, my thoughts are interrupted by a thwack in the face.

'We will have to ask the gardener to trim it for us,' Rory says of my rogue branch assailant.

'I could do it?' I offer.

'No, the gardener might have a special relationship with that particular bush, and you can't interrupt that.' He flashes me one of his vacant smiles, opening into a laugh when he sees my bemused expression.

I recall being told by our guide on the first day that Findhorn gardeners will discuss any pruning or felling with the tree beforehand, giving warning, explaining why the action needs to happen and seeking reconciliation. Even the household appliances here are given human names and treated as individuals.

Rory is still laughing. 'And I can tell you exactly what he will say' – he points at the homecare nest in front of us – 'he'll say, "It's your hut that's in the way, not the bush!"'

The next two days whizz by in a sea of hand-holding, meditation, cups of herbal tea and a 'nature bathing' session where we literally spend three hours hugging trees in the rain. Then, before I know it, I am sitting back in the Beech Tree Room with my group for our final tuning-out session. We are each asked to share something with the group: a song, a poem, a dance, a lesson in how to make origami hearts.

When I am finally passed the 'sharing stone', I find myself close to tears again. I had come here for what I thought would be a relatively transactional experience but am leaving with much more. I have learned how important community is, enjoyed the warm, fuzzy feeling of being part of this group, and realised the deep connection you can build with other humans if you are brave enough to be vulnerable with them.

The people of Findhorn are full of compassion, gentle and thoughtful. They are never too proud to dance around like a child or cry at the beauty of a sunset. They allow themselves to feel and do not fear judgement.

I have enjoyed getting to know each and every one of my fellow experience-weekers and we have spent so much time together I feel a remarkably strong bond has developed between us all. Often when I refer to people as 'nice', this is shorthand for 'as dull as an episode of *Cornwall with Caroline Quentin*' (sorry if you love this show; I use it to send myself to sleep), but this group are some of the most interesting people I have ever met; full of intrigue, warmth and passion, and open to anything, even crawling around with their eyes shut while honking like a goose.

I know, I know. One week in the commune and I'm all hand-holding and tree-hugging. Well, not quite – there were a few things I struggled with. Like asking forgiveness from the hedge in need of pruning, asking Helen the Hoover if she minded helping me with the task of cleaning the meditation room, or the countless stories of community members having lengthy conversations about the meaning of life with birds, moles and various other woodland creatures.

The community is operationally dysfunctional, I have no idea how it works, and any management consultant would have an absolute field day here. I know that if I lived here, this is what I would struggle with the most. I would buckle at the inefficiency of it all. I would want to make things work better, stop the pointless cleaning and re-cleaning of everything, and the endless talking just for the sake of it. But despite its inefficiencies, it all just, sort of, works.

'What does the future look like for you?' I had asked Yvonne as I was packing up after our interview on day three.

'I don't know.' She looked disoriented. 'But I don't want to be a part of the slick world out there. It has no heart. I could have lived a very selfish life, just looking after myself, but I like helping to facilitate the evolution of human consciousness. I am too nourished by being here to leave.'

I too felt nourished at Findhorn, a community where I believed anything, trusted everybody; a holiday from my pride, my cynicism, my black-and-white view of the world. I genuinely feel that I was supposed to come to this place and that a small miracle did happen. Even if that miracle was as simple as a newfound love for folding sheets.

J is for... Jack Duckworth

*They were so moved by the heart
stuff of that little pigeon*

OK, OK, I'll just come out and say it – J is a really hard letter, like *really* hard, and as much as I am sure you would love to be reading about jousting, judo or joinery, I'm not sure that any of those can really be described as a subculture. And for those of you who don't know who Jack Duckworth is, shame on you. Despite the occasional wrestle with intellectual snobbery on this journey so far, there is one thing I am not embarrassed to admit: I bloody love *Coronation Street*. As something that my mum and I would watch religiously together three times a week since I was tiny, the TV series has a real nostalgia for me. Jack Duckworth was one of the show's leading characters from 1979 to 2010, and what Jack was most famous for, before his penchant for 'booze and barmaids', was his love of pigeons. So I ask you to forgive the creative licence here, and travel with me to the peaceful village of Pilton in Somerset to find out more than anyone ever should about pigeons.

My hosts for this adventure are Terry and Jane Williams, owners of Somerset One Loft Race, a highly successful and stunningly located pigeon-racing business. The place has a relaxed and organised feel, sitting just over the hill from the Glastonbury Festival in the otherwise sleepy village.

Terry is a retired builder whose final project was to build the 1,000-berth loft on the land that sits directly behind us. He and Jane set to work explaining their world to me in their beautifully restored farmhouse, while Barney the Border collie busies himself with a bone under the giant oak table.

Pigeon owners (known as 'fanciers') send their birds to Terry at just twenty-eight days old, at which point he becomes responsible for their care and training for a one-off fee of £100 per bird.

'They arrive in a little box, and we learn 'em how to walk, how to feed and how to fly,' Terry explains in a charming West Country accent that reminds me of home.

'Then, when they're forty days old, we starts training 'em to go in the baskets and fly into the traps. It's all done with food. We take 'em down the garden and let 'em fly back into the lofts, then we take 'em five miles, ten miles, twenty miles and so on, building 'em up, like.'

Tomorrow is a big test for the birds. They will be released ('liberated') from Kent to race the 122 miles back home. This is all building up to the final race of the season in August, where they will be driven to Ypres and asked to navigate the 300-mile journey back to the lofts.

'This year we're also donating a thousand pounds to a local park for disabled children in Ypres,' Terry tells me. 'And an oil painting of the landscape, with a World War I pigeon transporter superimposed on top, to the Ypres museum. So people can see what it'd of looked like during the war.'

Before meeting Terry and Jane, I had treated myself to a copy of *British Homing World* magazine – page after page of middle-aged men proudly holding up their pigeons and pulling their grumpiest faces for the camera – and became engrossed in an article on messenger pigeons. It explained how the incredible homing instinct of pigeons was vital when they were used to carry messages during the war; every loft in the UK would give a few pigeons to France, and vice versa. When they flew back with a message, someone would pick it up from the pigeon and run it to the local messenger office, sometimes saving hundreds of lives in the process.

I can see a copy of the same magazine on Terry's work surface, peeking out from under a pile of unopened letters. Through the window next to it, the immaculately manicured lawn is punctuated by a big white marquee, erected in anticipation of the big race next month.

Terry follows my gaze. 'Everyone comes up 'ere on the big race day,' he explains excitedly. 'We have five hundred pigeon people; rich, poor, women, kids, millionaires, people on the dole, people in caravans. There is a whole mixture of life becoming one community, having a laugh and a joke together, until the first pigeon appears in the sky from Belgium. Last year it was all loud and jovial, then someone shouted "pigeon" and it was coming over the trees, a little dot about a thousand feet up. Then it all went silent.'

'You could hear a pin drop,' Jane jumps in, her eyes glued on Terry, willing him to continue.

'Then the pigeon circled and dropped down and the crowd erupted,' he says, gesticulating wildly with his arms. 'They didn't care whose pigeon it was, they threw their caps in the air and – "rrraaayyy" – they all cheered, 'cause that little pigeon had the bravery to come all that way by itself. Twenty minutes in front of the others, it was. We had Scottish people down – hard as nails, they were – and they were so moved by the heart stuff of that little pigeon, they had a tear in their eye. It was incredible!' He beams at the memory.

We have another cup of tea, and Terry explains that pigeon racing is typically, although not always, a blue-collar sport (despite the Queen having a royal loft). The 'cloth cap and whippet' pigeon fanciers – i.e. the Jack Duckworths – are still around, but that scene is gradually dying out. There used to be 300,000 fanciers in the UK, but now it's dwindled down to about 30,000 and the sport in this form continues to decline.

But the Williams' business is far from waning, as they keep abreast of the latest technologies and continue to adapt their business to cater to a younger crowd. The return traps are fitted with automated devices that recognise each pigeon's microchip as they return from a race, and the results go straight up online. A lot of the older fanciers didn't even know what a computer was until the Williamses went digital – but they all have one now, just so they can see the race results.

'I think those computers only get turned on for the racing season,' Jane says. 'One of the old boys used to phone up all the time and ask about his pigeons. Anyway, last year he phoned me up and said, "You'll never guess what, Jane... I've got an iPad!"'

'I write on the website every day,' Terry says. 'Pigeon bullshit, you know. It's all jovial stuff.'

'What are pigeon people like?' I ask.

'Most of 'em are really lovely, but some, specially the older ones, can be the grumpiest people you'll ever meet.' He laughs at Jane as she makes a 'watch what you're saying' face. 'It keeps older people alive, see.' He looks back at me. 'Gets 'em up and out in the morning, instead of watching the telly.'

Terry explains that a 'back-garden fancier' wouldn't spend

more than £150 on a pigeon, but those who want to win the big races will spend thousands of pounds, with the aim of selling the eggs of that pigeon afterwards. The record price for a pigeon changing hands is £275,000.

'Years ago, they would bake a loaf of bread, and use that to transport the eggs inside. Keeps 'em warm, see,' Terry says.

I ask him about a day in the life of a pigeon while he leads me outside for a tour of his lofts.

'We clean 'em out at five-thirty in the morning,' he begins. 'Then we let 'em out to fly around, stretch their wings and have a bath.'

'Do they enjoy it?'

'Oh yeah, this is what they are bred for,' he says.

Jane becomes animated. 'They go out and zip, zip, zip, all around the sky, playing and tumbling around. We let them out at six-thirty yesterday morning, and one group were enjoying it so much they didn't come back until two in the afternoon.'

Terry jumps back in again. 'If they didn't enjoy it, they'd just sit on the roof.'

He stands in the middle of the field and does an impression of himself whistling. 'I stand in the field – whistle like that – and then they all comes in. I train 'em that from day one. I whistles all the time, me – bit of disco tunes, bit of pigeon stuff.'

We walk into the loft and my eyes take a few seconds to adjust to the darkness, giving me time to drink in the smell of sawdust and warm earth. The pigeons coo softly, some perched on small wooden pegs while others busy themselves pecking at nothing on the ground. The birds don't look like the feral pigeons you see on the street. They stand taller, look leaner and their feathers lie flat, in a silky and seamless veneer that shines silver, green and blue. There is something almost regal about them.

'Are these pigeons different breeds to the ones on the street?' I ask Terry.

'No,' he smiles at me, 'but they are like the Olympic athletes of the pigeon world; bred for speed, fed a very specific diet and trained hard, so they look very different.'

In the outside area next to the lofts, yet more pigeons eat from a long metal tray filled with birdseed. It seems like quite a nice life, really. I wouldn't mind being one of Terry's pigeons. He hands me one to hold; it is calm and warm between my hands and I can feel its tiny heart beating through its soft chest.

On race day, Terry explains, the pigeons are driven through a gap out of the loft and into crates. Then he takes them out one by one, puts a green microchipped tag on their leg and scans them into the computer to be registered. The crates are then loaded onto a transporter van for the journey to the liberation site. He demonstrates this for me with one of his birds.

'They know it's race day tomorrow' – Terry looks back over his shoulder at me – 'because the routine changes a bit. Some of 'em are quiet, and some of 'em are big mouths, ya know' – he puts on his pigeon voice – '"I'm gonna win this, I'm gonna win that!"'

'Then I'll drive 'em up tonight, park up and give 'em a long rest. I open the curtains on the van at about five o'clock to let the light in – they're all asleep' – he makes a snoring noise – 'snoring away in bed. Then suddenly the door opens and they all wakes up and starts cooing. By about half six the noise gets really loud. Banging on the doors, jumping up and down' – he puts his pigeon voice back on – '"Let me out. Grrr. Let me out!"'

I look one of the pigeons in the eye as it is being held upside down for tagging, unsure whether or not to feel sorry for it.

'What happens to the pigeons after the race?' I ask Terry.

'Most fanciers will continue to breed and look after their

pigeons until they fall off their perch,' he says, 'but it depends on the owner, really.'

Of course, controversy is never far away, even in the world of pigeon racing. PETA launched a campaign against the sport a few years ago, dubbing it cruel in the way it forces the pigeons to travel so far over long stretches of water. Races incorporating a Channel crossing are high risk for the birds, and some will be consumed by the water as they fly too close to the sea to avoid the winds, or even fall into the sea from exhaustion. According to PETA's website, the loss of pigeons over the Channel is so high that the stretch of water is often referred to as 'the graveyard' in pigeon circles, although it is difficult to distinguish between those that have perished and those who have lost their way or chosen to take up residence on the steps of St Paul's.

The PETA campaign caused a lot of drama in the community, but it has since calmed down. Despite the relatively high mortality rate of these races compared to dog racing and horse racing, the sport gets less attention from anti-cruelty campaigners. I wonder if this is because we don't seem to empathise with pigeons the way we do with horses and dogs. Probably because humans have domesticated horses and dogs for thousands of years and our relationship is one of mutual interdependence, whereas pigeons are typically seen as vermin in urban settings, and food in rural settings, and so we offer and withdraw the protection of animals at the whim of our sentiment. Such is the paradox of humanity.

Hawks also take a significant number of pigeons, each able to consume up to three a day. Terry explains that Sunday is the safest day to let his birds out for a long fly, because all of the racing clubs release their birds on a Saturday – when there can be up to 30,000 pigeons in the sky at once – so by Sunday, the hawks are all full up.

The following morning I get up ludicrously early and meet Terry at 6 a.m. for the liberation in Kent. Low-hanging cloud delays the release (cloud can panic the pigeons), so we sit in the van, drink coffee from a thermos flask and put the world to rights for three hours while we wait for it to clear.

'How do the pigeons navigate?' I ask him, suddenly realising that these pigeons have never made this journey before.

'Well, the honest answer is we don't know', he says, 'and I hope it stays that way. Bit of mystery, ya know? The theory is that they've got a magnetic system in the white bit just above their beaks, so they use the magnetic fields and the ley lines of the earth to navigate.'

By 9.30 a.m. the sky is bright blue, and I stand back to video the release. Terry pulls down the lever and the pigeons fly from their baskets, meeting as a group in the air and circling a couple of times to get their bearings. Within five seconds they turn into dots and disappear over the trees, taking my vicarious sense of freedom with them as they swoop and curl gracefully out of sight.

I look back at the man standing in the field next to me, his mouth wide and his eyes locked in awe on the open sky above him, and decide that my new goal in life is to find something that moves and inspires me half as much as these birds do Terry. The ultimate dream. I wonder if my FOMO truly could be cured by finding such contentment in a pleasure so apparently small as a pigeon. I would love to think so, though there must be an easier way. One that involves a lot less... self-work. But perhaps I'll come back to this later

on, after I've crossed off another sixteen versions of myself.
God, I'm ridiculous.

K is for... The Kabbalah Centre

You need to scan it for twenty-six minutes

I open the doors of the London Kabbalah Centre, a huge Victorian building set back from Bond Street, convinced I am walking into a cult. Will I ever be the same again? Ever see my friends and family again? Ever think for myself again? I take comfort in the fact that at least I am following in the footsteps of that well-balanced and grounded celebrity Madonna.

Having done my research beforehand, I already know that Kabbalah is a branch of Judaism based on the Zohar, a thirteenth-century holy book that is alleged to reveal the hidden secrets of the Torah. Although Orthodox rabbis traditionally maintain that the study of Kabbalah be limited to married Jewish men who are over the age of forty and highly learned in Jewish law, the founders of the Kabbalah Centre, Rav Berg and his wife Karen, disagreed entirely, declaring it their life mission to bring this wisdom to the people. And so the first Kabbalah Centre was born.

My eyes are greeted with brilliant white walls, high ceilings, antique furniture and tables wrapped in crisp white cotton. Above me hangs a blue crystal chandelier.

'Great to meet you.' The girl behind the welcome desk reveals a pristine row of teeth with a well-rehearsed smile. She guides me to a large meeting room, where eighty or so young, glamorous-looking men and women sit around circular tables. The room is filled with expectant faces of varying nationalities, diverse in skin colour but not in their outward displays of wealth, revealed in designer handbags, soft leather suitcases, sharp suits, neat hairstyles and flawless complexions.

I am here for a ten-week introductory course in Kabbalah – 'Kabbalah One' – paid for by the grace of previous students who have gained from the course and wish to support the learning of others. Despite not fitting with the other chapters' format of spending one block of time with each community, this felt like my best access point into this world, so I jumped on it.

We take our pre-assigned seats around the circular tables, matching the place settings to our sticky label name badges. Our leader, John (not his real name), talks with an Israeli accent. 'Welcome to Kabbalah One,' he says. 'Each of you has been assigned an experienced Kabbalah student who will act as your mentor for the duration of the course. Please ask them questions; they are all here to help you.'

I look around the table and spot a round-faced lady waving at me. Elegant with a dark bob and a black fitted suit, she introduces herself to us as Lana. Each mentor is asked to share with the room what Kabbalah has done for them so far.

A smartly dressed man with a sharp beard stands up. 'Since studying Kabbalah, my relationships have improved, especially with my family.'

Lana is the next to take the floor. 'Kabbalah has brought me tranquillity and happiness,' she says, revealing a subtle Russian accent.

We are asked to stand up and introduce ourselves to our groups, to share our star signs and a quality about ourselves beginning with the first letter of our names. For some reason, I always panic in these situations. I feel my mouth going dry and my pulse at my temples. 'My name is Lucy,' I say. 'I am a Virgo... and I am... er... lovely.'

The woman sitting next to me, who wears a tight black dress and red high heels, takes her turn. 'I am Anna,' she says. 'I am a Scorpio, and I am... all right.' Phew, the bar is low.

When we have all finished our icebreakers – relentless Ryan being my favourite – John retakes control of the class.

'Kabbalah is not a religion,' he begins, 'so stop looking so worried.' He smiles at us, sparking a ripple of nervous laughter. 'It offers tools to help us to expand our consciousness. It is wisdom. It doesn't contradict any other belief system; in fact, it can be supplementary.'

Consciousness is here defined as a separate part of our awareness, not from our brain, not from the senses or logic, but from the soul. Lower consciousness is of the body, and higher consciousness is of the soul.

'Everything that happens to you in your life is a blessing,' he explains. 'Gravity pulls us down to our lower consciousness, where we only see the day-to-day, the pleasure and pain. We call this the one per cent. Kabbalah teaches us to try and elevate ourselves into our higher consciousness, to the ninety-nine per cent.'

This seems to contradict what I was taught at Findhorn and during my Vipassana meditation course, where the aim is to occupy the here and now as much as possible, grounding yourself in your senses and bodily experience. This New Age spiritual stuff is bloody confusing.

'Happiness shouldn't come from reacting to what happens to you from the outside,' John explains. 'Happiness should come from taking responsibility for your actions, from being proactive.'

This sounds about right to me. I often want to blame unhappiness on something or somebody else. I want to point and say, 'She is making me unhappy', or 'That situation is making me unhappy', when, if I think about it, I am almost always making myself unhappy.

After class Lana tells me the positive effect Kabbalah has had on her life. 'Kabbalah has changed my life for the better in so many ways', she says, her face glowing. 'You know, most of the teachers at the Kabbalah Centre gave up high-powered jobs to come and work full-time at the centre. One teacher used to work for Goldman Sachs, but now he is so much more fulfilled.'

I leave my first class feeling as if I have just stepped out of a self-help class, positive about all the big changes I am going to make in my life.

Between classes, I do more research on the Kabbalah Centre and its founders. After splitting from the wife and the mother of his seven children, Rav Berg married his secretary Karen in 1971. At the time he was an insurance salesman in Brooklyn. The pair then moved to Israel, where they began to extend the teaching of Kabbalah to anyone who showed interest.

They moved back to the USA in the early 1980s and launched the first Kabbalah Centre. Since then, the growth has been significant, and the organisation now boasts centres in over seventy countries, with tens of thousands of students. This growth propelled the couple from a modest income to extreme wealth, allowing them to acquire a mansion in Beverly Hills and to travel between the various centres in private planes. When Rav died in 2013, Karen was left to continue running the organisation alone.

After reading a few more articles on the subject, I sit down with a cup of tea in my beloved earthenware Findhorn mug to try and figure out how I feel about all of this. My overarching emotion is suspicion, but I can't work out whether or not this is fair. Does profitability automatically make an endeavour untrustworthy? I decide to suspend my judgement and continue the course with an open mind. After all, I was pleased with the first session and had already decided that, rather than blame my boyfriend for not emptying the dishwasher this morning, I would blame myself for not having done it the night before. That felt like real progress, despite still having to empty the bloody dishwasher.

Battling driving rain and unnerving wind on my rickety old bike, I arrive at Bond Street for my second session looking like a dishevelled cat that has been wrestled into a bath. Seeing my course mates looking pristine, arranged around the white cloth tables, makes me feel hostile. How are they all so perfect? Are they even real people?

Over the course of the next hour, we are taught that the word Kabbalah means 'to receive', and that Kabbalah teaches us how to be the cause of everything we receive through being proactive and taking responsibility, as opposed to being reactive and playing the victim. To receive light without earning it is known as 'bread of shame'.

Like some kind of New Age Thatcherite, John concludes the lesson by telling us that you can also impose bread of shame on others by doing too much for them and not letting them be their own cause. 'Kick away the crutch and let them fend for themselves,' he says. Well, he didn't, but that was the gist of it.

His speech had been punctuated by regular sips from a bottle labelled 'Kabbalah Water'. I stay behind after class to quiz Lana about this magical elixir.

'Kabbalah water is very powerful,' she explains.

'How is it different from normal water?'

'It goes through a process.' She looks me straight in the eye. 'It is meditated over to give it energy, so it has healing powers.'

She registers my unsubtle sceptical expression. 'It's been proven,' she says, 'water takes on the properties of its environment. They tested it. They compared water left in a room with music, candles and love with water that was left in a room with people arguing. They looked at it under the microscope, and it had completely different properties.'

It costs £3 a bottle. The Kabbalah Centre website calls the process 'Quantum resonance technology' ('changing the intermolecular properties of the water through meditation to give it spiritual and medical properties'). Did I mention it costs £3 a bottle?

Fast-forward one week, and we are introduced to the concept of 'the opponent'.

'The opponent typically manifests itself as a negative or bitter feeling,' John says, 'telling you to do things that aren't good for you. It makes you feel bread of shame and causes us to doubt and question everything.'

He explains that the opponent is part of human nature. Whenever you make a bad choice, it is because you have listened to the voice of the opponent rather than the soul. The role of the opponent is to strengthen your connection with the light, the idea being that if you beat the opponent, you will be happier than you would be if you had never been tempted at all.

I recognise this feeling as the elation of finishing an early-morning run, having defeated the voice in your head that tried to convince you of how much you deserved to lie in. That smug feeling you get when you look at your colleagues and think, I was running while you were still in bed, you lazy bastards. There is a chance I may have missed the point here.

'Kabbalah has nothing to do with religion,' John continues, 'nothing to do with dogma. People ask me, why do I wear a kippah?'

'Why do you wear it?' a tall, handsome man shouts out.

John looks irritated. 'You learn that in Kabbalah Three!' He laughs and absorbs the silence, taking a few moments to realise that we are all still waiting for an answer.

'It's because you want to keep it all in,' he says. 'You don't buy a bottle without a cap. That's why I need a head covering, to keep it in.'

'But a baby isn't born with one,' handsome man retorts.

John is visibly losing his patience. 'And a bottle isn't made with a cap; it comes later, once you have filled it, like the head,' he says. 'Now we move on.'

By week six, the routine has become familiar. I rush to the centre, invariably late, scan the room for faces I recognise and take a seat next to a cynical Brazilian called Erica. We sit for an hour being talked at by John, who is really starting to lose me.

'The number seven connects us to the frame of physical existence,' he says. 'That's why there are seven days in a week, seven continents, seven notes in music and we have seven holes in our face.' Oh, that's why. I always wondered why we had seven holes in our face. We have thirty-two teeth in our face and two eyebrows – why aren't those numbers important? Also, are ears really part of our face?

'Ten is the number that connects us to the spiritual,' John continues, without an explanation, 'and Jerusalem is the energy centre of the world.'

I resign myself to the fact that all religions and spiritual movements disappoint me in the end. They start off well, promising me the tools to help live a happier life, and then they start to link universal truths to random beliefs, drip-feeding in the dogma while our guard is down.

As if reading my mind, John looks right at me. 'You might have doubts, but it is human to doubt. Doubts are just fog. The less fog you have, the more open you are to the light. We work all our lives to get rid of the doubt and open ourselves up to the light.'

In other words, just go with it.

After class we are each offered a copy of the Zohar to take home for the week, so we can all 'experience its energy'. Originally written in the ancient language of Aramaic, the Zohar is sold in twenty-three volumes by the Kabbalah Centre.

'You won't understand it,' John says. 'You just have to connect to it in your own way' – similar, I decide, to the Findhorn concept of 'tuning in'. 'You can download energy from it by scanning the letters, as you would a barcode. If you want to feel something from the Zohar, you need to scan it for twenty-six minutes.'

We are instructed to leave it on our bedside table or sleep with it under our pillow and to let it 'affect us' in whichever way it chooses. The three rules for scanning the text are as follows:

1. Do not scan or read the book when you are in the 'private room' (translation: while you're having a poo).
2. Do not scan or read the book while you are sitting on the floor.
3. Do not scan or read the book without wearing clothes.

I put my hand up. 'Why the rules?'

'It's an energy thing,' John says. 'If you break the rules you will be attracting the wrong kind of energy.'

In my eagerness to connect with the book, I 'scan' a chapter in bed that evening. Half an hour passes before I realise with a panic that I am not wearing any clothes underneath my bedcovers. Shit. I slam the book shut.

The next day I fly out to the French Alps for a ski holiday. On the first night of the trip, we get broken into while we are sleeping, and between four of us we lose about £2,000 worth of stuff, including a €500 food and drink kitty we left in an alluring bowl on the entrance table. On the third day, my boyfriend breaks his collarbone. On the fifth day, we all get sick. On the sixth day our flight home is severely delayed, and when we finally do get home a carbon-monoxide scare forces us to evacuate the flat at 1 a.m.

Of course, this could all be a coincidence.

I suppose the Kabbalist would tell me that all of these events were sent from the light and that I should say 'thank you' for them. If I think about it hard enough, I can deduce that all of these events taught me something: to remember to lock the door when I go to bed, to warn my boyfriend not to ski so fast, and not to panic when a carbon-monoxide alarm bleeps because, IDK, it probably just needs new batteries. Ahem. But I can't lie to myself – I still wish these things hadn't happened.

I tell Lana about this before our next session.

'Well, you are probably paying a debt for something from a past life,' she says. I take my seat quickly before I accidentally punch her in the face.

'Kabbalah is not a self-help course,' John says. 'It teaches us how we can bring about peace on earth through the decisions we make.' He explains that the year 7000 is the deadline for peace on earth, according to the Kabbalists. The year at the moment is 5774, calculated from the birth of Adam and Eve, and therefore humanity.

John senses the tension in the room. 'Kabbalah is not against the idea of dinosaurs,' he reassures us, 'but that doesn't matter, because, according to the Kabbalists, time cannot be measured without human consciousness.'

Very clever, John. Very clever indeed.

A week later I decide to attend a Friday-night celebration to mark the beginning of the Sabbath. This week's event is extra special because Karen Berg will be attending. 'So there will be a lot of good energy,' Lana promises.

I am greeted at the centre by a lady wearing bright red lipstick and shown to a seat in a crowded room full of chairs. The men sit on the right, and the women on the left, with a ratio of around one man for every three women. I seem to be the only woman not wearing high heels.

The men are dressed head to toe in white, missing only the red leather balls and multicoloured sunscreen for the full cricketing ensemble. Lots of the men look like they have just grabbed anything white in their wardrobe and thrown it together. The heavily scented woman next to me kindly explains that the men wear white to 'attract good energy'. Some wear white kippahs, and those who don't wear white baseball caps with the peaks facing backwards.

According to Lana, tonight we will be treated to a 'connection' and a series of 'meditations'. I am excited by the idea of this, expecting to be holding hands and reflecting in silence as we did at Findhorn, so I am disappointed to find out that a 'connection' actually means a Kabbalah service, during which the 'meditations' are Hebrew prayers and songs.

After ninety minutes of singing and praying – sorry, meditating – we are to wash our hands before meeting in the dining room for dinner.

'Why was that called a meditation?' I ask Lana when she comes over to check on me.

'Because we don't want to scare people off by calling it prayer,' she says.

I have to admire her honesty.

Another week later I meet Lana for lunch in an Italian restaurant just off Oxford Street.

'Did you enjoy the course?' she asks me, as we wait for our salads (I really wanted a pizza).

'I liked the tips for living a happy life,' I say, dribbling over the pizza being delivered to the next table. 'But I struggle with the arbitrariness of some of it. Like why Hebrew is the "language with the most light", and why men have to wear backwards white baseball caps when they meditate. I mean, why should I just accept all that stuff?'

She nods stoically as I talk, delicately pushing salad leaves around her plate.

'You want to see things in black and white,' she says to me, shaking her head. 'You want to put a label on things, and that is natural because it is the way our minds work. We like facts; you are either this or this, one way or the other. We like to analyse things and put them all in boxes. This makes us comfortable. But this is what separation is, and what you are doing is trying to separate everything. In Kabbalah, we call this "tree of knowledge".

I think about this for a while and decide she is right. I do need to rationalise everything, and if something doesn't make sense to me, doesn't fit my model, I won't accept it. I am suspicious of anything I am told to believe without a rational explanation. This means I cannot commit to anything without having all of the facts, without exploring all of the options. But there are times in life when you simply don't have access to this information. So what do you end up doing? Well, you end up running around Glastonbury Festival like a mad person, catching half a show here, half a set there.

'Sometimes you just need to take a leap of faith,' Lana says, as if from inside my mind. 'Spirituality is everything we know is there but cannot explain. Like good energy. We can all connect to it, but it cannot be rationalised. This is what we call "tree of life".'

I can see why anyone would want to be a part of this community. The people here have an air of success, they are beautiful, and there is a genuine sense of camaraderie, but I just don't seem to 'get it' in the way they do. I wonder why I let Findhorn get away with a lot of irrational things, like the Angels and talking with animals, forgiving their nonsense as harmless eccentricity, yet seemingly hold the Kabbalah Centre to a much higher standard of logic. I think I just find the Kabbalah Centre a bit too slick.

The couple has been accused by the media of preying on the rich and vulnerable – a simple google throws up numerous articles and reports about how the Bergs built an empire, making themselves rich in the process – but I don't think the centre is a cult. I think it's more likely that wealthy people are drawn to explore their spirituality when money doesn't bring the happiness and contentment that our capitalist culture promised it should. Each of them has a compelling story about how Kabbalah has changed their lives, and the people here seem genuinely happy. Lana would say this is because of the unconditional love that the centre teaches, 'worships', even, and perhaps I simply didn't dig deep enough to feel this love in the way that others so clearly do. Perhaps if I were to linger a little longer in this world, it would all fall into place, and perhaps passing judgement on an entire community based on a ten-week course is both unfair and lazy.

Lana looks me dead in the eyes with genuine kindness. 'Kabbalah doesn't require you to accept blindly; it just requires you to open yourself up. To try it out, to practise, and see how it can affect your life. You will see that there is no negative; everything comes from the light, and what you think is negative at the time has happened for a reason, to bring you a lesson. If I look back on my life, I can see why everything has happened the way it has; everything I thought was bad at the time I was just interpreting the wrong way.'

'But isn't that just adjusting the facts to fit the situation retrospectively?' I challenge. 'You can justify anything by saying "it got me to where I am now", but that is necessarily true; of course it did. But that alone doesn't imply the existence of a Divine plan or allow you to assign a positive or negative to it. It just happened.'

I am arguing for the sake of arguing, of course, because that's what I do. But if I am honest with myself, I think she is right. A rational being isn't any happier than an irrational one. In fact, most of the hyper-intelligent and 'rational' people I know are pretty unhappy. To believe in this would probably make me a happier person, and isn't that what it's all about? I just can't seem to trick myself.

L is for... LARPers

Not twats

'Where are you off to, then?' Dave the plumber scans his eyes over my camping gear as I load myself up for the trip down to the car.

'Oh' – I make a waving gesture with a bottle of port – 'something called LARPing. You probably haven't heard of it, but—'

'No way!' He retracts with a start from the bowels of our misbehaving dishwasher, bumping his head on the way up. He looks me in the eyes for the first time. 'Are you going to the Renewal of Magic?'

I nod dumbly, my eyebrows almost reaching my hairline.

'Well, if you see Savjenni Nightwing of the Dragons faction, tell him that his head mage sends greetings, and begs forgiveness for his absence.'

I had presumed the world of LARP to be a clandestine community, known only to the super-geek – up until a few months before this event I hadn't even heard the word before – but not only did my ultra-cool plumber Dave know what it was, he was one of them. Mind. Blown.

Four hours later I join 900 fellow LARPers at a Scout camp in Buckinghamshire, arriving to an assembly of men with long hair wearing band t-shirts and baggy jeans, greeting each other with enthusiastic bear hugs. I unpack my tent in an area signposted as 'OOC' (out of character) and get talking to Dave, a friendly Scot with a welcoming smile that puts me instantly at ease.

Dave leads me into the 'IC' (in character) forest, teeming with dwarves, elves, goblins and orc, complete with pointed prosthetic ears, painted skin and mysteriously attached horns. Sounds come from speakers hanging in the trees; suspended lights give the path an eerie green glow and smoke flows from dry-ice machines hidden in the bushes.

Hang on a minute – let's take a step back here – what the bloody hell is LARPing? Well, have you ever watched a fantasy film, like *Lord of the Rings*, and thought to yourself, I wonder what it would be like to actually *live* in that world? Well, live action role play (LARP) gives you that opportunity. Affectionately referred to as 'cross-country pantomime', it is pretty much *Dungeons & Dragons* acted out in the real world, complete with foam weapons and elaborate costumes.

As we walk, Dave gives me the rundown of what to expect this weekend.

'People usually sleep off-site,' he says, pointing to the field we had just walked out of. 'But you are supposed to stay in character between ten a.m. and two a.m., and everything inside the forest – including the faction camps, the tavern and the trader tents – is in-play for those sixteen hours.'

Deciding that I wouldn't make a very convincing orc, I had chosen to join the Lions faction, a group of chivalrous and earnest knights. Once at the Lions' camp, Dave hands me a latex sword and a dagger.

'So, how does the fighting work?' I ask him, marvelling at the detailed paintwork and overall craftsmanship of the weapons.

'Well, there is a point count for each location,' he explains, 'head, torso and limbs, and that point count is defined by how magical or strong you are, or how much armour you are wearing.' I nod, sort of following. 'And every time a player receives a hit, they lose a point.'

'Like in a computer game?' I risk, my mouth opening into an 'I might have just said something offensive' grimace.

'Exactly,' Dave nods. Phew. 'And when the character's head or torso locations reach zero, the player falls to the floor and counts down from one hundred and twenty. If they finish the "death count" without being healed by someone with the right magical skills, their character dies and they have to create a new one.'

Feeling frazzled by this barrage of information, I look down at the scorecard Dave hands me. It contains a shopping list of skills to pick from, each one with an associated point cost.

'As a new character, you have twenty points in total,' he says, before wandering off to help erect a huge round table in the main tent behind us.

'How on earth do I choose when I have no idea what this stuff means?' I ask Rufus, a fellow Lion who is busy wrestling his two young kids into their costumes.

'Well, what kind of character do you want to be?' he asks calmly, sensing my exasperation.

'One that does a bit of everything.'

'How about a ranger?' He looks hopeful. 'That way you can fight, do some magic and go off on scouting missions.' I picture Strider from *Lord of the Rings*, and my eyes widen. I have always wanted to be Strider from *Lord of the Rings*.

'OK, then,' Dave says when he sits back down and learns of the latest development. 'You will need a one-handed weapon, a shield, a "contribute to ritual", shaman magic, medium armour...'

I try and keep up with him, adding up all the points as I tick the boxes on my sheet.

'How about a wild ranger who has been taken in to be civilised by Queen Cersei?' Rufus suggests. I nod encouragingly, excited by the prospect of embracing my inner scamp.

'Do I need a surname?' I look back at Dave.

'Not really, especially if you're wild.'

'Ooo, how about Luna?' I sit up onto my heels. 'Maybe I was raised by wolves?'

'Yeah, that works.' Dave nods. 'But you will need to be careful because that's a bit unnatural, and the Lions are straight down the line when it comes to things like shapeshifters and werewolves.' He gives me a serious look.

Is he for real? I can't tell and decide to play it safe. 'OK, so not Luna, in case I'm mistaken for a werewolf. What about Storm?'

Everybody nods in agreement as I stand up, ready to head for GOD (the Game Organisation Division) to register my new character. Dave calls me back in a panic. 'Hang on a minute,' he says, 'you didn't pick the numeracy skill, so you won't make a very good scout.'

I look back at him blankly.

'You can't count if you don't have numeracy,' he says, in the same tone you would use when explaining something simple to a child. 'So, if you are asked to go out and count the enemy on a scouting mission, you're screwed.'

'Maybe I can ask somebody else to count the enemy for me and hand me the appropriate amount of stones to bring back as a message?' I ask, trying to hide any trace of sarcasm from my voice.

Dave shakes his head, 'No, that won't work. You can't trust just anybody – it's too risky.'

Apparently, you can never take LARP too seriously.

After registering Storm, I head to a newbie briefing where around a hundred people gather, most now in their character costumes, to be bombarded with yet more information on how the game works. Some bring pads, madly scribbling down the commands. I spend the entire session stifling an overwhelming urge to giggle.

I make it back to camp just before 'time in', dressed in leather leg guards, jodhpurs, an oversized canvas shirt, a borrowed scabbard and belt housing a sword and dagger, and a leather character cardholder containing six pieces of paper that read 'Shaman 1'. Every time you cast a spell you have to rip one of them off for the spell to take effect, limiting the amount of magic you can use during a day.

'Time in', a passing ref shouts from the front gate. The atmosphere changes immediately. Suddenly everyone becomes confident, talking in Olde English and catching up on the latest in-character gossip, some of it made up, some of it fed from the plot team, via the three planted non-player characters (staff members) in our faction.

'Storm.' Queen Cersei walks over to me. It's a little awkward because we had been mid-conversation when 'time in' was called, and I hadn't finished explaining my character. She is unperturbed and regards me sternly. 'Storm,' she repeats, 'you must be introduced to the High King. Come, follow me.' I bound over to her, too nervous to say anything in case I get it wrong.

We approach the High King, who sits in his lion-engraved throne, ready to be counselled and meet with the new arrivals. He has long auburn hair pulled into a ponytail, a goatee beard, a prosthetic scar on his cheek, and kind eyes. Around his head is a simple gold band. He seems detached, in a regal sort of way, but offers me an encouraging tilt of the head and a faint smile. I decide in that instant that I am terrified of him.

My mouth feels like sandpaper as Cersei gestures toward me. 'Your Highness,' she says, 'this is Storm. She is of the forest and I have taken her in as a hunter.' I bow uncomfortably, not knowing what the protocol is for such an interaction.

'Lady Storm, is it?' The King looks at me expectantly.

'No, sir,' I say, 'not yet, anyway. Although Queen Cersei is helping me become worthy of such a title.' My face flits between confusion and surprise. I have no idea where that came from.

'Very well,' he says, 'you are most welcome. I will be announcing a new master of the hunt shortly, so you must introduce yourself to her and offer your services.'

'Yes, sir,' I say, taking a step back, relieved that this interaction is over.

By the time the High King calls all of the Lions together, about fifty in total, for the 'opening parliament', the place is really coming to life. Everybody has gone to extraordinary lengths with their costumes and I feel like an extra on a film set.

'Welcome, Lions, to Teutonia,' the King roars to the surrounding circle. 'We are here for the great ritual of the Renewal of Magic, to aid our allies, to trade and to learn. Be safe in the Black Forest – anything could happen. Now, will those of you who are new to the Lions please step forward and introduce yourselves.'

A few of us step forward as he looks at me to start things off. Shit. What on earth do I say?

My voice shakes uncontrollably. 'My name is Storm of the Albion forest,' I manage, turning to look at Cersei. 'My Queen has taken me in to teach me what it is to be civilised. I am a hunter. Please find me if you need me to... erm... catch you anything.'

I step back and take a much-needed breath, feeling morbidly self-conscious.

'Well met. Thank you, Storm,' the King says, moving on to the next person.

Over the next half an hour I am introduced to a series of other characters, some of whom appear half human, half animal. They all ask me about my past, where I am from, how I learned to hunt. My answers are fumbled and brief. I hadn't given this much thought – I just hadn't had the time – and it turns out I am terrible at improvising.

I am rescued by Dave (now Jonny Diamond), who takes me for some fruit wine in the IC Tavern, the Crimson Moon. On the way we bump into all manner of characters: centaurs, warriors wearing huge animal skins over their shoulders, and sand people in yellow robes.

When we get back to camp, it is time for me to perform 'gate duty', a two-hour stint during which a small group of us are responsible for the safety of the camp. 'Monsters' run riot down the forest paths, attacking, enchanting and kidnapping the players as we watch helplessly. Our first attack at the gate is a lady with bedraggled hair and a white face, surrounded by a group of stiff-looking creatures who drag themselves along behind her, wearing rags dripping with what looks like blood.

A referee walks past and whispers 'fear' into my ear. I flick my mind back to the newbie briefing, remember what I have to do and run away screaming for thirty seconds. I stumble and fall deeper into the darkening forest. By the time I reach zero and come around from my fear enchantment, I have no idea where I am, but I seem to have been spotted by a group of goblins. With green faces and red eyes, wearing cobbled-together rags, they look at me, cock their heads and start to walk over. I am backed against a tree. Nowhere to run.

'What's this 'ere, then?' one of them says, pushing to the front of the group and sniffing the air menacingly.

'A Lion. Saw 'er come from down there.' Another points back in the direction of our camp.

The air-sniffer pulls out a gnarly-looking weapon and walks towards me and I don't have to act being scared. Instinctively, I draw my sword, but bottle it completely and decide the best course of action is to run for it. Heading straight to the group and pushing them aside, I feel a spongy thwack in my back and one of the goblins squeals in rage. I feel like I am supposed to lie down now and go on to my death count, or do I have enough magic to protect myself? How many points is the torso again? Sod it. I keep running, driven on by genuine fear, and make for the safety of the gate.

When I arrive back at camp, everything seems to have returned to normal. Breathing heavily and still shaking, I walk back over to Jonny Diamond on the gate. 'What the hell was all that about?' I splutter, trying to regain my composure.

'Lady Fear and her minions,' he says matter-of-factly. He looks around furtively at the trees around us. 'I think she was using the trees to teleport.'

Fin, another friend from pre 'time in', senses my confusion. Leaning over, he whispers, 'If you don't know what someone is talking about, the best thing to do is to nod, and say "indeed".'

'Indeed.' I nod in the direction of Jonny Diamond, fighting the smile from my lips.

Towards the end of our shift, while Fin disappears to top up our tankards with some sort of whisky cocktail, a man arrives at the gate screaming in pain with bleeding prosthetic guts protruding from his stomach.

I panic. 'What should I do?' I wail at a passing, nonchalant Lion.

'Take him to the alchemist to see what can be done to help,' he says, before losing interest and wandering off.

I try and comfort the screaming man as I ask random people around me if they know who the alchemist is. Without my noticing, the maimed man walks past me into the camp. As soon as I realise what has happened, a passing ref yells, 'TIME FREEZE!' and everybody, including me, dutifully closes their eyes and starts humming.

The idea of time freeze – another learning from my newbie briefing – is to simulate things appearing from nowhere. So, when you open your eyes, you are to pretend no time has passed at all and react accordingly. I close my eyes for a while, opening them just a fraction to see about fifty people dressed in black with red-painted faces flood into our camp.

'TIME IN!' shouts the ref.

The chaos is instant. 'AAAAARRRRRHHHHH!' The demons surround us. Shouts of 'Healer!' reverberate around camp as Lion after Lion falls to the floor. Those with magical powers rush around, bending over bodies and mumbling two-minute-long spells to revive the fallen, ripping paper from their character cards for the spells to take effect.

After a few minutes, I am the only one alive at the gate. 'Healer, healer!' I shout for my fallen friends as I am backed into a corner by two demons. I try to defend myself with my shield, but they hit me on the arm, then on the leg, then on the arm again. I'm not sure if I have reached zero on each location yet and worry they are going to think I'm a cheat if I don't do the right thing, but I just don't know what that is. How on earth am I supposed to keep count?!

In a sudden flurry of activity, we are rescued by the Wolves, our neighbouring faction, who flood into our camp, flailing their

YEAR IN THE LIFE

weapons at the demons. Overwhelmed in number, the demons flee, leaving behind a field of fallen bodies.

'What the hell was that about?' I repeat, this time to Marcus, a young, floppy-haired bard who carries a guitar on his back.

'We think the tortured man was a bomb, planted by a druid,' he whispers back hurriedly. 'When he exploded, the demons were released from his body.'

The night ends in the candlelit tavern, drinking mead and talking about the history of Albion as a group of travelling minstrels play their instruments and sing folk songs in the corner. I sit quietly and listen, feeling overwhelmed and exhausted by the spectrum of emotions I have experienced today.

For the first few hours of the day, I felt daft. Like we were the kids in *Lord of the Flies*, and at any moment a grown-up might come along, break it all up, and tell us not to be so silly. But it wasn't long before I was having a lot of fun in spite of myself.

'Time out!' a ref calls into the tavern at 2 a.m., as everyone cheers and starts talking in their normal voices. Although a little surreal at first, a wave of confidence sweeps over me as I realise I can be myself. All of a sudden I go from shying away from conversation to holding court. I take the opportunity to ask people what they do for a living and am told this is a rare question to be asked in the LARPing community.

'People don't really want to know,' Mark tells me, a line straight from the battle re-enactors. Nevertheless, I manage to meet a vet, a doctor, a banker, a lawyer, a police officer, lots of IT people, a chemist, an accountant, more IT people, a teacher, and a few more IT people.

The High King comes to join us, and I fall silent again. Even out of character, he terrifies me. Maybe LARPing is a microcosm of the real world, of celebrity culture and the arbitrary hierarchy we put on things. Just as I am too afraid to go and talk to a celebrity on the street, I am too afraid to talk to any of the main characters here. I am reminded of my conversation with hill-bagging Alan: 'It's all just made up,' I'd said to him. And it is. Power lies in the hand of whomever people believe it does. LARP is no different; in fact, it offers a mirror to society, forcing it to look at itself, mocking the 'reality' it represents. Rank here is as real as rank in the real world; it only exists as long as people are there to support it.

I wake up in my tent the following morning, confused and covered in leaves. I think I must have fallen asleep on my feet while walking back. Dusting myself down and pulling my hair into a raggedy side plait, I dig out a cereal bar and wander back over to camp. Once there, I am surprised to see hundreds of LARPers from other factions gathered on wooden benches around a marked-off arena in the middle of our camp.

In a scene borrowed from *Robin Hood* (the fox version, of course), the High King, Queen Cersei and the higher-ranking knights of Albion sit on wooden thrones at the head of the arena, draped with yellow and red flags.

A man wearing eyeliner and a yellow headscarf informs me that the Lions are hosting a 'tourney' (tournament). I take a seat next to him and watch the ladies of Albion give speeches and hand out 'favours' to the knights of their choosing. I realise with dread that I am supposed to be doing the same, vaguely remembering being given a handkerchief to use as my 'token' the previous evening. I consider entering the ring but can't bring myself to do it. What would I say? I am just too shy. I don't have the confidence to go up there in front of hundreds of strangers and improvise. I worry too much about getting it wrong. Whatever that means.

'I am surprised by myself,' I say to Rufus, in a brief OOC conversation later that afternoon as he tends a copper kettle hung over a fire. 'I am normally happy to talk to anyone, but I feel so shy and exposed here.'

'LARPing is excellent for you psychologically,' he says, pausing to sip from a ceramic goblet. 'It gives us the chance to play, which we tend to suppress as adults. In the twenty-odd years I've been doing this I've seen so many people come out of their shell. I used to be shy as well, but LARP has given me a lot of confidence.'

I consider this for a moment, wondering why I seem to be having quite the opposite experience. 'But if you're confident anyway,' Rufus jumps back in, 'you don't need the mask of playing a character. LARPing is all about escapism.'

The camp steward looks up from his seat across the other side of the fire. 'LARPing is a holiday from yourself,' he says, continuing to look into the flames like a contemplative wizard, 'an escape from the monotony of life.' He nods, satisfied with his interjection.

A holiday from myself seems quite refreshing – after all, we are all stuck playing the character we have created in our real lives: the 'skills' we've developed, the role we have assigned ourselves to play, our 'phys reps' like fashion choices and hairstyles, and the anxieties we all carry around with us about made-up stuff that other people aren't even thinking. So LARPing is an opportunity to create a new character, to act, dress and even think differently; the chance to *be* somebody else, if only for a weekend.

I realise that I am still not really in the mind of Storm; I am not reacting to things in a different way, not truly playing the part. I am just Lucy, dressed up and attempting to say things in Olde English. Perhaps this is why I am struggling to interact in the way others seem to find so natural.

*

'Rank is attractive in LARP,' Queen Cersei confides in me later that evening as I accompany her to visit other camps to be plied with hospitality wine, mead and a delicious pig roasted on a spit above a glowing fire. I agree with this, finding myself attracted to the senior-ranking people here, not in a sexual way, but in a way that draws me towards them. I also quite fancy the elves.

When we arrive back at camp, the mood is low. I soon discover that we have lost three members of the Lions faction to an enemy called the Lady of the Forest. A wake is held and women collapse in fits of tears as Marcus the Bard sings songs penned for the fallen heroes.

I stand next to Rufus during the ceremony. 'Do characters die often?' I ask him, as the songs come to an end and we all start to peel away.

'Yeah, we typically lose one or two at most events; sometimes lots more if we lose the battle.'

'And how long have you been LARPing?'

'About seventeen years now.'

'And how old were you when you started?'

'Are you trying to work out my age?' He gives me a sideways smile.

I laugh at him. 'I can't count, remember?' I flash the character card hanging around my neck. 'I don't have numeracy!'

Oh God. I just made a LARP joke.

Feeling accomplished, I head out of camp to use the loo and recognise Neil on my way. With a green painted face and cropped jet-black hair split by moulded horns, Neil is still wearing his 'monster' costume from the hour both of us had spent together as ogres earlier this afternoon. 'Monstering' is something most people volunteer for during the course of the weekend, and it involves spending an hour playing the part of a loosely scripted malevolent character or as one of an army of organised creatures that create chaos around the camp, thereby providing role-playing opportunities for the players.

'What would you say are the defining features of a LARPer?' I ask him as we settle down for an interview.

'Not twats,' he says, visibly pleased with his answer. We sit in silence for a while, testing each other's will before he finally accepts I am looking for more. 'LARPing involves a lot of face-to-face co-operation,' he goes on. 'At its heart, it's a social game. It is quite touchy-feely – a lot of hugging, and pathos – so people have to be open with their emotions. It gives people a sense of belonging, in a geeky way.'

He takes a long breath and looks up at me. 'I love geeks.' He shrugs his shoulders. 'Non-geeks bore me; they don't have anything interesting to say.'

'How do you define a geek?' I wonder aloud.

'Someone with a special interest they pursue passionately,' he says. 'But that doesn't include football. That's too mainstream to be interesting.'

'What advice can you give me to get the most out of this?' I ask.

'It's all about interaction,' he says. 'If you just play the rules you might as well be playing a computer game. You have to take it with a degree of seriousness if you're going to get anything out of this; you have to suspend your disbelief.'

So that was why people were taking it so seriously; everyone knows it's a game, but everyone also knows that the best way to enjoy the game is to take it seriously. This is what I was doing wrong. I was enjoying myself, but I wasn't suspending my disbelief enough to properly get into character.

*

On the morning of the final battle, the sky opens and rain floods down. We gather in a circle and listen to a rousing speech from the High King, concluded with a rendition of the 'Lions' Prayer', recited from memory by all.

> To this duty are the Lions beholden:
> Only the weak lie, cheat and steal.
> ...
> In this, and in the service of Albion,
> To stand against evil wherever it is found.
> We are the Lions
> And we shall not falter!

As we trek up to the battle, I force myself to consider what Storm might be feeling right now, to get into her head, to inhabit her body.

I look around to find myself surrounded by a fighting unit of knights, elves, beast-men, trolls, ogres and orcs. I take a deep breath, my chest filling with moist air that stings my lungs. Do I have the strength I need to get through this? To finally complete my lifelong mission? The one I have been preparing for, training for, yearning for these last fifteen years?

My mind flicks back to a memory. I am sitting on my mother's knee in our stone hut, deep in the forest of Albion. The fire dances in front of us, as the wolf pup we rescued that spring gnaws on the bone of some poor creature it's just devoured.

'Have I ever told you how your father died?' My mother strokes my wild, tangled hair.

I look into her deep-set, troubled eyes. 'No, Mama.'

Her eyes narrow, brimming with venom. 'He was killed by the Steppe Alliance.' She spits on the floor next to us. 'For nothing more than piercing a goat that strayed into the Great Wood. We were starving, my child, all-but-lifeless waifs. You must grow up to be big and strong. You must learn the art of battle and the true meaning of courage. For only you can avenge your father.'

We march deeper into a wood that smells strongly of pine, the mud thick and sticky under my boots. The enemy is in sight, red-faced, with pointed teeth. I can hear their disgusting breath beyond the bracken. I bang my shield with my sword and run at them roaring. My time has finally come.

M is for... Morris Dancers

We refer to it as the darker side of Morris

'You have to use your hankies to help you really leap into the air,' our teacher Merv explains as she throws up her arms and jumps with surprising height. Today we are learning a 'caper'. It doesn't look that difficult when I watch the other women do it, but when I try it, I look like a cartoon penguin slipping on ice.

I have been a member of Dacre Morris, a women-only side based in Blackheath, for three months now, much longer than I had planned. I had only expected to come along for a few rehearsals to have a go at the dancing and interview people, but something has kept me here; the sheer abandonment of ego required as you skip around with bells on your feet, feeling utterly ridiculous, but all with an enormous grin on your face.

Rewind three months.

At first the community was surprisingly difficult to infiltrate, and I spent hours emailing and calling various sides around the country to figure out how I could get involved.

'We are a men-only Morris side,' came the response each time. One side even added, 'Sadly, if we started to let women in, too many people would leave.'

It was as if the ancient folk-dancing tradition had been frozen in time, rejecting societal change and occupying its own separate bubble like the circus families. Perhaps driven by the desire to preserve something – to retain Morris in its original male-only form – or simply the desire for one night a week away from the missus.

I resolved to set about finding a women-only side and happily discovered Dacre Morris, which happened to be on the lookout for new recruits. Good old Google pointed me in the direction of a 'Have a go at Morris' day in a little church hall just outside of Blackheath, and I arrive to find a group of twelve women dressed in red pinafores. They look pleased to see a group of just as many potential newbies, gathered to try their hand at a bit of hanky-flinging.

Two smiling gents with life-weathered faces pick up their melodeons and start to play a familiar folk song as the ladies usher us into 'sets' of six to begin learning our first dance.

Over the course of the next hour, we are taught a series of skips, hops and leaps – known as a 'hay on the side', a 'tree tops' and a 'half-jip'. We are also taught how to wave our hankies 'with conviction', flapping them in the air while our bodies flood with a unique combination of humiliation and joy. I find the entire thing hilarious and laugh inwardly while the rest of the class channel their energy more productively into perfecting the moves.

During the half-time break, a group of four young people turn up to join in. The place becomes increasingly rowdy, and Merv loses her patience with one of the new arrivals, who is ad-libbing with her stick and having a bit too much fun.

'It's anarchy!' shrieks a voice behind me.

After the rehearsal, we head for a pint of Bishop's Earwax, or something equally as British-sounding, at the pub opposite the church hall. I am beginning to wonder if British subcultures are just an excuse for people to get together and drink, perhaps in a bid to escape that overtly self-conscious Englishness so deeply ingrained in all of us.

We are taught about the history of Morris dancing, and that there are lots of different accounts of where it came from, with references to the tradition dating back as far as 1448. Some historians believe it may have come over from the Moors of North Africa. Others believe the word simply refers to a folk dance, developed from the French *morisque*, which became *morisch* in Flemish, then the English 'moryssh', 'moris' and finally 'morris'.

I make it through the audition phase (showing up) and attend my first official rehearsal with Dacre on a Monday evening, drinking in the familiar church-hall atmosphere of bright lights, musty smells and plastic chairs that reminds me of the many hours spent in our village pantomime rehearsals as a teenager. (I feel I must take this opportunity to apologise to all of my friends and family for dragging them along to sit on small wooden chairs in a draughty church hall to watch these three-hour embodiments of pure British eccentricity. My God. Sorry, guys.)

I am paired up with an older lady called Susan, who tells me every time I do something wrong. I feel like the baby of the group, as they all take it in turns to put me right when I get it wrong and praise me when I get it right. It feels strange to be back in an environment with such a mixed age demographic, surrounded by so many older people. It reminds me of my weekend with Rawdons Regiment, and how much I enjoyed spending time with such a wide variety of people spanning different generations. I guess that living in a faceless part of London shelters me from this part of family and community life undoubtedly so familiar to others, so being in this environment comforts me.

After an hour of dancing, we gather to talk about upcoming gigs and it is decided that I am allowed to 'dance out' with the side at the Rochester Sweeps Festival in a few weeks, presuming I can pick up the dances in time. I start to feel the pressure as I attempt to learn a stick dance during the second half of rehearsal and accidentally stick myself in the face. I resolve to practise with a broom at home.

In the meantime, on the morning of 1 May, I drag myself out of bed at the ungodly hour of 4.30 a.m. and head for the open common in front of Greenwich Park. I drive around precariously in the dark, hoping I don't get stopped by the police as I squint through an open window, cruising menacingly along the pavement in my black BMW. What would I say if they pulled me over? 'Oh, hello, officer. No, nothing untoward. I'm just trying to find a group of men who look like they might be about to perform a dawn dance of fertility.'

I finally spot them on the far side of the common and pull my car onto the side of the road next to them.

'Good morning!' I say, recognising Mike, who plays the melodeon for Dacre.

'Hello there!' comes the chorus of happy responses, with far too much energy for this time of the morning. Dressed all in white, with thick ribbons secured at their breast by a leather 'Greenwich Morris Men' badge, the men are here to perform a sunrise dance, a May Day tradition that numerous other Morris dancing sides from across the country will also be taking on this morning, on the pagan festival of Beltane.

They look striking, their white costumes and thick leather straps against the grey morning sky. The men dance for about half an hour, vigorously flinging their hankies until they are rewarded with a stream of light that pokes through the clouds and dries the damp grass below their frolicking feet.

During the dance, we are continually blasted with beeps from passing cars and lorry drivers. 'Oi-Oi!' they shout out of their windows, grinning and waving. I feel a real sense of community, proud to be a part of this ancient tradition still so close to the hearts of the British people.

Before I knew it, and certainly before I was ready, it was time for the Rochester Sweeps Festival.

'Will you help me make my Morris dancing dress?' I had sent a text to my mum in the weeks leading up to the event.

'Help?!' she said, followed minutes later by 'Send me the pattern.'

A 6.03 a.m. on 4 May I wake up in a good mood, before realising I am about to go Morris dancing. My swelling nerves are heightened as I get dressed, fuelled by a mild sense of embarrassment at what I am pulling onto my body: a long red smock with leather badges and tricoloured ribbons running over the seams, complete with strips of bells around my wrists and across my red-tasselled shoes. I don't think it is possible to look any less cool.

My boyfriend does nothing to help my embarrassment. 'You look ridiculous,' he says, looking me up and down and shaking his head, as I musically emerge from the bedroom in full ensemble. 'Most people are probably watching a Sunday-morning film on the sofa or having brunch. But I'm off to a Morris dancing festival with the bastard offspring of Little Red Riding Hood and a Christmas reindeer!'

I sink my head and walk towards the door, jingling with each step.

*

In Victorian times the chimney sweeps of Rochester would take to the streets and dance to make ends meet during the summer months. Begging was illegal at the time, so they would cover their faces in soot to avoid recognition from the authorities. The tradition outlived the open fireplaces, and over the years the sweeps were replaced with Morris dancers, and the festival slowly evolved into what it is today, attracting over fifty Morris sides, who travel from as far afield as Nottingham and Stockport to represent the various traditions within the Morris family.

Dacre is a Cotswold Morris side, a style of dancing that originated from the villages of the wider Cotswold region. Dress is typically conservative in style, and dances involve bells, sticks, hankies and lots of lovely jumping. Another heavily represented Morris tradition at the festival is Border Morris, a style that originated from the Wales/England border country. Most border sides are dressed in 'disguise' with blackened faces and strips of fabric sewn into jackets, known as tatters. The blackface element of the Border costume is naturally controversial, with some arguing that, regardless of whether or not the history of the tradition is racist – perhaps inspired by the mummer tradition, or the American minstrel shows from the Victorian era, or perhaps stemming, as most who adopt the tradition claim, from the act of disguising dancing faces from the authorities – to continue this practice is no longer appropriate.

Border typically attracts a younger crowd, and a lot of the groups are mixed gender. The tradition uses simple steps, accompanied by deep drums and a lot of 'whooping'.

'We refer to it as the darker side of Morris,' Susan tells me.

I count seven Border sides in total that have a gothic theme to their costumes, complete with top hats and brass goggles. Most are in their thirties and forties and consider themselves part of the wider goth community. One side in particular, Steampunk Morris, look like they have stepped straight out of Whitby.

Something about this festival feels earthy, real and connected – the music from acoustic folk instruments, the traditional dancing, the costumes – not much has changed in this world in the last century, maybe longer – and I feel as if I am at a medieval festival. It strikes a chord somewhere deep in my psyche. Perhaps I have lived a previous life as a Morris dancer.

Our first designated spot to dance is shared by Boxhill Bedlam, a 'Border gothic' side. One of the dancers, who wears an oversized pirate hat, lends me his tambourine to play along with the music while they jump and crash their metal sticks in mid-air. The dancing is impressive, which does nothing to ease my nerves as my first dance with Dacre edges closer.

'Next up are the ladies of Dacre Morris,' announces one of the officials. Colin picks up his melodeon and begins the rocking melody for the 'Upton Hanky'. I tentatively approach the performance area. 'This time!' yells Susan, and we all swing into action, skipping on the spot (always left foot first) and tossing our hankies high into the air.

Everything seems to go relatively well until I tree top the wrong way in the second movement. For the next few bars, my confidence is shot, but it only takes a perfectly executed hay on the side to bring me back to form. As we gather in a circle to end the dance, one leg cocked and our hankies in the air – 'Woooooo' – the audience erupts into applause. Boxhill Bedlam join in with whoops of encouragement.

I go over to thank them.

'How long have you been doing this for, then?' One of the younger guys makes polite conversation.

'Oh, only a couple of weeks,' I say nonchalantly. 'This is my first dance out.'

'Wow.' He looks impressed. 'I've never known someone learn to dance that quickly. This is a big event to be making your debut!'

I decide that I'm probably not taking this seriously enough, which seems to be a recurring theme of this project. I like to think this is down to the sheer volume of new worlds I am venturing into, with only enough bandwidth to skim the surface of each. I'm sure I could write a whole book on any one of these chapters, there is just so much to learn. Well, perhaps just a short book on Morris dancing.

For the next dance we down our hankies and pick up our sticks, ready to dance my nemesis, the 'Adderbury Bluebells'. First, I don't remember which number in the set I am supposed to be. The roles are different for each dancer, depending on where you stand in the set, so it is important to stand in a position you have practised before. I remember that I am supposed to be second in the line, but I can't remember what number that translates to. Susan looks visibly annoyed with me and goes into a mild panic, moving my position back and forward in the line and asking me which one feels more natural as we scramble to make a decision. A mere few seconds before the music starts, we finally work out that I am supposed to be number five in the set and breathe a mutual sigh of relief.

I begin the routine in a fluster, but manage to make it to the chorus before the shit really hits the fan. First, I start one of the skips with my right foot first (God dammit, Lucy, left foot first, always left foot first!) and then I have to correct myself with an awkward double hop that nearly sends me flying off into the crowd. Then, by the time the second chorus arrives I have another mini meltdown and get the sticking the wrong way round, stopping myself just in time before I hit Susan in the face. Without saying a word, she grabs my hand and yanks it back the right way round so we can complete the rest of our stick routine in harmony.

'I'm so sorry!' I say to her, mortified, when the performance is over.

'Don't be silly,' she says in a brisk Mary Poppins manner, 'and sorry to be so brutal with you. It wasn't a time for words, it was a time for action.'

'Oh, it's fine – I needed it,' I say, genuinely grateful for the abrupt correction.

'You also need to remember that it's your responsibility to know where you need to stand in the set,' she says, before nodding her head sternly and lifting my hand in the air.

'A big well done to Lucy,' she yells, 'for a successful first dance out!' Everyone cheers as I turn bright red, grinning at my boyfriend, who I had lumbered with filming duties. He smiles and waves at me, mouthing 'yaaaay'. I give him an enthusiastic thumbs-up, conscious of how much he would rather be watching the football right now.

N is for... Naturists

I accidentally just touched someone's bum with my bum

'I'm not being the first one out there,' my friend Tori declares as she scurries over to the peephole to scout the corridor for naked bodies. She squashes her nose against the door and glues her eye to the small bead of glass. 'Oh my God,' she says, spinning her head around to beam at me, her face alive with tipsy excitement – 'a willy!'

And why, I hear you ask, was Tori so excited about seeing a willy?

Rewind the scene an hour, and we are standing in the lobby of a famous water park in the north of England, our senses assaulted by the smell of chlorine and glaring aquarium-themed wallpaper. I look around the room, trying to imagine the scene when 'clothing optional' commences in less than an hour. Oh God. Less than an hour. A feeling of dread washes over me and I forget how to breathe.

'It'll be fine,' Tori tries to reassure me in a voice two octaves above her usual pitch, her blonde hair framing an increasingly reddening face.

I reach for Tori's hand as we walk up to the welcome desk. 'We're here for the naturist weekend,' I manage to squeak, convinced that the young, fully clothed reception workers are inwardly laughing at us. I feel an overwhelming urge to tell them all that we aren't *actual* naturists, but I had made Tori promise that we wouldn't do that on the drive up. 'No disclaimers,' we agreed. That would be cowardly.

According to the British Naturist (BN) website, there are as many as 4 million naturists in the UK, 10,000 of whom are signed up as members of the national organisation. We will be spending the weekend with 420 of their most active members, here to enjoy an annual holiday of 'fun, in a non-judgemental environment'.

After check-in, we head straight for the bar, a novelty Caribbean-themed room with a warm stone floor, wicker furniture and fake palm trees. The air is sticky, and there is a buzz of anticipation in the air as people mingle from group to group, hugging and shaking hands. We order a bottle of wine to numb the awkwardness of our impending disrobing session and take it up to our room.

Fifteen minutes and four glasses of wine later, we both set to work lowering expectations before the big exposé, describing the intricate details of our anatomy to each other in preparation for what is about to be unveiled, like schoolkids sheepishly saying, 'It's not very good,' before revealing their art projects to each other. We take it in turns to remove one layer at a time, our nautical-themed hotel room – complete with bunk beds and SpongeBob SquarePants welcome packs – providing a surreal backdrop to our platonic striptease.

Once naked, we begin to fire panicked questions at each other – what do we do with our phones? Do we wear shoes? What if I have to bend down to pick something up?

Cue the peephole willy scene.

By 6.03 p.m, we are walking down the corridor, completely naked but for our towels around our necks, our social norms shattered and our dignity left somewhere in the discarded pile of clothes under our bunk beds. According to our research, the first rule of naturism is to always carry a towel, for hygiene reasons in case you want to sit down. We also discover, to our delight, that they make convenient boob covers for nervous first-timers.

We walk past the cartoon fish wallpaper lining the corridor, trying to avoid looking at each other to maintain our poise. At the end of the hallway, we call the lift, which takes approximately four months to arrive, and bundle into it next to a couple who look to be in their sixties. He wears nothing but a pair of Crocs, carrying his first-rule-of-naturism towel and a newspaper in his weathered hand. She wears a pearl necklace, her hair in a neat bun behind her head. They grin at us.

'Hi.' I raise my voice to be heard over the blaring *Captain Pugwash* lift music.

'Hello!' The lady's smile widens. 'Lovely day, isn't it? I can't remember the last time we had such a sunny November.'

The lift takes us down to the water park, where we make straight for the water and start to feel a little more comfortable, presumably because swimming is an environment we naturally associate with a certain level of nudity. I look around me and take in the scene. There really are all shapes and sizes here: old, young, fat, thin, tall, short, willies that are all shrunk and wrinkled, barely visible, even, willies that stretch down to mid-thigh and the odd pair of boobs that make it down just as far. The scene is completely at odds with what we are fed by the media as being normal, and I feel instantly more confident in my own body. I am humbled by a slender man who walks past us with a nude-coloured colostomy bag hanging from his stomach, happily displaying what I assume can be a confidence-denting affliction and translating it into something that is completely acceptable and normal.

After a few minutes of swimming (hiding), we emerge from the pool and wander past the fully clothed lifeguards to queue for the flumes, employing the trusty British technique of pretending everything is totally normal as we jabber away about the last season of *The Great British Bake Off*. Once at the front of the queue, we realise with horror that we have to sit in our rings and wait for the green light, policed by a uniformed teen lifeguard who has to step in and stop our floats with his foot at the top of the slide. I wave to him as I sit naked and exposed in my rubber ring, trying to break the awkwardness. He looks away in embarrassment, which fills me with an unexpected sense of power.

An hour later we are back in our room preparing to head down for dinner, which is, horrifyingly, in buffet form. We straighten our hair, apply our make-up and leave the room with a niggling feeling that we've forgotten something. After pointing at the beef to the clothed meat-carver, who painstakingly avoids our eye contact, we sit down at the table with our full plates, the surrounding room full of willies, exposed vulvas and wrinkly bums now positioned perfectly at eye level. I don't make much of a dent in my parsnips.

We walk back up the stairs to the disco in the bar, where a pub singer is wooing the crowd with jukebox hits as the surrounding masses goad him to strip. Hundreds of naked bodies groove on the dance floor, a pulsating celebration of flesh. A pair of flip-flops and a couple of bum bags are the only pieces of clothing in sight.

Lost for words, we snake our way across the dance floor and through the surrounding beer-clutching crowds, and make for the bar.

After a few more minutes of staring, Tori finally breaks the silence. 'Why?' She shakes her head in disbelief, eyes wide. 'Why do they want to be naked *all* of the time?' I reflect on this – perhaps the burden of proof should be on the other side, because being naked is natural, isn't it? We are born naked, after all, and we die naked. And I get why we would wear clothes to protect us from the elements, but why do people wear clothes inside? Is it just societal convention?

Before I can launch the debate out loud, the commercial manager of BN, Andrew Welch, approaches us. Despite wearing nothing but an official BN lanyard, Andrew has a white-collar look about him, with a thick head of shiny chestnut hair, a round, cheerful face and rimless glasses.

Andrew is the first recipient of Tori's question.

'Because it makes me feel free, relaxed and happy,' he says. 'I have even been on *This Morning* and *Daybreak* to promote the cause.' He looks across at Rob, who has also joined the conversation.

Rob is a thirty-four-year-old accountant. He puts me in mind of a naked Chris Evans. 'It is the ultimate in inner confidence,' he responds when Tori asks him the same question, 'a middle finger up to conventional society. It completely disassociates me from my day job, as if I am removing my mask and really being myself for the weekend.'

I see my opportunity to ask the question that's been plaguing me all day. 'How do you disassociate seeing a naked woman on a naturist weekend from seeing a naked woman in a sexual context?' We all know what I'm asking here, don't we? And no, we haven't seen any yet.

'It's not about disassociating,' he says. 'I never associate it in the first place. Just like I don't associate a woman in clothes with sex. Genitals aren't about sex in a place like this. The size of the genitals here is the same as the size of an arm or a leg.'

'Have you ever had an involuntary erection at an event?' I brave. We got there in the end.

'No, never,' he says, poker-faced.

Tori heads to the bar for another round, as I confide in Rob. 'I feel painfully self-conscious here,' I tell him.

'I'm not surprised,' he says, 'because all the time we are being told that there is something wrong with the human body, usually by companies that make money out of selling us something to fix the problem.' He opens his hands, gesturing at my frame and causing me to instinctively recoil, my body almost folding in on itself. 'This is especially true for women,' he says. 'You are pushed everything: liposuction, Botox, anti-wrinkle cream. The media shows you pictures of flawless women and says "you can look like this too", even though these images have been airbrushed and manipulated.'

He takes a sip of his drink. 'So women are shown unrealistic objectives that they can never obtain, to keep them spending money on beauty products, clothes and even cosmetic surgery, in more extreme cases. A lot of people have fallen for it and now people will look at you if you don't comply and think you don't care, or that you are slovenly. This is why so many people are so self-conscious of their naked body because they compare themselves with unrealistic ideals.' He pauses to take another sip of his drink.

'There are all shapes and sizes here,' he says, gesturing to the crowd around us with an enlightened smile. 'These people have decided to be comfortable with the way they look and accept it. If other people don't like it, fine, it's not really any of their business.'

Tori and I had not escaped the issue of body-consciousness in our preparation for this weekend, spending hours poring over the quarterly BN magazines we had signed up to receive, researching an important question – to wax, or not to wax?

'She has nothing', 'She is very hairy', 'He has nothing', 'She has trimmed'. The consensus was that most of them had gone the whole hog and had no hair at all, which proved an accurate assessment when we arrived. This surprised me, as I had associated naturists with wanting to be natural – 'how God intended', as it were – but this doesn't seem to be the case here at all.

I had decided to go for a halfway house and got a landing-strip style Brazilian wax, but regretted this when I realised that I was the only one here with any kind of 'style'. I am reminded of my experience in Essex, as the thread of feeling embarrassed that people might notice I have put effort into my appearance rears its strange head again. Although I doubt anyone else thinks it, with nothing else to label my identity I can't help but worry that I look like a bit of a tart. Thank God I don't still have my vajazzle.

I pose the question of pubic hair decision-making to Rob.

'Naturism has nothing to do with personal grooming choices', he says, looking confused and frustrated by my question. 'It's just like deciding whether or not to have a beard.'

Fair.

I decide to change the subject. 'Do you tell your friends where you're going when you come to an event like this?'

'No', he looks down at his hands. 'Because even though they're happy to get naked in the nightclub to the *Baywatch* theme tune, or to do a "naked quad run", they would be mortified by the idea of going to a naturist beach.' He shrugs. 'It's funny, really.'

'Why do you think they feel that way?'

'A lot of the prejudice naturists go through today is the same stuff homosexuals had to go through in the seventies. What they were doing was seen as sinful, or even criminal, but now we have legalised gay marriage, so we are progressing.'

He continues, 'People still see the body as something wrong or obscene. There are arbitrary rules about what is and isn't acceptable. Men are allowed to walk around in public with their shirts off, but women aren't. But at the same time, the *Sun* newspaper runs its Page Three pictures of women with their breasts exposed, sexualising them. [It's important to note here that this feature has since been scrapped. Thank God.] It's just depressing and should have been banned years ago. This sort of thing permeates into the national consciousness.'

I am impressed by Rob and think he is an excellent advocate for the cause. Why are we so ashamed of our naked bodies? Perhaps a hangover from the Christian concept of sin. Can it really be that, thousands of years on and post the Nietzschean death of God, we are still carrying this societally ingrained shame around with us?

He interrupts my train of thought, cradling his pint with one finger outstretched. 'You see, naturists take it one step further and say that there is nothing rude about genitals. There is nothing obscene about them – fifty per cent have male genitals, and fifty per cent have female genitals – it shouldn't be shocking. Then you go to other European countries, and they are completely nonchalant about nudity, which makes it even more arbitrary.'

'Why do you think nudity is more acceptable in places like France and Germany?'

'We are more conservative as a culture. We are still titillated by the naked body. It is a very British thing – just think about the *Carry On* films – it is all part of our cultural identity. Nudity is seen as naughty.'

'Oooh, Matron,' I say in my best Kenneth Williams. Rob looks blankly back at me, and we stand for a few minutes in awkward silence.

'What do your parents think about the whole thing?' I change the subject again.

'My parents don't know I am a naturist; they don't know I'm here,' he says, revealing a glimmer of self-consciousness for the first time. 'My mother had a very traditional upbringing, and she would feel strange about it, so it's better she doesn't know.'

I deflate. For somebody so evangelical about the naturist plight and so against societal prejudice, it seems a little hypocritical that he has avoided confronting these prejudices in his own parents. But maybe I should give him a break.

Tori re-enters the conversation, and I take the opportunity to try and convince myself that standing here naked is completely normal and that there is nothing in any way sordid about it, but I can't help but worry that the people around me are looking at me in a weird way. Ogling. Perving. Am I just imagining it?

After one more drink, Tori and I congratulate each other on making it this far and allow ourselves to say our good nights and escape for the evening. It has been a long day, and we are very excited by the prospect of wearing pyjamas.

The next morning, I drag myself out of bed early for a 'bareobics' session in the bar. A plump lady with blonde shoulder-length hair, wearing nothing but a pair of pink flip-flops, makes her way to the front of the group and introduces herself as the leader. In a group of around twenty, I am the youngest participant by at least thirty years. While I am adjusting my ponytail, the group are asked to take a step back, leaving me exposed in the front row, where I am promptly papped by a man taking photos for the BN website. FML.

'I use the exercises we will do today as a warm-up for children at the start of the school day,' Mrs Pink Flip-flops tells us, as Aqua's 'Cartoon Heroes' kicks in. I have a momentary out-of-body experience as I ponder the absurdity of my current situation.

Aside from having to hold my boobs for the star jumps, the routine is gentle, with lots of grapevining and arm waving. After every song, we have to stop and 'catch our breath', perhaps unsurprising given that the majority of attendees here are retired couples. Outside of this, the demographic is broad: there are gay people, straight people, transgender people, a few younger people who are here with YBN (Young British Naturists) and many families with young children. The only age group who seem to be missing completely are those between twelve and twenty-five, presumably when we feel the most body-conscious as we battle with adolescence.

After a quick breakfast, Tori joins me for the next event of the day.

Naked yoga.

Running a little late, we walk into our yoga studio (the bar, again), now lined with crowds of people sitting around the edge of the room, reading their morning papers, drinking coffee and preparing for the spectacle about to unfold. The class has already started, so the only spaces left are on the outside edge, mortifyingly close to the audience.

As first-timers, Andrew had warned us the previous evening

that we might want to wear pants for the yoga. We took his advice and brought them down with us, before arrogantly leaving them on the back of a chair like abandoned bow ties at a wedding reception.

We copy the rest of the group and lie on our backs on top of our mats, making the numbers up to around thirty. Once again, we are the youngest in the group by a significant margin.

The teacher is a wrinkly older gentleman with neatly trimmed white (head) hair and a moustache. He looks healthy and has an energetic glow.

'OK then,' he says. 'Let's start with some gentle stretching.'

He takes us through a series of stretches: touching our toes, which no one can do, obviously; reaching up tall on our tiptoes, which makes a few of the group topple over; and twisting our spines to look behind us, which fills the room with hideous clicking sounds. Unaffected by the inflexibilities of the group, the teacher weaves his way in and out of the class smilingly, straightening a back here and adjusting an arm position there.

'Now everyone get down on your hands and knees, push your arms out in front of you and raise your bum in the air.'

Oh no. Downward-facing dog.

Tori and I catch each other's eye and collapse to the floor in a fit of giggles. Luckily no one seems to mind.

The next position is a body fold. I manage to complete it and grab my ankles from behind, now so exposed, I worry onlookers may actually be able to see inside my body.

'Oh lovely,' I hear the teacher say. 'Now everyone stop, turn around and look at this lady.' The whole class goes silent, and it takes a second for me to realise that the entire room is staring at me.

'No, no, no, please don't!' I squeal, turning an unnatural shade of purple and recoiling back into a standing position so dramatically my boobs do a dance of their own. 'I'm not that good, you don't all have to look.'

Tori has collapsed on her front again, her whole body shaking. I'm glad someone finds it funny.

The final move is a shoulder-stand and 'plough' pose, which involves pulling your legs apart and pushing them over your head to touch the floor behind you. There now isn't a single part of my body that hasn't been exposed to the audience in its entirety. I curse myself for being too proud to wear the pants.

After yoga, we allow ourselves a short break, returning at 3 p.m. for a belly-dancing class. Again, true to form we are a little late on parade, which means all of the coin belts have now been snaffled. Tori is devastated and decides to use her first-rule-of-naturism towel instead. Not wanting to be the only completely naked one, I join her, but my towel is bigger than hers, so it just looks like I'm wearing a comically oversized nappy.

The teacher is a large lady with short bleached-blonde hair and rosy-red cheeks. She insists on showing us the entire three-minute dance routine on her own before she will teach us anything. So we all stand staring for an uncomfortably long time as she shakes her hips and thrusts to Middle Eastern music in a coin belt that doesn't cover anything significant. When the show is over, she teaches us some simple moves: hip slides, figure eights, thrusts, lifts, drops and shimmies, shaking our wobbly bits to the omnipresent audience around the edge of the bar. Some of the women are mainly made up of wobbly bits, so the scene is reminiscent of a tray of wobbling pink blancmanges.

When we are finally released from belly-dancing class, we

decide to warm ourselves up in the outdoor hot tub, where we promptly discover that most people here have lied to their friends and families about where they are this weekend.

'We use code names here,' one man tells me, his arm around his wife's waist, fiddling with the strap of her waterproof bum bag, or at least I hope that is what he is doing. 'We like to keep our lives separate. No one here knows who we are in the real world, and vice versa. I wouldn't want any of my naturist friends to add me on LinkedIn. Imagine that!' Oh dear, I had already added Andrew.

One of the only people completely open about his hobby is Clive, an avuncular sixty-two-year-old who was inadvertently outed as a naturist on national TV.

'I remember signing a release form,' he chuckles, 'but I thought I was too far away for anyone to recognise me. Didn't realise they had zoomed in on me, did I?'

After the programme was aired, Clive received call after call from his friends and family. 'We had no idea!' they told him. Some even said they were envious.

'It was one of the best things that ever happened to me,' Clive says. 'I wouldn't have had the guts to tell them myself, and now everything is out in the open.'

I instantly like Clive. He puts me in mind of a naked Father Christmas. In a non-creepy way.

'I have always considered myself a naturist,' he continues in a deep voice with a soft Yorkshire accent. 'I enjoy being naked and have never had a problem with it. I would often sneak off to the naturist beach without my wife knowing. We just never really talked about it.'

His voice quietens and he starts to wring his hands. 'Then when I lost my wife ten years ago – it was a hard time – I thought, I can either give up now, or I can go out there and get my own life. So, I thought, why not? I'm going to do it!'

'What do you like about it?' I ask him.

'Well, my first experience was at Cap d'Agde in France, a beach town that is pretty much the naked capital of the world. You can be naked all of the time there. It's a lovely sense of freedom. Getting out of bed in the morning and going straight outside into the sunshine. The warm sun on your body.' His eyes light up, and he nestles deeper into the hot tub, like a dog snuggling into a warm blanket. 'It's exhilarating.'

'Since I got involved, I have made a huge circle of friends. By their very nature, naturists are less inhibited and more game for a laugh.'

'They definitely seem less bothered about self-image.' I nod in agreement.

'Yes,' he says, 'and I'm not bothered about being a bit...' – he looks down at his belly, searching for the right word – 'portly. People don't care, they just look at my face and try to get to know the person behind the body.'

'If naturism was banned tomorrow, would you continue to socialise with the community?' I ask him.

'There would be a hell of a stink kicked up if—'

'Hypothetically speaking,' I interrupt as Clive puffs himself up.

'Of course, naturism creates a particular type of person. I was a lot more closed-minded when I was a textile.'

I raise my left eyebrow, and Clive takes his cue: 'Oh, textile is the word we use for people who aren't naturists.'

So now I am a private (non-circus), a mundane (non-goth) and a textile (non-naturist). Oh, and a Muggle, sadly.

He continues, 'Well, back then I was a bit homophobic, I think because of the way I was brought up. But coming here I meet all types of people: gays, transgenders, business people, artists. You learn to take people as they come. All that matters is if they are nice or not.'

I ask him a question I had been wrestling with for a while. 'Are you ever worried about the kids here, Clive?'

'No, not at all.' He shakes his head. 'It's so safe because everyone is looking out for them. Each club has a child-protection officer. I am one at my club and have done a course on how to identify abuse, but it's rare in a naturist situation, because it's far more visible, of course.' When I work out what he means, I wish I hadn't.

The evening activity of the day is body-painting, which we throw ourselves into, overjoyed by the prospect of covering ourselves up in some way. I paint Tori like a mermaid, complete with a shell bra and a scaly tail. It is strange how comfortable we are painting each other's boobs, never once thinking about anything remotely sexual.

During the body-painting, a chap walks over and kindly hands us the two pairs of pants we had left behind after yoga this morning, as if returning a child's toy that had fallen from a pram.

After the body-painting Tori takes herself off to bed to read a chapter of her book, and I find myself wishing I was going with her. Forcing myself to stay, I order a pint of Guinness and watch the room around me transform back into the disco from the previous evening. The lights start flashing and the band open with 'Don't Stop Me Now', which is enough to tempt me to cast off my remaining inhibitions and venture onto the dance floor.

On my way back to my seat at the bar I have an awkward cheek-to-cheek moment with a woman as I try to squeeze past her.

'I accidentally just touched someone's bum with my bum,' I confess to Andrew when I get back to my seat.

'Oh, don't worry about it,' he says. 'Sometimes my willy pops over someone's chair and hits them in the back when I am squeezing past. It's inevitable.'

The band finish playing at midnight, when I somehow get cajoled into singing the opening karaoke number with Andrew. We burst out a tuneless rendition of 'Come What May' from *Moulin Rouge*, after which my co-star announces to the room that this is my first time as a naturist and hands me the microphone. I have no idea what to say, so I start to list off everything I've done naked this weekend. 'Yoga, body-painting, belly dancing and… errr… karaoke.' For some reason, this gets a roaring applause.

After another couple of hours of dancing with inflatable guitars, and an enthusiastic butchering of 'Ernie (The Fastest Milkman in the West)' from Clive and me, I clamber happily into my bunk bed at 2 a.m., wondering if the evening would have been any more or less fun if we had all been wearing clothes.

It had been a hilarious but incredibly challenging weekend. Breaking through the social barrier of nudity was extremely difficult at first, although, as with most things, the human mind has a wonderful way of coping and both Tori and I were surprised how quickly we became desensitised to it all.

I was also surprised how separate nudity and sex could be. Nothing about the weekend felt remotely sexual to me. Having said this, I did feel that, while most people were there for the atmosphere and the sensation of nudity, there were probably a few people around with seedier intentions. 'You get the odd weirdo,' Andrew had told me on the first evening, and I think that's probably fair.

As with most of the other communities I have spent time with, although the touchpaper for joining is a shared interest, the social bind of the group is what keeps most people coming back. 'Naturism turned my life around,' Clive told me during our interview, happy to have found that sense of belonging and identity we all crave.

So, would we do it all again? Having gone from being nervous about changing in front of other women in the gym, I can safely say that I would now happily go to a naturist beach or a naturist spa resort without too much cajoling. I am a convert, in that sense, because I see the value in being naked in these environments. However, I do think that being naked has its place, and it just didn't feel like that place is at a theme park, in a restaurant or dancing to 'Sweet Child O' Mine' in the small hours, using a deflated plastic guitar to maintain my modesty. Being naked in this environment just feels like a bit of a novelty.

On the plus side, not wearing clothes is certainly a leveller. Clothes are an extension of your personality, and expression of your social status. So by removing them, you strip away these labels, avoiding any prejudice or preconceptions. You have no idea what anybody does for a living, where they're from or how they orientate themselves in society, which does allow for more open-minded relationship building.

Tori and I agreed that we both gained a lot from the weekend: self-confidence, a better relationship with the body we were born in, and a deeper comfort in our own skin. Having been raised in a generation where people pay thousands of pounds to achieve the looks that are dictated by the various fashion, beauty and fitness industries, which make money out of sowing seeds of dissatisfaction with our outward appearances, we realised within the first hour of being there that the human body comes in ALL shapes and sizes. Nothing is right or wrong, and nothing about the human body is obscene. We all have the same bits, so why the big secret?

The most common reply from the people I had told that I was coming to this weekend was: 'I don't have the body to do something like that.' When, really, that couldn't have been more irrelevant. 'You have a body,' Clive rightfully retorts, 'that's all you need!'

O is for... Otherkin

*Trying to organise unicorns is like
trying to herd fickle, glittery cats*

When I was about eight years old, I had an alter ego: a dog by the name of Uffie. I would spend a lot of time as Uffie, exploring my house and garden on all fours, lapping juice from a saucer, clambering over rocks on family walks and drinking from the occasional stream. My mum indulged Uffie to the point of buying me a collar, a lead and a water bowl for my bedroom floor. I'm still not sure whether or not this was good parenting.

Then, one day, Uffie disappeared.

So what happened? Did I just grow up? Or did I suppress Uffie, bowing to a societal norm that tells children that if they don't look like a dog, they probably aren't one? If the latter is true, I may already be a member of this community.

I can't remember how I initially uncovered the world of otherkin; probably down an internet rabbit hole on one of the many days I have lost to YouTube. In simplistic terms, otherkin believe themselves to be 'other than' or 'more than' human; although most accept that their current carnation is human, they believe that their spirit is either entirely or partially non-human.

The most common otherkin are either mythical creatures – like elves and faeries – or animals ('therians').

This may sound fanciful, but many otherkin would argue that what they experience is a genuine spiritual and/or physical dysphoria; a feeling that they have been born in the wrong body.

Although uncertain of his true identity, Kiaan, who I meet at a bustling bar in London's financial district, is currently 'flirting' with the idea that he might be a star (as in a celestial body). You may already be writing him off as a nutcase, but don't do that just yet. With a degree in psychology and sociology, he is now a successful information management consultant who meets me wearing a smart suit in the financial district of London. 'I have no right to sit here and say you are a woman if you tell me you are a man,' he said. 'Just as you have no right to sit there and tell me whether or not I am a walrus.'

He looked up and met my gaze. 'I'm not a walrus, by the way.'

For some, it's not necessarily about being in the wrong body; it is about expressing another part of themselves. A week later I explore this idea with Shaft, the founder of 'The Fabulus of Unicorns' in London – a subculture of people who dress as unicorns and live by the mantra 'spread the sparkle.'

Shaft is not strictly otherkin, and would probably be referred to as a 'furry' within the community because, rather than believing he is a unicorn spirit in human form, he sees the unicorn as his 'power animal', in the same way a Native American has a 'totem animal', and a Druid has a 'spirit animal'.

'Some people have mythical power animals,' he tells me, 'like mermaids. I have always been attracted to those people.'

Shaft freelances as an artistic director for a major TV network and uses big arm gesticulations when he talks. We meet in a park in Shepherd's Bush during his lunch break, where he is dressed in a sparkly top, a purple shell-suit jacket and skin-tight trousers, his mid-length hair clinging to his face in dark tendrils.

'Since I hit thirty, I started going to Burning Man festival,' he tells me. 'I have a beautiful white bike that I call my unicorn. Everyone just decided "you are a unicorn", and I realised I was. That's when I bought my first horn.'

He leans back and picks at the grass. 'It was always me on my own until recently. My mantra was "famous at festivals, lonely in London". So I gathered this group of super-hot, fabulous individuals who are crushingly insecure and lonely, and created my own subculture.'

There is something vulnerable about Shaft, his raw honesty piercing holes in his charismatic armour.

'But things are different now,' he goes on. 'We are a positive force of glittery energy. Born from the stars, each unicorn contains within them the sparkle of the UniForce that binds us all together. We live by the Ten Principles of Unicornia, which came to me in a vision I had in the Old City of Jerusalem.'

I don't know where to start.

'How many unicorns do you have in your Fabulus?' I try.

'Hundreds all over the world,' he says whimsically. 'There are many types: Pure Bloods, Homoeroticorns, Light Warriorcorns, Tantricorns, and there are always new breeds of unicorns rising every day. My dream is to create a subculture of mythical creatures, but trying to organise unicorns is like trying to herd fickle, glittery cats.'

Following a traditional Bangladeshi upbringing in Bexhill-on-Sea, Shaft turned his back on the faith of his Muslim parents at the age of seven. They are fine with him being a unicorn, so long as he realises that he will have to 'come back to reality' at some stage.

'I am not always going to be a unicorn,' he reassures me. For a moment I presume he is taking his parents' advice. 'After living a life of loneliness, depression and addiction, I found tantra as a form of healing. So now I'm a Tantricorn, and I travel the world empowering men and women to find a deeper love for themselves.'

When his lunch break is over, I walk him out of the park, sad that my time with this colourful character is coming to an end.

'Never stop being YOUnicorn!' he says, a parting gift as he waves me goodbye.

Two days, fifteen hours of otherkin-related internet research, and countless YouTube documentaries later, I meet Karen Kay at the Labyrinth Faery Ball in Glastonbury. It is the morning after the ball, and we are tucking into breakfast at a vegan café.

As the organiser of the now popular 3 Wishes Fairy Festival (which pulled in over 1,000 attendees this year), Karen is a prominent figure in the British faery subculture and the producer of the internationally successful *FAE* magazine. A tattoo of a sunflower decorates her right arm, and her thick wavy hair flows down to her lap, framing a gentle face.

For Karen, being a faery wasn't a choice – it was a calling; an innate part of herself.

'My whole life has been completely taken over by faeries,' she says. 'Faery people are quite shy and reclusive, so to get them to come to an event was difficult at first. But when they did come, there was a communal feeling of coming home; a sense of belonging and reconnecting with your family.'

'Are you a faery?' I get straight to the point.

'Well, I feel like a hybrid of human, faery and mermaid. So I call myself a MerFae, but I am obviously dwelling in a human body at the moment. I definitely have mermaid in me because I like to be near the sea. It makes me feel invigorated. I am not a great swimmer, but I like to put my feet in the ocean.'

Organising the faery events and the publication of *FAE* magazine is now Karen's full-time work.

'The festival grows every year,' she explains, 'and I now organise faery events in Glastonbury and the magical location of Tintagel, home of King Arthur.' (Who you'll meet in the next chapter.) 'Obviously it has to make money, because you have to adhere to certain rules in the human world, but we are very conscious that we don't want it to become too commercial. So it's a balance.' I am reminded of the same conflict at Findhorn; the ever-present tension between a distrust of money and the impossibility of living without it.

'It feels right, so I go with it,' Karen says, smiling gracefully. 'Some people think I'm bonkers, but, usually, it's in a fond sort of way. And I don't care what people think: it's my incarnation, my life and I am having great fun working with the otherkin, and with the fae realms.'

'So faeries are in a separate realm?' I venture.

'Yes,' she says, 'but it exists alongside our realm. You can find yourself in it if you go through a faery portal – they're all over the place. Every flower and tree has a nature angel/faery watching over it too, helping it to grow – just like a parent would raise a child.'

I can't help but wonder where all this stuff comes from. 'Is your knowledge of faeries from folklore?'

'A lot of it is folklore, yes,' she nods, 'wives' tales, and legends, but it's all steeped in truths.'

'Do you know any non-faery otherkin?'

'Yes, there are quite a lot of merfolk in the UK. A lot of elves as well. You look at these people and think, "You are an elf, of course you are, I can't deny it." It's awakened within them. And hobbits. I know a lot of hobbits too.'

I can get on board with the idea of being a faery, or a mermaid, perhaps even a unicorn. But I wonder why it is that the otherkin community is full of fabulous mythical creatures, beautiful and fierce. And yet there aren't any slugs. Why aren't there any slugs?

Back in the City bar, I pose this question to Kiaan (you know... Kiaan the star from the start of this chapter).

He thinks for a while. 'Well, I think there wouldn't be a strong cognitive recognition of being a slug. The memory would be too simplistic, too weak. It wouldn't influence your being.'

Articulate and self-confident, Kiaan is softly spoken with an unidentifiable accent, his face framed with tight blond curls. 'Although I do struggle a little when people say they are Japanese anime characters or those who say: "I am Optimus Prime" – not "I identify with him" (who wouldn't), but "I am Optimus Prime". I find that difficult.'

When we first meet, he is adamant that he cannot represent the community in any way because he doesn't want his experiences to be seen as forging a path for others. He laughs. 'I'm a useless otherkin for you, aren't I? There is no headline for you, "Walrus Speaks" or "Star Speaks" – I am an enormous ball of gas; hydrogen smashing into helium.' He smiles, enjoying the image in his head.

'There are stereotypes, like "I always knew I was different", or "I didn't recognise the life I had been born into". Then you will get the feeling of being slightly out of sync with your dearest friends, or any group you try and fit into.'

I am surprised to hear Kiaan say this; he doesn't come across as odd or socially awkward to me. I leave a silence, willing him to continue.

'Before the internet, I didn't have the word "otherkin". But I always felt out of place. I was trying to work out why even my best friends had concerns about me, wishing I was a little bit more "same-o, same-o". Then you ask questions: is it because of my religious upbringing? My conservative parents? Or because I was fighting being gay in a small town? It was an intersection of a few rigid ideas.'

'And was it?'

'Who knows.' He looks resigned. 'But you start to think, "Oh that's why," and you end up congratulating yourself. Then the internet comes along, and maybe you are being influenced or maybe you just "click"; the word "otherkin" is there, and it's associated with magic, elves, vampires, and you think, "Ooh, this is interesting."'

Kiaan explains to me that, for him, otherkin doesn't mean 'other than' human, it means 'more than' human; acknowledging your human incarnation, but going further than that when it comes to identity.

'There have been reported investigations online into whether or not otherkin tails show up on Kirlian photography,' he explains. For the uninitiated – i.e. me, before I googled it – Kirlian photography is a technique for creating contact print photographs using high-voltage current and a metal discharge plate, said to be able to capture the electromagnetic field around an object or person, otherwise known as their 'aura'. He continues, 'Maybe that's bull, but the point is, that's not looking for a sense of identity any more; that's looking for objective truth. People in forums will say, "I've had my blood tested and I'm deficient in iron," but that doesn't mean you are a vampire.'

I decide that, if I were otherkin, I would be this way: wanting to prove everything; searching for the hard facts, the objective truths. I explain to Kiaan about my experiences with Kabbalah; that I am too much in 'tree of knowledge' and want to put everything in a box.

'Yes!' he nods enthusiastically. 'I studied Kabbalah for a while. The Tree of Life is a great model for anything. I am the same as you. My friends don't like watching films with me. Like the Hulk – I can't just enjoy it, because I can't work out where all that extra mass comes from! It's just not possible, so it distracts me.'

We both laugh.

'But I enjoyed suspending my disbelief for a while,' he continues. 'During the early web, when I wanted to find my identity. I flirted with my body, trying to feel for things, hoping for an epiphany. Like headgear; hair that turns to bone, like rhino horns. Or wings, maybe a tail, maybe fingers like this' – he puts his middle two fingers together like a Simpsons character.

He looks down. 'But I am too self-doubting. I worry I am tricking myself and just want to believe. That's why I am flirting with the idea of "star" as kin because we are all stardust, aren't we? So maybe I am just being poetic.'

There is a pause while Kiaan goes to the bar to get us another drink. When he returns, it is as if he's just remembered something really important. 'I have a friend I work with who came out as elven when she recognised the "kin" in my email address,' he says.

'Do elves speak in Elvish?'

'With each other?' he clarifies.

I nod.

'Oh yes. They write it too. My elf friend, for example, she knows the vocabulary. So, often she will think of the elf word for something before the English word.'

'But where do the languages come from?'

'Well, Tolkien has laid down the basis for two different elf languages, but they are always remembering new words as well. They remember the feeling of the words in their mouths.'

I decide to tell Kiaan about Uffie.

'So, as a kid, I was always a dog, on all fours,' I explain. 'My mum even bought me a collar and lead.'

'OK, well that really is something.' He leans forward in his chair, hands clasped in his lap like a therapist.

'I would lap from streams and stuff...' I start to feel embarrassed.

'LUCY!' he says, looking shocked. 'What are you saying?!'

I laugh, not sure whether or not to take him seriously. He smiles but continues to look straight at me, eyes wide, as if I have just revealed something life-changing.

'But I was a kid!' I say, feeling the sudden need to defend myself. 'Kids have imaginations!'

He laughs, 'Ha, yes! I would dress up as a lollipop man.'

'Exactly,' I say, relieved he hasn't locked me in the otherkin box, 'and imaginary friends and stuff. So I don't know if all this was suppressed because society told me to act more like a little girl, or if I just grew up.'

He nods. 'There is nothing wrong with saying a lot of people like dogs.'

'Have you considered how a psychologist would interpret the otherkin phenomenon?' I lean forward, mirroring his pose.

'Yes, just look up "magical thinking",' he says. 'It's when, instead of finding the logical cause for the effect you are experiencing, you embroider it so that everything has significance. But it's irrelevant, really; if something has significance for you, it doesn't matter whether or not it was a coincidence.'

He looks at the ceiling and takes a deep breath, searching for an example. 'If I see a sign in a twig or a feather or the sky, that's my meaning, and if you want to discount that as magical thinking, that's fine. There are a lot of psychologists out there who understand that you are modelling the world, and your model is just as relevant as anything else. Psychologists can be quite groovy in that respect. You can poke every occultist with the "magical thinking" stick. But you are right to query the trap; you are right to query what a psychologist would say.'

I left our meeting feeling like my brain had been wired to an electric current. The idea of modelling fascinated me, challenging me to step outside of my own map of this world and consider how others might experience it. Life is much harder when you can't put people in boxes, when you can't write them off as crazy when they don't conform to your model. To negate a belief system by labelling it a cult; to vilify fox hunters, yet poison rats because society happens to deem the latter more acceptable; to patronise hippies for experiencing a breadth of emotions not accessible to all of us. I realise that if I am truly going to understand the communities I am exploring, I need to let go of my fanatical quest for 'the truth', for objective fact, and realise that life is full of grey areas, full of the inexplicable and the unverifiable, as is the very nature of human consciousness.

Don't misunderstand me here: I bloody love science – just look at where it has got us. But if you aren't careful it can become a tyrant in its denial of the flexible, the changing, the poetic and the subjective. I have always been obsessed with debating, with proving people wrong, with debunking and smugly pointing out logical fallacies, as if all communication and human interaction can be boiled down to a mathematical equation.

You can find fanatical otherkin, who want to prove the world wrong with scientific evidence, just as you can find fanatical naturists who want to convert everyone to their way of living, and fanatical circus families who refuse to allow their children to integrate with the 'private' world. But you can also find trolls who flood the otherkin forums with 'logic bombs', conservatives who protest the opening of naturist beaches, and progressives who campaign against those who choose to live by old traditions. Both sides fight with a dangerous rigidity, rejecting all that is shaded grey, that uncertain place where human beings hate to linger.

I only wish I could fully immerse myself properly into this world, perhaps by spending the week in the body of a dog (it would definitely be a dog, not a slug), rather than sitting on the sidelines as an observer for this chapter, as if I were back in the big top. Kiaan had helped me to understand that lurking beneath what may seem like an Americanised 'fad' is a far deeper, far more considered community of people who are asking interesting Cartesian questions about identity and what it means to be human.

Kim, who shares her body with the spirit of a wolf called Luna, helped me further in this realisation. I meet her for lunch the next day in her local town of Chichester.

Arriving late, and all a fluster, I buy us both a pint of cider. The Wetherspoons pub we have chosen for our meeting is dimly lit and smells of bleach.

Kim 'awakened' – the otherkin term for realising your true identity – when she was fifteen years old. Her short bob tucks neatly behind one ear and is pinned down by thick-framed glasses.

'Everything just clicked into place,' she tells me as we order food from the dog-eared menus. 'All of the feelings and weirdness, and the phantom limb sensations – all of it made perfect sense.'

'Phantom limbs?'

She smiles patiently. 'A lot of otherkin get the same sensations as people who have had an amputation, but in the animal parts we don't have in this body. Like, teeth. I would feel like I had sharper, longer teeth, and pointed ears and claws and things like that. Tails are also very common.'

Kim feels that she and Luna are two parts of one soul. 'When I was younger,' she explains, 'there was more of a divide between us. My friends would notice; I would speak in a different voice and say things out of character. But now we are much more balanced.'

'Do you know what Luna's body looks like?'

'Oh yeah,' she says confidently, 'when I dream and meditate, I am often in my wolf body. It's very intense.'

I picture Bran from *Game of Thrones*, wondering how his ability to port himself into the minds and forms of other creatures compares with Kim's experience.

She continues, fingering a silver wolf pendant as she speaks, 'I don't know how long we've been together. I think it's a while. She is a spiritual, intelligent being as well. I think, if she were ever on her own, she would have been a creature of another realm, an astral realm, perhaps.'

'Is there much of a community in this country?'

'Online, yes, but real-life community not so much, although I have friends who are otherkin. We just find each other. It's creepy. You somehow know, and you fall into these situations – something tingling on the edge of your senses – you just get the feeling they aren't quite human, you know?' I nod, but I don't really.

'The last otherkin I met is a teacher,' she goes on. 'She just started behaving in a telltale way. Then she told us that she was a cat, and I was like "ah yes". My husband is a wolf too. We have been together since we were sixteen. We just instantly bonded, and I could sense what he was.'

'It seems like a massive coincidence that you are both wolves...'

'Yeah, but it was meant to happen.' She purses her lips into a tight smile and shrugs. 'We found each other for a reason. Wolves are probably the most common otherkin. Maybe it has something to do with the way humans domesticated dogs; we spent so much time with them and developed such a deep relationship with them.'

This excites me. 'Yeah, maybe we spent so much time together, our souls became permeable?'

'Maybe,' Kim sticks out her bottom lip and nods slowly.

'Are you happy you awakened?'

'Of course. It was hard to adjust at first, but it doesn't affect me so much any more. There are still times it pops out. Like when I am hurt I will growl, especially when I am surprised. Also, I am very scent-orientated. Smells distract me. I'm not saying I have a better than average sense of smell, but I pay more attention to it.'

Our food arrives, and I have a momentary fear that Kim is going to put her plate on the floor and eat as Luna. She politely picks up her knife and fork and puts her paper serviette on her lap.

'My husband and I can be wolves with each other,' she continues, 'especially when we communicate. It's so normal for us, and we have to be careful in public. We communicate in noises, growls and grunts, and our body language. It's just natural for us. When we are out in public, we say to each other, "We need to use our people words.'"

'Do you ever think that everybody is otherkin?' I ask, my mind desperate to weave its narrative. 'You know, like maybe we are all a mixture of souls in one body, but some people are more sensitive to this than others?'

Kim smiles at me, enjoying my enthusiasm. 'I have thought about that,' she says. 'Maybe some people are born to see, and others aren't. Children can see faeries and into the other worlds, but they get told by adults that it's not real, so they stop seeing over time. They are so pure, they have no filter like we do, and they haven't been corrupted by a standard they have to abide by to fit into society.'

I can't help but want to figure out the cause of all this. Surely there must be something that connects Kim, Karen and Kiaan?

'Have you seen a thread that connects your otherkin friends?'

'Well, a lot of otherkin I know are pagans,' Kim says, picking at her chips. 'But then again I know a lot of pagans. Most otherkin are creative and in touch with who they are. Sometimes you know someone is otherkin before they do, but you can't tell them. It feels wrong, like breaking a sacred law. So there is a stage when you have the awkward feeling of "I wonder if they are going to figure this out…"'

Like Kiaan, Kim is far from the 'crazy' I had expected. Friendly, intelligent and spiritual, she is completely open and comfortable with her realised identity. I trust her enough to let her in on my secret.

'You know, I used to pretend I was a dog when I was a kid. I had a lead and everything.'

'I did exactly the same thing!' She smiles knowingly, ever so slightly raising an eyebrow.

P is for... Pagans

*It's just the final burning of the Wicker
Man that's a bit of a bummer*

I listen to the *Wicker Man* album on repeat as I journey north for a Pagan Pride march through Nottingham city centre, anticipating the aesthetics I hope will surround me when I finally arrive. I am not disappointed. The men shroud themselves in long robes and carry staffs, while the women wear long, flowing gowns, their heads crowned in flower garlands and animal horns.

'We are pagan. We are proud!' I join in the chant as we parade in a long snake a hundred metres long and five abreast. Passers-by display a spectrum of emotions at the spectacle – from looks of unreserved delight to bewildered stares – probably wondering why these strange fairy-tale folk are parading through their unassuming town.

In 2010 the journalist Melanie Phillips wrote an article in the *Daily Mail* entitled 'Druids as an official religion? Stones of Praise here we come'. The commentary is openly mocking and talks of her anger at the prospect of paganism being recognised by the National Charity Commission. 'Someone tell me this is a joke,' she says, before going on to call Druidry a 'cult' and a bunch of 'totally barking mumbo-jumbo'.

What she doesn't acknowledge is that Christianity – 'the bedrock creed of this country' as she affectionately terms it – is predated by paganism. Christianity was a foreign religion, brought in and imposed on the country by the Romans, who reported the indigenous religion of this country as Druidry.

The original pagans had little organised religion per se, but generally adhered to a collection of beliefs including a reverence for nature and a pantheistic view on divinity. These days the word pagan typically refers to a person who worships nature, the elements, the seasons and the natural cycle of life and death, represented by the associated gods and goddesses inherent in the natural world. The modern pagan movement, known as neopaganism, is believed to be the fastest-growing religion in Britain, and it has been estimated that there are around 250,000 practising pagans in the country today.

The rousing chanting snake grows in volume as our rally progresses, and I get quite carried away by the whole affair. In fact, by the time we reach our final destination, the festival itself, I have pretty much convinced myself that I am pagan, and I am proud.

The venue of the festival is a large park, now packed full of stalls selling floaty dresses, books, horns, staffs, robes, trinkets, pottery, dragon ornaments, bunches of dried herbs, psychic readings, wings and incense. I peel off to wind my way around the stalls, talking to people and taking photos. I feel a little out of place in my black shorts and woollen top, and decide to buy a green, elven-looking dress to change into, my subterfuge ushering in a renewed sense of confidence.

Underneath a giant oak tree, Kerry, a full-time pagan priest, delivers a talk about priesting in the modern world to a group of around fifty.

'I think of myself as the Vicar of Dibley of the pagan world,' she says. 'I make tea and give hugs.'

Kerry performs public rituals, handfastings (pagan weddings), naming ceremonies (pagan christenings), passing-on ceremonies (pagan funerals), and hospital and prison visits.

'We go into schools sometimes too,' she says, 'for multi-faith assemblies, and we always get all of the attention because of our robes. The kids stare at us, wide-eyed, thinking we're from *Harry Potter.*'

She explains that pagan priests are also known as Druids, a name derived from the educated and professionals among the pre-historic tribal Celtic people of Britain. Modern Druids (Neo-Druids) are modelled on these ancient Celtic priests, wearing the same white robes as depicted in the accounts of Cicero, Pliny and Julius Caesar.

One such Druid is Damh the Bard, a famous pagan musician who had kindly agreed to a Skype interview with me the previous weekend.

His friendly face stares back at me from my computer screen, smiling eyes framed by the archetypal cascading grey hair. He is sitting in the office of the Order of Bards, Ovates and Druids – OBOD – an organisation with a membership upwards of 19,000, for which he is a global ambassador. With an average of 44,000 downloads of its monthly podcast at the time of interview, official membership of OBOD is growing by about ninety heads a month.

The office behind his wizardly face is disappointingly normal-looking. Strewn with piles of paper and coffee mugs, with a modern bookshelf and a round clock, it looks nothing like Dumbledore's office, which feels like a real missed opportunity.

Damh (born Dave Smith) explains that he initially found the occult through heavy-metal music, Ozzy Osbourne and the like:

'I guess I'm the reason they put those warning stickers on CDs,' he laughs. He first found the pagan traditions via studying magic, before moving onto Wicca, folklore and Druidry. His life had always been about music, poetry and art, so in 1994, when he received the intro booklets for OBOD, and they started to talk about 'the bard', it all clicked for him.

I realise I have no idea what his organisation does, so I ask him about the benefits of joining.

'Well, anyone can call themselves a Druid,' he admits, 'but there is so much information out there, you can become very confused, like you are clawing your way through a blackberry bush. So OBOD is a teaching order. The course isn't academic – it's experiential. The idea is to get people out of their houses and into the woods, doing stuff.'

I can't help but picture Eglantine Price from *Bedknobs and Broomsticks* poring over her course material from the Correspondence College of Witchcraft. I think about the old book that all the spells come from and wonder if OBOD is the same.

'Where does the knowledge for the course come from?'

'A number of sources,' he says. 'One is archaeology, so whenever there is a new finding at a site, it can influence what we do now. Another is the writing from classical sources like Julius Caesar and Siculus. But the biggest influences are the old stories and poems.'

He takes a sip of his tea. 'The way we like to explain it is with the metaphor of a restaurant. Some people like a menu, with ready-made options as choices, like Islam or Christianity; they are "religions of the book" and come fully formed and delivered to them. But pagan religions are so fragmented – we don't have a book, we have nature and stories – so we like to think of ourselves as being in the kitchen, and all the learnings are like ingredients, so we can make our own dinner. For me, that's what makes paganism so vibrant and relevant, and for some people that makes it fake and made-up.'

This analogy makes sense to me, but I can't yet decide which camp would work best for me. I have always considered myself a spiritual tourist, but I wonder whether this is just another symptom of my FOMO: walking down the aisle of a spirituality supermarket and struggling to choose from all the options. Like when you go to an all-you-can-eat buffet and end up with a bit of everything because you can't decide on one dish. I can tell you from experience that pizza, spaghetti and sweet-and-sour chicken does not work well together; sometimes I just need the chef to make these decisions for me.

'Do you have a daily practice?' I ask.

'Yes, because you can get swept along with technology and everyday life,' he says, gesturing at his computer. 'I need my daily dose of remembering what I am doing. So every morning when I wake up, I go out into my garden and offer a prayer to the four directions and a blessing on my day ahead. It's short, but it's grounding.'

I could do that, I think. 'Is there anything else that makes your life different to a non-pagan?' I cross my fingers for some kind of magical powers.

He laughs, 'Well, I've been working in the OBOD office since December 1998, and my music is directed towards the pagan community, so I haven't existed outside of this bubble for years. I don't know what's normal for everyone else any more.' He gives another big belly laugh. 'Some pagans are vegetarian; some aren't. Most eat ethically, so if they do eat meat, they will make sure they know how it's sourced.'

Dammit. So I would probably have to become a vegetarian. I recall the endless lentils at Findhorn and decide this probably isn't the religion for me.

'I have been a vegetarian in the past,' he says, 'after watching a film called *Earthlings*, which is a film everyone should watch if they eat meat.'

I desperately want to ask about human sacrifice, so I opt for a more subtle and cowardly version of the question. 'What was the response in the community to the *Wicker Man* film?'

'Weirdly enough, it is positive,' he says. 'It contains a lot of lore. And, in their hearts, apart from the human sacrifice bit, most pagans would love to live on Summerisle, to be part of a permanent community whose underlying principles are a belief in magic and a love of nature. It's just the final burning of the Wicker Man that's a bit of a bummer.'

The interview comes to an end, and Damh signs off with a cool 'see you along the road sometime'. As soon as he disappears from my screen, I watch *Earthlings* online. Holy shit. Suddenly the lentils don't seem so bad.

The pagan year is represented as a wheel, divided into eight significant festivals: the four seasons, the spring and autumn equinoxes (with equal days of light and dark), the winter solstice (celebrating the shortest day), and the summer solstice (celebrating the longest day). And where do you go to celebrate the summer solstice with the pagans? To Stonehenge, of course.

Although surprisingly little can be confirmed about their heritage, other than that they are thought to have been erected about 2500 BC (and holes have been found nearby that may have held stones which are dated to 7500 BC), many pagans claim the site as a spiritual home. Probably because they sit in the middle of the densest complex of Neolithic and Bronze Age monuments in England, offering a meaningful place of connection with our ancient ancestors.

I arrive at Stonehenge campsite on 21 June and immediately get stuck into a conversation with 'Jamie, Jamie Brown', a fifty-five-year-old surf instructor from Australia. After having a heart attack last year, Jamie became acutely aware of his mortality and decided to save for a three-month trip to tick things off his bucket list.

'I just thought I'd come over and poke around a bit, ya know, Lucy,' he tells me, in his Aussie drawl. 'I don't really have a plan. Just to meet some good people and see some great stuff.'

Spending the night at Stonehenge over the summer solstice is now the seventh most popular bucket-list entry in the world, another great example of the human obsession with ticking things off a list.

I explain to Jamie why I am here. 'Then you'll wanna talk to King Arthur,' he says. Luckily, I had already been in contact with this legend and arranged to interview him later that evening in exchange for a can of cider.

Arthur, born John Rothwell, was a biker and general odd-jobs man until one night, in a squat, his friend told him that he was in fact not John Rothwell, but a modern-day reincarnation of King Arthur. After realising his friend was right, John changed his name to Arthur Pendragon the following week. The first group of people to accept Arthur were the Druids, raising him as an 'Honorary Pendragon' in the Glastonbury Order of Druids.

His first battle in this order was to release Stonehenge from its shackles. The site had been fenced off to the public since 1977 due to concerns around preservation, provoking outrage in the community, who felt that their right to practise their ancient religion in a place that is sacred to them had been compromised. And so began a decade of protests from Arthur and his loyal 'Warband'.

Regularly returning to the site, Arthur was arrested and imprisoned every year between 1990 and 2000 for 'challenging the legality of their exclusion zone' (attempting to break in). He took on the British government in the European Court of Human Rights, pleading his religious right to worship at Stonehenge as a Druid. After continued negotiation between the authorities and the Druids, it was agreed that, from the year 2000, Stonehenge would be open to the public for the summer and winter solstices, and the autumn and spring equinoxes.

I arrive at the stones at around 11 p.m. to find the place packed with 36,000 revellers. Strewn with litter and hawker vans selling burgers, the place looks more like a festival than the spiritual sanctuary I had been expecting.

I step over the sleeping bodies and squeeze through the throngs in the middle of the giant stone formation to arrive at the Heel Stone, my pre-arranged meeting point with the king.

'Hi, Arthur, I'm Lucy.'

He looks at me with piercing eyes, his wizardly white hair held in place by a thin silver crown. He wears a tabard bearing a red dragon over a white robe, his sword – Excalibur – sheathed at his waist.

'What did I say to you in the email?' he says to me in a surprisingly high-pitched voice.

'To bring you cider,' I say, handing him a can of Thatchers Gold.

'That'll do.' He opens it and takes a swig.

'I have been relentlessly fighting for peace for the last twenty years,' he begins unprompted, as if giving this speech for the hundredth time. 'At the moment I'm fighting the "English Heretics" to return the remains of the ancestors they dug out of the ground, instead of putting them in a display cabinet in their visitor centre. I gather signatures every day. I'm a right pain in the neck!' he says, laughing. 'But I'll win in the end. I always do.'

It's true – he has been remarkably successful, even when it came to securing his right to legally carry Excalibur in public, and to wear a crown in his passport photo (for 'religious reasons').

Arthur sees himself as a true knight of the Round Table, put on this planet for a reason: to fight the good fight. It is romantic, and I can see why anyone would revel in this sense of purpose.

'What will you do when there is nothing left to fight for?'

He laughs in a high-pitched shrill. 'I'll leave!' he says with a resigned shrug. 'My work here will be done. I always say I fight for peace, and when we get it, I'm not interested any more. I'm outta here.'

I guess we all need something to fight for, a reason for our existence. With the decline of organised religion, in the UK at least, the thirst for purpose inherent in the human psyche searches desperately for another outlet. Something to fight for: Justice for Harambe, a favourite contestant on *The X Factor*, the right to be naked, the success of a beloved football team; desperately searching for meaning in a meaningless life.

Arthur looks back up at me. 'Do you have any more cider?'

'Yeah, I have another one back up in the circle. I'll bring it down later,' I reassure him.

A lady walks over. 'Ah, there you are, Sue,' Arthur perks up. He turns toward me. 'This is Lucy. She is a writer.' She takes this as her cue and leads me away from Arthur.

'I am Arthur's High Priestess,' she tells me. 'My full title is Dame Knight Commander of the Arthur Warband.' She wears a long crimson cloak, her dark red hair covered by a black hat decorated with a garland of flowers.

'I've followed Arthur for twenty years now,' she says, 'even visited him in prison.'

'What was he inside for?'

'Oh different things,' she says. 'Protests, drunk and disorderly...'

The king wanders back over and starts laughing. 'I defended myself on that charge,' he says. 'Stood up and spoke. Wasn't supposed to, but I just said, "You've got it all wrong – yes, I was drunk – but I am always disorderly." That's just me, ain't it? Nothing to do with the booze!' He bends double, his laugh like a machine gun.

'He is the Lord of Misrule,' Sue says, gazing at him affectionately.

Arthur decides to talk to me again, relaying his theory on the three different types of Druids.

'First there are the elitist Druids who are pious, think they are better than anyone else and want to keep sacred places for themselves. Then there are the learned Druids, who spend decades studying the books and learning about all the different gods. Then there's my lot, the warrior Druids, who are more intuitive, fight for peace and get their education from the world rather than books.'

People continually walk up to Arthur to say hello and introduce themselves. He is like a celebrity here. He engages with everyone in a kind and authentic manner, even the drugged-up teenagers who struggle to construct a sentence.

The night progresses, and I speak to a few more Druids, dotted irregularly among the sea of partygoers. Among the 36,000 people, the Druids are insignificant in number (fifty or so), with some now refusing to attend because they disapprove of what the event has become: a drug-infused festival, or a tick on a bucket list.

I keep accidentally stepping on passed-out people every time I want to get somewhere, and the floor is strewn with empty beer cans. I can't help but yearn for something a bit more peaceful, a bit more spiritual.

I wander back over to see what Arthur makes of it all. 'The pious Druids don't like it,' he says, 'but I don't mind at all. For lots of people, being here is just a cultural thing, like going to Times Square for New Year's, but for pagans it's a spiritual thing. We're here for the rituals. Doesn't bother me either way; we have our thing, and they have theirs, so everybody is happy.'

It is now four o'clock, and the sky is becoming lighter. Everybody stands to face the Heel Stone, their eyes glued to the horizon, waiting for the golden orb to make an appearance. The Druids begin their rituals and a big circle forms around them. Rollo Maughfling, the Archdruid of Glastonbury, stands up to lead the crowd in a chant against hunger and fracking, clinging to his crooked staff like an old wizard.

'May there be peace in the south,' he says – raising his hands as if doing an upright press-up.

He motions for us all to copy him; we do.

'May there be peace in the north.'

'May there be peace in the west.'

'May there be peace in the east.'

His sentences come out in flurries, his wild silver hair and long beard blowing in the light morning breeze.

'And most importantly,' he says, pausing to assume his wisest face, 'may there be peace throughout the world.'

A few minutes later the sun finally arrives to cries of jubilation from the crowd. I feel as if we are all rolling towards it, tipping closer and closer to the sun. It gives me a sense of connection with the earth and the natural order of things. Although that could also be the cider. The group behind me burst into a rendition of the 'Circle of Life'.

After the sunrise, I go off to find Arthur, who has promised me a knighthood. I kneel before him in the middle of a large crowd while he unsheathes Excalibur. A man in full Druid tabard plays the drums at the head of the circle.

He places the flat of his sword lightly on my head. 'Do you swear to speak the truth?'

'Yes,' I say, with false confidence.

He touches the sword on my right shoulder. 'To honour your spoken word.' He moves to my left shoulder. 'To be just and fair in all your dealings.' He begins reciting some words in a language I don't understand as he repeats the action with Excalibur. When he gets back to my head, he pauses.

'If I take your head off, it's because you forgot the second cider!'

Shit. I did. I instinctively stand up and back away from the huge sword. Thankfully his face opens into a grin as he says, 'Arise, Warrior Priestess...' – giving me a bear hug as he completes my new title – '... the Ciderless!'

Q is for... (Drag) Queens

*Tucking my old man away
and all that business*

My phone rings. It is an unknown number.

'Hi, Lucy, it's Dave here,' the voice says. 'I was given your details by a friend. Apparently you want to find out more about drag queens.'

'Oh, hi, Dave,' I say, elated to have finally hurdled my drag-queen brick wall. Although drag is undoubtedly an open and friendly culture, I didn't know any drag queens personally and hadn't had any responses to my Facebook messages, tweets and emails to the various artists I had found online, so I was really struggling to make any inroads here. That was until a friend put me in touch with a helpful Brighton bar manager (thanks, Kat), who must have shared my details with Dave. Of course, the Brighton drag cabaret scene is just one small element of a much broader and thriving drag culture across the UK – a subculture within a subculture, as it were – but I hoped it would at least offer me a glimpse into this vibrant community.

'Did your friend tell you what I'm doing?' I ask.

'No, not really,' he says.

'Well, I'm writing a book about British subcultures and—'

'Oh no!' – he cuts me off – 'We're not a subculture, dear. We are an enormous, thriving community, not some seedy underworld. We're out in the open, as big as West Hollywood. Have you even heard of West Hollywood?'

'Yes,' I lie, 'I—'

He interrupts me again. 'Well, if you are looking for a subculture, then you're looking in the wrong place.'

I somehow manage to persuade him, in the short bursts of words he allows me to shoehorn in, of what I mean by a subculture. 'Not the typical British mainstream,' I land on.

'Well, when I think of subculture, I think of lowlifes, you know, and murderers.'

'No, no,' I laugh. 'I'm not spending time with any murderers.'

'Well, you wanna be careful with that word,' he warns me. 'Some people won't like it.'

I haven't had any trouble using it so far. In fact, a lot of the groups I have spent time with have even worn it as a badge of honour, proud to be different from the mainstream. But I can see why those who have had to fight for acceptance from society might take offence at being dubbed non-mainstream, and vow to rid the word from my vocabulary for the next week.

Dave lowers his hackles. 'Well, let me start by telling you that drag queens are professionals; they're not just men who dress up as women – that's trannies, darling. Nothing wrong with trannies, but they aren't the same thing. Drag queens are men who make a professional living as entertainers. There is a big difference.'

'Got it, thank you.'

He continues, 'Lots of pubs pay thirty pounds for amateur drag queens to host karaoke nights and crack a few jokes, but they aren't the real deal. Drag artists are comedians in wigs.

There are five main acts in the Brighton scene at the moment.' He pauses. 'I hope you are writing this down?'

I scrap around in my backpack for a pen, balancing my iPhone against my shoulder.

'There's Davina Sparkle – that's me, darling – then there's Maisie Trollette, who is the oldest drag queen in the country at over eighty, then there's Miss Jason, Dave Lynn and Lola Lasagne.'

I scribble the names on the back of a rejection letter from the Estate of Kate and Wills (it was worth a try...).

Dave continues, 'I was in a TV thing a while back. But they all want to sensationalise it. So they cut and paste their videos and they end up making you look like a dick.'

I reassure him that I do not plan on making him look like a dick, and we agree to meet at Legends ('Brighton's Biggest Gay Hotel') the following weekend.

Eight days later I carry a suitcase of sparkly clothes through a sea of immaculately dressed men and make for reception. Once checked in, I head straight to my room, put on a jazzy top, force myself out of my room and head back down to the bar full of strangers to try and make some friends.

'They are only strangers until you talk to them,' I mutter to myself, probably looking like I've lost the plot, before ordering a large glass of wine from the bar.

With my glass of confidence in hand, I make for a middle-aged, smiling couple sitting by the stage.

'Hello,' I say, waving gormlessly, 'I'm Lucy.'

'Hi, Lucy,' the lady says, a short bob framing her friendly face. 'I'm Kim.' She smiles, stretching out her arm to encompass the man sitting next to her, 'And this is Graham.'

I take a big gulp of wine. 'I'm on my own – do you mind if I join you?'

Graham pulls out the chair next to him, and I collapse into it, relieved to have some company.

'We come out to see Davina quite a bit.' Kim points at the empty stage. 'She has recently had an operation on her knee, so I've been doing some of her washing and ironing.'

'Yeah,' Graham rolls his eyes and smiles. 'Cheeky cow!'

'Do you always refer to a drag queen as a "she"?' I ask, cringing at my naivety.

'Oh yes,' Kim says, 'I always call Dave Davina. But it depends. Maisie Trollette, for example. Now she hates anyone calling her "she" when he's not in drag. But most don't mind either way.'

I hope I don't mess this up.

With that, Davina appears from behind the bar in dramatic make-up, a huge blond wig, a black sequinned jacket and velour trousers. She weaves through the crowd as the soundtrack switches to show tunes. It is around this point that I start to feel a lot more relaxed. I bloody love show tunes.

Davina makes for the stage. 'Now, I do swear a lot. So if anyone is easily offended, I suggest you fuck off,' she begins.

After an hour of observational comedy, filthy jokes and cabaret songs, she points to me and beckons me up on stage. I have no idea how she identified me: I guess I look much more out of place than I'd hoped.

I walk up the few stairs to greet her, shielding my eyes from the burning lights.

'Everybody, this is Lucy,' she says to the audience. 'She is writing a book on drag queens.'

Hmmm, sort of true.

She looks back at me. 'Are you straight, Lucy?'

I nod.

'Well, watch out for all the lesbians.' She points to the back of the hall. 'They'll be after you.' She fills two glasses with a black syrupy drink and passes one to me. I decide to try and link my arm through hers for a dramatic down-in-one.

'Oh no, we're not going to do any of that, darling.' She pushes my hand away. 'You've got a vagina.'

After one more cabaret number, the show ends to rapturous applause, and Davina invites me up to her hotel room to talk.

I sit in silence and watch her remove her wig and saturate a cloth in baby oil to wipe away her make-up.

'See, in Brighton,' she says, unprompted, 'they have a drag cabaret circuit.' She hands me her wig and gestures for me to put it on a polystyrene head sitting on top of the wardrobe.

'The main scene is: start here at four o'clock sharp, then get to the Queens Arms for six o'clock, then on to Charles Street for seven-thirty. It's a tradition. Each venue will give the main drag queens four bookings a year. Are you with me?'

I nod, wondering when my narrative should switch from she to he; at what point Davina becomes Dave.

'Is this what you do for a living?' I ask.

'Yeah, this is my full-time job, four to five nights a week,' she says. 'But I also manage a male striptease company called the Adonis Cabaret Show, so on a Saturday night, I do that. It's a bit daunting because you have a little bit to drink as well, so you have to watch your health.' She pats her belly and raises an eyebrow. 'But I love it. Wouldn't want to do anything else.'

Davina now moves onto scrubbing at the layer of plastic that keeps her thick eyebrows pinned down. The change is dramatic.

'Do you feel different when you take your make-up off?' I ask.

'No, I don't feel any different in drag or out of drag.' She takes a sip of water and rubs the sides of her face. 'We don't dress as women; we dress as drag queens. A lot of straight girls don't get that. They think that we are all trying to be women, but it's not true. I look like a parody of a drag queen, really, like a pantomime dame.'

'Do you enjoy dressing in drag?'

She looks at me in the mirror, as if noticing I'm there for the first time. 'Not at all,' she says. 'I hate dressing as a woman. Hate it. But I love the show.' She looks back at her reflection with a joyful longing. 'The gays wouldn't accept you as a man doing jokes, you see. They want a drag queen. The audience like you being camp with them' – she turns her head and winks – 'because we all like a bit o' camp.'

She gestures for me to pass her jeans.

'Even in the old days with Kenneth Williams, *Round the Horne* was a popular radio programme. They used to come out with all the gay speak – like "bona lallies on the omi" – and people would laugh because they didn't know what it meant.'

She looks at me expectantly. I smile and raise an eyebrow, willing her to continue.

'Nice legs on the man!' She grins before turning her attention back to the mirror.

I did know what Davina was talking about. Known as Polari, this code language was used in the early twentieth century by gay men to communicate safely when homosexuality was still a criminal offence. It was a mixture of different slangs and argots, containing elements of French, Italian, Yiddish and Romani languages as well as back slang (pronouncing words as if they were spelled backwards), Cockney rhyming slang and Elizabethan thieves' cant. It was also widely used by circus and fairground people (hence the Romani), theatre actors, sailors and sex workers. Its use faded after the Sexual Offences Act of 1967 decriminalised homosexuality, but some of its words have become part of everyday English. It is saluted in the name of the Polari Prize, which is currently the only literary award that celebrates writing that explores the LGBTQ+ experience.

'But there is so much equality at the moment,' Davina continues. 'People can go anywhere, get married, all that stuff. So we're losing our identity as a gay scene, you know? People just go, "Oh, he's a poof. Seen it all before."' There is a pause. 'Equality is a good thing, of course, but all I'm saying is, be careful what you wish for.'

She wrestles with her flies while I wrestle with what she has just said. I have honestly never thought of this before. Does equality somehow make us less unique? Does something lose its appeal as it becomes more mainstream, more accepted? Perhaps that's why many pagans have abandoned the summer solstice at Stonehenge as tens of thousands flock to join them, the experience somehow losing its value. There is something nostalgic about Davina bringing up Polari here that speaks to a sense of her version of the old gay culture being somehow lost or dissipated.

'If you could command the same audience performing out of drag,' I try, 'would you prefer that?'

'Well, some people do,' she says. 'Like Miss Jason, and Lola as well. They've done stand-up. But I don't because the make-up is a cover, it's a "you can't hurt me, I'm a character". When I am Dave, I'm just Dave, but when I am Davina, I am outrageous, and a little bit naughty. So that's the difference.'

I am reminded of the LARPers; the escapism of taking on another persona and the freedom it gives you to do things you believe yourself incapable of in your other identity.

'So it's like something to hide behind?'

'Course it is,' she says. 'It's a mask that you put on.'

Now fully Dave again, he takes a final look in the mirror and narrows his eyes. 'Oh God, I'm a bit pissed!'

When we arrive at the Queens Arms together to watch Lola Lasagne's show, the crowd is full of familiar faces from Legends, including Kim and Graham. Lola has a powerful, pitch-perfect voice, and between her and Davina, I am impressed with the level of vocal talent and showmanship I have seen on this scene so far. The crowd love her, especially the very loud front circle of black-shirt-clad women, out for a social with the local skittle club.

During the performance, a trio of Dave's friends take me to the back of the pub to look at pictures of all the big local queens like Mandy Gap and Tanya Hyde.

'Where are you off to next?' I ask the guys. 'Charles Street,' is the unanimous response.

'Can I come with you?'

'Of course!' Dave joins in, introducing me to the wider group. 'Everyone, this is Lucy. She's coming with us, and she's writing a book about drag queens.'

'Well, it's about lots of different subcultures really,' I pipe up, emboldened by my third glass of wine. 'But Dave doesn't like that word.'

'Yeah, we had a bit of a barney about that on the phone, didn't we, darling?' Dave winks at me.

On the way to Charles Street, I tell one of Dave's friends what my book is about. 'So I have been living with different communities, like hippies, pagans, circus performers, goths,' I explain.

'Ohhh.' He screws up his nose. 'I don't know if I like the idea of drag queens being in a book with all that lot.' I sidle away from him as we enter the bar, unwilling to entertain his prejudice, and not sober enough to be polite about it.

I stumble home at around eleven, and fall into a dreamless sleep, pissed as a fart. I am sure some interesting stuff happened over the course of the evening, but I honestly can't remember any of it.

I spend the following day writing and people watching in the bar, enjoying the strong sense of community as people come and go, sharing their gossip and making plans. A few of the regulars come over for a chat, curious about my writing, and, more likely, wondering what somebody wearing a fleece and hiking backpack is doing in Brighton's Biggest Gay Hotel.

Four o'clock sneaks up on me, and so does Miss Jason. 'I'll be the one with the laptop just inside Legends,' I had texted him to say.

He texted back immediately: 'I'll be the fat camp one. Lol. X'

I love him already and wave manically as he walks over. He has a rosy face with spiky brown hair and a button nose. He buys me a pint of cider and orders himself a soda water. 'I'm trying to lose a bit of weight,' he says, presumably to excuse himself from not drinking alcohol. I'm sure this must be a British thing.

'I've been doing this for seventeen years this August,' he begins after we have settled in the corner of the bar.

'What did you do before drag?'

'I worked in the House of Lords, as a researcher and constituency officer' – he makes a bet-ya-weren't-expecting-that face – 'I was also the youngest county councillor in the country, elected at twenty-one.'

'What did your ex-colleagues think of you becoming a drag queen?'

'Some of them were quite accepting of it, and I'm still in touch with them. But others just finished with me there and then. I think they just didn't understand it; it was too different for them, so they shut down.'

I remember the battle re-enactor telling me about her colleagues reacting in the same way. I guess some people just don't know how to respond to someone who is different; so afraid of something they don't understand, they simply block it out and pretend it doesn't exist.

We pause to stroke a passing dog. 'She likes me as a man,' Jason says, tickling the dog's chin. 'But she can't stand me in drag. Barks her head off!'

He starts to sing along with the music, swaying his head from side to side and raising his eyebrows. 'We always sing as kids, don't we?' he says. 'Oh, I'm a vain old queen, though. Sang in the mirror, din' I? With a hairbrush.' He laughs.

I pick up on this. 'Now, you used the word queen there, but that doesn't necessarily mean a drag queen, right?'

'Oh no, it just means another gay man.'

I picture one of my gay friends, wondering how long it would take for him to talk to me again if I called him a queen. I try to clarify: 'A certain type of gay man?'

'Yeah, a camp, effeminate man. But I do tend to refer to all men as she, even the butch ones. It winds some people up like nothing else, but that tends to make me want to do it more.'

The dog wanders back over and jumps onto the bench between us. Jason strokes its head absent-mindedly. 'The essence of drag is disappearing,' he continues, his tone softer. 'The young 'uns coming up through now are more like female impersonators.'

'Why is it changing?'

'I think one of the reasons is to do with how much gays have moved on in the last decade,' he says. 'Now we can go anywhere we like. We can be as camp as we like and get away with it. So our scene is disappearing, and as our community has moved on, it has become more popular on the telly – Graham Norton, Alan Carr, Paul O'Grady – so there is less demand to have the outrageous camp on stage.'

I am reminded of my time with the circus, of the decline of nostalgic, live performances like this, in the face of modern-day entertainment beamed straight into our living rooms. Of course, this is where you can also catch the fabulous *Ru Paul's Drag Race*, a show that has grown from a small, fervent fan base to regularly clocking up more than 700,000 viewers, sweeping the Emmy Awards for Reality TV year after year. The show has no doubt done a huge amount to popularise drag and bring it to a wider audience, but perhaps it has also changed the face of the more traditional drag-show scene, forcing performers like Davina and Miss Jason to either appeal to nostalgia or adapt with the times.

'Evolve or die, that's what people say, isn't it?' Jason interrupts my thoughts. 'Well, I'm doing a bit of work as a man soon. Stand-up comedy. I hope the stand-up grows, because I am desperate to get on the telly.'

I think about the transformation of Paul O'Grady from his drag alter ego Lily Savage; it's almost difficult to remember him as Lily now, but she was the one who stole the nation's heart, then Paul came in and sealed the deal. But would he be as successful if he went back? I would like to think so.

'Are you nervous about performing as a man?'

'Yes, I shall wear these glasses' – he holds up black, thick-framed glasses – 'because I won't have my make-up, the wig, the frock and the jewellery. It's all armour you see, dear. Emotionally, dressing in drag is fantastic, because it brings me fun. But physically it's a nuisance, squeezing myself into tights and Spanx, tucking my old man away and all that business.'

'Would you do this for ever, if you could?'

'I think my longing for stimulation, attention and adulation—' He puts his hand over his mouth. 'That's terrible, innit, but it's true. Something like that always stays with you, because if you've had it once, you want it again. You always want another applause, and you want it to be bigger and louder each time. I don't think I would ever lose that.'

It's time for Jason to go up to his dressing room and transform into Miss Jason. I picture yesterday's experience of Davina's dressing room in reverse. Before he goes, I have time for one last question.

'Why do you want to be on the TV?'

He pauses for a few seconds and then grins, 'Because I'm an attention-seeking poofter, darling!'

R is for... Racing

It used to be all about the dogs

'You'll have to excuse the mess,' Barry shouts back in a thick, south east London accent as I habitually take off my shoes at the front door. I step over the body of an outstretched greyhound in the hallway and swerve to avoid a pile of toys en route to his lounge. The enormous room is lined with hundreds of rosettes, shelves bursting with dog-shaped trophies. My nose is overwhelmed by the potent combination of dog, wood smoke and rich pine.

'Come on, then.' He stands by the fire with his arms crossed and looks at me expectantly. 'What do you want to ask me?' Like a grown-up Artful Dodger, Barry's glowing cheeks, oval face and round nose give him the look of a loveable rogue.

'Um... well, a lot of stuff, really,' I say, taken aback. 'Like... um... how did you get into dog racing?'

'Oh, that's easy,' he says, 'me dad was a trainer, wunt he.' He pauses and looks at me again, his eyes saying 'next'. I don't have a next, so we stand in silence for a moment, before he beckons me out to the hall.

'Look this is 'im 'ere.' He points to a black-and-white picture of a handsome man kneeling proudly between two greyhounds.

'And this is the house.' He points at another picture on the wall, a bird's-eye view of the house with what looks like a massive racetrack in the back garden.

'Wow.' I look at him wide-eyed. 'You have your own track?'

'Course we do, mate.' He beams at me. I like that he calls me mate.

Barry is the trainer of just over a hundred dogs, all of whom live in the kennels behind his house. Contracted to run at least thirty-five dogs a week at Crayford Greyhound Track in Dartford, his kennel is the biggest in the county and the only one with its own track and dog swimming pool.

He takes me out to show me around. The kennels are bright white, surprisingly clean, and ear-shatteringly noisy. The dogs live in pens of two, spread across three wings. Each has a bed filled with shredded paper and a small space for the dogs to walk around. As I walk past each pen, the dogs go crazy, jumping up at the bars and wagging their tails wildly to compete for my attention.

'Can I touch them?' I ask Barry.

'Of course' – he nods and smiles at me, as enthusiastic as his dogs – 'greyhounds are very friendly.'

I nervously put my hand through the bars into one of the kennels, where it is greeted by a warm tongue and a soft furry head.

After helping Barry to load up eleven dogs into the wire crates of a large van, we head to Crayford for the evening's racing. I ask Barry about his livelihood as we make the short journey to the track. He explains to me that his contract at Crayford gives him a modest and sustainable income, which he supplements with training fees of £7 per dog, per day, and renting his track out to other trainers.

'Do you enjoy doing this?'

'Yup,' he says. 'Love it. But it's hard work, and you get fed up sometimes, just like any job. You never get a day off, and it takes over your life. But you got to step back, take a chill pill and say, you know what, I would much rather be doing this than sitting in a bloody office.'

'What are your owners like?'

'It varies. They can come from all over the country, sometimes from abroad an' all. One of me owners even 'as an MBE!'

'Do they ever come up to visit the dogs?'

'Most of 'em do, yeah. Sunday's the day for that. They come down the kennels, walk the dogs, give 'em tidbits, pet 'em.' His voice breaks into laughter. 'Drive me mad with "why didn't it win?"'

For Barry's greyhounds, the day starts at 6.30 a.m., when they are let out into the paddocks while their kennels are cleaned. Then they are 'galloped' round the track, taken for a swim if they need it – usually as physical therapy – groomed, let out twice more and fed before bedtime.

'How do you "gallop" a greyhound?' I ask him.

'Easy.' He smiles at me. 'One man stands at the top of the field, and one stands at the bottom, and we take it in turns calling 'em.'

This makes me laugh.

'What?' Barry grins, laughing along with me, neither of us really knowing why.

When we arrive at the races, I am not allowed through the dogs' entrance because of anti-doping regulations, so I go through the main entrance and head for the cafeteria. The room feels sterile and dated, flooded with intense artificial light. The smell of fried chicken and chips makes me hungry as a smiling woman with a tattooed arm and a hand full of gold rings hands me a Styrofoam cup of tea through a serving hatch. Groups of middle-aged men sit around in tracksuits and children play tag between the tables. Most of the younger crowd look like they are dressed up for a night on the town.

I am surprised by how many people have ventured out on a Tuesday night and I pose this thought to the man next to me as we queue to place our bets on the dog with the most ridiculous name (that's definitely what everyone does).

'Well, you know, greyhound racing used to be the most popular spectator sport in the UK,' he says, his hands buried deep in his tracksuit bottoms. 'There were over eighty different tracks, and each could attract up to fifty thousand spectators.'

'What about now?' I ask him, struggling to choose between 'Jabberin Jackie' and 'Iruska Tomtiggle.'

'Well, it ain't in its prime no more,' he says. 'It's still popular, but a lot has changed in the sport over the decades. It used to be all about the dogs. People were passionate. It's all they would talk about. But now it's mainly young people who come here for a bit of fun before a night on the town.' He gives a dramatic 'what ya gonna do?' shrug, presumably accepting of the fact that, without this new line of business from the young revellers, the track simply wouldn't survive.

During the races I stand outside on the steps with Barry and his fellow trainers. They are a mixed bag; some in tracksuits, others in tweed suits and trilbies. The lady next to me wears a black bomber jacket.

I lead with an ingenious icebreaker. 'Hi, I'm Lucy.' (I know, right? Sometimes I amaze myself.)

She looks at me, forces a smile and nods before turning her attention back to the race.

'Is there anything you don't like about being a trainer?' I ask, pushing through her obvious reluctance to engage.

'People think it's cruel,' she says, her eyes not leaving the track.

'Why do you think that is?'

'Oh, I dunno,' she shrugs. 'Probably because they think we kill our dogs. But we don't. We love our dogs. We are so proud of 'em. When they win, there's no feeling like it.'

'Have you ever killed one of your dogs?' I hold my breath.

Her head snaps toward me as she takes me in for the first time. 'Never,' she says, 'and we've 'ad 'undreds.'

The crowd start to roar, and she turns her attention back to the track as the dogs round the bend in front of the stands. 'Come on, girl,' she yells. Everyone joins the cheer, the sound reverberating around the track as the dogs zoom past us, transfixed by the orange windsock masquerading as their prey.

'Sometimes they have to be put to sleep, mind you.' She continues to stare in the direction of the dogs as they disappear onto their second lap. 'You know, if they're old and sick.'

'Would you ever want to do anything else?'

'I couldn't. None of us could. It's a passion.' She looks over at Barry. 'It's in our blood, innit, Bar?' He nods, smiles, and flashes me a wink.

It hasn't been a great day for Barry, particularly compared to the night before, when he won three out of four races. We come away with one win and a handful of seconds and thirds.

It has been a great evening for me, though; I won £2.50. We debate what I should spend my newfound wealth on during the journey home, before unloading the sleepy dogs back at the kennels and dishing out their well-deserved kibble.

*

The following morning, I drive back down to Kent and walk around the back of Barry's house, through the adjoining greyhound rehoming centre – Dunrunnin' – and find him at the helm of his hare machine. The 'hare' is a brightly coloured windsock that he operates at varying speeds as the dogs chase it around the sand track.

'You all right, mate?' He smiles and stretches his hand out as I walk towards him. 'I wondered when you'd be 'ere.'

Today Barry is controlling the hare and timing the runs for various owners and trainers who have brought their dogs in for training.

I wander over and join the group of men at the side of the track to watch. One of the dogs lies down in the traps for an impromptu nap, completely ignoring the hare as it zooms past. 'She is just a bit confused, that's all.' Her trainer leaps to her defence as the other men do nothing to hide their amusement. He walks over and rescues her from the traps, bringing her back out to join us at the side of the track. 'She'll get there in the end, won't ya, girl?' He rubs her all over, bending down for her to lick him on the nose.

Chloe, Barry's daughter, joins us. She is training to be a vet at Liverpool University, 'So my dad can get free treatment for his dogs,' she tells me in her outside voice. A faint chortling comes from the hut.

'Do you want to come and meet the pups?' she asks me. I nod vigorously, and she leads me over to two big grass pens on the other side of the track. 'You always keep pups outside,' she explains on the way over, 'so they can run around. It helps them to develop properly.'

The pens are full of gangly, happy dogs, whose whole bodies lean from left to right with the swinging of their tails. She introduces me to Trigger, Boycie, Cassandra, Del Boy, Rodney and Uncle Albert.

It's time for their daily exercise, so Chloe opens the gate and the dogs bound past us, barking and leaping in the air like gazelles. They pelt out onto the track and start to gallop madly, round and round, stopping to play now and then, before accelerating off like coiled springs.

The manager of Dunrunnin', a lady called Karen, walks past the edge of the track and Chloe beckons her to join us in the middle.

'They make such wonderful pets,' she says, as one of the dogs comes over to greet us. 'The only problem is that they get a bit institutionalised when they are racing. Most of them will have never been in a house before, never seen a cat, never seen a glass door,' she laughs, 'so they tend to run into 'em, full pelt.'

'Are some of them too vicious to rehome?' I ask.

'It is almost unheard of for a greyhound to be human aggressive,' she says. 'But they can sometimes chase smaller dogs because they don't know what they are. Most will be rehomed but occasionally they are too nervous, and no one wants them.'

My face screws up. 'What happens to those ones?'

She rolls her eyes. 'They end up hogging my bloody sofa!'

S is for... SF Super Fans

I've got Bran three times now

Like Hansel and Gretel, we follow the trail of bearded men wearing printed t-shirts through the Wellington Park Hotel in Belfast. The smell of ale fills the convention floor. Groups of people wearing dark shapeless clothing huddle around small tables bursting with pint glasses.

Armed with little more than patchy Tolkien knowledge and Converse trainers, my trusty geek-curious friend Lynsey and I are attending our first-ever 'con' (convention). Fans gather at cons all around the world to explore common interests related to Speculative Fiction (SF), an all-encompassing label that includes science fiction, fantasy and supernatural horror. Our event of choice is TitanCon, focused on the epic fantasy adventure and cult HBO TV series *Game of Thrones*. With around 200 attendees, this is a more intimate convention and, as fans of the show, we hoped we would be able to fit in here, or at least hold our own in plot conversations.

To calm our nerves, and give us something to focus on, we decide on a game of 'count the beards'. It runs out of steam when we get past fifty, so we decide to strike up a conversation with one of the beard-bearers instead. Dan is sporting a black Stetson and a pink t-shirt with a unicorn posing in front of a rainbow.

'Why doesn't he have wings?' I point at Dan's t-shirt.

'Unicorns don't actually have wings,' he explains patiently, 'you are thinking of a Pegasus.'

I attempt a retort: 'Ah, but some unicorns do have wings; wings and horns are not mutually exclusive.'

'True,' he nods diplomatically, 'but the wings are irrelevant to the definition of a unicorn. It just needs to have a horn.' Everyone who has gathered around to be party to this conversation nods in agreement. I acknowledge my inferiority with a speedy retreat, glad to have learned an early lesson that I definitely cannot hold my own here, and I shouldn't embarrass myself by trying.

The next day gives way to a series of panel-led discussions that typically fill up the daytime hours of a con. The panels help me realise that, although I am a fan of *Game of Thrones*, I am not a 'convention' fan of *Game of Thrones*. The former has probably not read the books but might tune in to the series with a glass of wine on a Wednesday night, and may even discuss the more shocking plot twists around the water cooler with colleagues the next day. The latter has definitely read all of the books, wears t-shirts with obscure *Game of Thrones* quotes scrawled across the front, can describe the family tree of each minor character in intricate detail and has the theme music as their ringtone.

Each panel lasts around an hour, during which guest speakers – cast and crew members from *Game of Thrones*, authors, illustrators and comic creators – discuss assigned topics and answer questions from the audience. I get the sense that the backstage gossip is all anyone is really interested in, probably because it's all I'm really interested in.

The second panel of the day has the title 'What is it like to die on stage?' during which Ron Donachie recounts his twelve on-screen deaths, including *Taggart, Doctor Who, Titanic* and a gruesome beheading-scene-gone-wrong while playing Ser Rodrik Cassel in *Game of Thrones*. I bump into him walking around the fantasy art show after the panel.

'Hi Ron,' I say, all nerves in his broad, theatrical presence. 'Can I ask you a question for a book I'm writing?'

'Sure, go ahead.' His smile is warm.

'Do you find it intimidating to work in this genre? Given how...' – I search around for a diplomatic word – 'you know...' – I decide to go for it – 'obsessive the fans can be.'

Ron takes a few seconds to think about his answer. 'Not really,' he says, shrugging his shoulders, 'because I am a massive fan of the genre too.' He gestures around him at the hordes of people walking around us. 'You become very well connected with the fans, and they start to feel like your extended family. You see a lot of the same people at the various conventions, and the vast majority are very complimentary, and good fun.'

He stops to study a painting of a winged female creature riding some sort of giant bug. I hang next to him for a while, trying to pretend I'm interested in it, when really, I just want to get back to the next panel to find out what kind of sandwich Emilia Clarke eats between takes.

Ron looks up at me, clearly still ruminating on my question. 'I suppose it's more difficult for actors who are not fans of the genre,' he says. 'They might feel a bit more alienated here, like it's a club that they aren't part of.'

Outside the art show, a long snake of people holding posters, books and photographs wait patiently for something. Finally registering the sign on the door at the front of the queue, I realise they are in line for autographs from the cast members. I spot someone being escorted to the back of the queue for trying to push in and watch the glares from the queuing masses with a suppressed smile.

'I've got Bran three times now,' one guy says to me, his *Better Call Saul* t-shirt covered in pin badges from previous cons. He unrolls a poster pasted with illegible black scribbles and points at one of them. His eyes glaze with a look of distant hope. 'I wonder if he'll remember me?'

I decide against the queue and instead buy a pint for Dave Lally, the recently retired chairman of the European Science Fiction Society and a regular of the con circuit. With light brown, floppy hair and a six-o'clock shadow, Dave wears a green 'Sci-Fi London' t-shirt, cream chinos and sensible brown shoes.

'You have fantasy, anime, comics, manga, cosplay, gaming, SCA (Society for Creative Anachronism) and LARPing,' Dave begins, 'and they are all connected in some way. Nerds and geeks, they call us, and we all tend to get on very well.' Dave talks in rushed and enthusiastic sentences, like a man who views stopping for breath as admitting defeat.

'I call them my family; we all know each other and the different subjects we are experts in. I go to most of the European conventions, to socialise and catch up on all the gossip in the SF community.'

He takes a quick breath. 'My work colleagues in London think I'm a bit weird. They can't understand why I go off to all of these science fiction thingies. They all go off on their golf weekends or to their football matches, but to them, what I do is entirely different, and they just don't get it. It all just seems a bit unfair.'

His head sinks, and as it does, he notices his watch, jumping up with a start – 'Gotta go,' he says, turning around and scurrying off to prepare for a screening.

I take the time to look around me and soak up the scene in

the bar as I finish my pint. It strikes me that there are far more women here than I had expected. The balance isn't far off fifty-fifty. I am surprised by this, probably based on the depiction of this community in popular culture. After all, the leading characters of the genre tend to be male; Tolkien had few female characters in his books, and only 19 per cent of the characters he names in his Middle Earth series are female. The usual depiction of women in fantasy literature of a speculative past is either as evil villainesses who need to be stopped by a male hero, or helpless damsels in need of rescue... by a man.

I guess I'm not too bothered by this when it comes to historical fiction; after all, we are led to believe that it *was* typically the men who had all the fun back in the day – the adventure, the gory deaths and the epic battles – while the women were stuck at home sewing birds onto hankies. But when it comes to modern-day SF, it seems archaic that the social advancement of women, and the fact that we get to do fun stuff as well now, is not proportionally reflected.

For example, the Bechdel test is now globally recognised as one way of measuring gender equality in movies, which are given a 'pass/fail' rating based on three criteria: are there at least two female characters, who converse with each other, about something other than a man? According to Ellen Tejle, who uses the Bechdel rating system in her Stockholm movie house, the number of SF movies that completely fail the test is staggering, including the original *Star Wars* trilogy, the *Lord of the Rings* trilogy and all but one of the eight *Harry Potter* films (although this last one is the subject of some controversy online).

However, the balance in the fan base and the wider community does seem to be changing in line with the rest of society, albeit at a slightly slower pace. A woman is co-chairing this particular convention, and more than half of the current British Science Fiction Association board members are women.

Feeling thirsty, I swing by the bar to pick up another Guinness and head back up to the room, where Lynsey and I begin the preparations for the much-anticipated Saturday-night Masquerade. Costuming, or 'cosplaying', is a big part of SF culture, and the Masquerade – an on-stage costume contest where people compete for nominal prizes by assembling and presenting their own genre-inspired outfits – is the pinnacle.

After an hour of perfecting our Daenerys and Missandei (two characters from *Game of Thrones*) look, and my pint of nerve-steadying Guinness, Lynsey and I emerge from the lift in our home-made costumes. I had re-enlisted my Morris dancing costume maker to knock me up the blue dress worn by Daenerys in series two (thanks, Mum), ordered a wig online and invested hours sticking around 800 drawing pins into three Styrofoam balls to create my dragon's eggs. Lynsey needed an Afro for her character, so her preparation involved not washing her hair for a few days and sticking a few pins in a bed sheet to transform it into a cape. I had obviously picked the wrong character.

Once fully transformed, we walk self-consciously through the hotel and down to the bar, our confidence growing with every smile of recognition. What little confidence we have gathered by the time we reach the bar is suddenly sapped from us as we behold an entire *Game of Thrones* family of Lannisters, wearing period dress complete with full sets of lion-emblazoned armour. Tyrion has shoes sewed onto his knees, wears a shaggy wig and carries a book stuffed with Lannister family portraits. We had no chance.

Right before we are due to go on stage, Peadar, the compère, reminds us that we are supposed to have prepared an entrance skit. Shit. We haven't. Without waiting for our response, he walks into the auditorium and begins our introduction while Lynsey and I whisper a panicked scrap of a plan behind the curtain.

Seconds later I walk into the auditorium, shaking with nerves. The room is dimly lit, apart from a spotlight following me as I make my way up to the stage. I look around at the expectant faces in the audience and channel all of my concentration into not tripping over my dress. Luckily my trying-not-to-fall-over face is identical to my I'm-a-regal-mother-of-dragons face, so it seems to work quite well.

Once on stage, I turn and stand still for a while, gazing into the distance. 'Missandei,' I boom with all of the authority I can muster, 'where are my dragons?'

Just as I am running out of steam with my looking-round-the-room-fraught-with-worry act, Lynsey enters, subserviently carrying my eggs. She pretends to drop them on the floor. I gasp theatrically, but she rescues them just in time and delivers them to me, bowing at my feet. Having no idea what to say, I settle on, 'Well done,' and pat Lynsey on the head like some sort of cape-wearing dog.

With that we are ushered to the back of the stage to watch the other entrants, including a belly dance by the 'Sand Snakes' and a funny skit from the Lannister family, who we convince ourselves must have had far more time to practise.

A few minutes after the final skit, hands shoot into the air as the members of the audience are asked to vote for their favourite. The officials count the votes and reveal that there is a three-way tie for first place.

'OK, then it's up to the judges,' Peadar announces, gesturing towards the bar outside. 'Will the judges please withdraw from the room to deliberate and make their final decision?'

The atmosphere in the room heightens as we await the final result, the excitable chatter building as Lynsey and I share a desperately sweaty hug. Within a matter of seconds, the room falls silent as the judges walk back through the door.

One of them walks over to the microphone, slowly, enjoying the drama. 'And the winner is...' he says, leaving another pregnant pause, 'Drum roll, please.'

The audience hammer the tables with open hands.

He throws his hands in the air and in a booming voice yells, 'Daenerys and Missandei!'

The room breaks into applause as Lynsey and I stare at each other in disbelief. This has to be one of the best things that has ever happened to me, I think. A sentiment perhaps influenced by the nerve-steadying Guinness.

The enthusiastic judge beckons us over to the microphone to make a victory speech. At some point between leaving my corner of the stage and arriving at the microphone, I make the outrageous decision to try and earn some geek points by attempting to talk in a made-up version of Daenerys's mother tongue, Valyrian. I look out at the audience, in all their geeky splendour, and begin with an Elvish quote I remember from *Lord of the Rings*.

'*Natha dated dhaer.*'

'Thank you so much for bestowing this honour upon us,' Lynsey translates.

'*Ichsvill hacker struntite,*' I desperately begin to make up words.

'We... are... very happy to be here,' Lynsey starts to struggle.

I panic about what else to say and end up wildly confessing, 'This is our first-ever convention!' Thankfully, the news is received with a round of applause and Lynsey and I retreat from the stage with a self-indulgent bow.

The room settles down again as we take our seats for a set from the Hardbitten Fleabottom Swingtime Band, a folk-blues group who entertain us with a rendition of the *Game of Thrones* theme tune, followed seamlessly by 'Triffy, the Horny Prostitute'. After the 'filking' session (a musical performance inspired by the sci-fi genre, which we are reliably informed to be a favourite activity of the con scene), the night just keeps on getting better and better as we find ourselves passionately singing along to 'Star Trekking', dancing the Macarena (still in full Daenerys costume), and headbanging our way into the early hours with Rodrik Cassel, Myrcella Baratheon and Bran Stark, who have all emerged as if from nowhere to join the party. By 2 a.m. we collapse into a circle of chairs, drunkenly reciting quotes from our favourite shows and singing songs from the *Lord of the Rings* soundtrack. It feels good to be able to discuss my theory of how dragons breathe fire with a willing conversation partner for a change.

It doesn't feel quite as good when the alarm goes off at 8 a.m. the next morning for the early-departing coach tour of the local *Game of Thrones* filming locations. Nevertheless, morale is high, and the coach is filled with excitable chatter and stories from the previous evening. And so ensues a full day of tramping around the countryside to visit various filming locations, punctuated by scene re-enactments, fencing, archery and fire-eating lessons.

After a medieval hog roast in a banqueting hall lined with taxidermy deer heads and cast-iron candlestick holders, it is sadly time for Lynsey and I to make an early departure to catch our plane home. Peadar presents us with *Game of Thrones* action figures for winning the Masquerade, and we leave through the centre of the hall, taking the applause as our exit music and high-fiving everybody in our path to a great geekend.

*

A couple of months later, Lynsey and I meet Dan, Triffy and Phil – one of the event organisers – for a few pints and a catch-up in a London pub. It is great to see them again. Phil has travelled for an hour and a half to meet up with us, and I applaud his commitment as we walk to catch the train home.

'It's OK – I can have a lie-in tomorrow. I'm off work for two weeks now,' he reassures me.

'What are you up to?'

'The new PlayStation comes out tomorrow,' he says, in a 'you really should know this' tone, 'and I have it on pre-order!'

'You've taken two weeks off work to play computer games?' I ask him, convinced I must have misunderstood.

'Of course – the graphics are much better on this one.'

Of course, I think.

T is for... Trainspotters

When they realise I'm a trainspotter, they run a mile

Waiting at our rendezvous point in Surrey Quays, I reread an email from Simon, whose website I had stumbled onto when digging into a Google thread about trainspotting: 'In this cold weather, I am wearing green padded winter trousers, a red jacket over a grey fleece jacket and a black circular hat.'

Just as I am wondering what a square or triangular hat might look like, the conventional circular-brimmed hat floats along the windowsill and walks into Starbucks.

'Simon – over here.' I beckon to him.

He sits down opposite me and stares expectantly from behind 1980s glasses, which magnify his eyes and give him a look of permanent surprise.

'I know this station well because I used to come here a lot to film the trains when it was part of the London Underground.'

Carefully pronouncing each word and talking in a steady chug, Simon explains that he was born in east London and still lives there now at the age of fifty-four. He can't recall when his love for trains began, but distinctly remembers holidays in Europe in his early childhood, when all he wanted to do was take pictures of his three loves: trains, trams and trolleybuses. It got to the point where his parents had to confiscate his camera.

'Do they like trains too?'

'No,' he laughs, 'they thought I was nuts. I'm not a number taker,' he explains, almost defensively. 'I take pictures and videos, or just observe. I go to special events like historical carriages running, or new carriages that use old routes. I have been stopped by police a few times, but when they realise I'm a trainspotter, they run a mile.'

Simon has volunteered at an old people's home every Saturday for the last thirty years. Aside from this, he spends most of his time making his YouTube videos. He doesn't have a job at the moment, but he hopes to make some money producing a DVD mixing his old footage of trains and trams in Berlin with new footage he will take later this year.

'I got very annoyed when they stopped supplying the zone-two-to-six travelcard,' he says, pushing his glasses up his nose. 'It's all part of a wider government plan to stop us moving around so much. They want to control us.' He pushes his glasses even further up his nose, squashing his eyelashes against the lenses. 'They are moving in, bit by bit, to keep us under control.'

'Who are "they"? The New World Order?'

Something seems to come alive in Simon. 'Exactly! They are trying to keep us away from life force.' His eyes widen, and he leans in closer.

'We have all been enslaved by the New World Order,' he continues. 'They steal kids and take them away on ships to film snuff movies and perform satanic rituals. The Galactic Federation of Light are planning a rescue mission.'

He looks around furtively, and, remembering we are in the middle of Starbucks, lowers his voice. 'If you type "Zero Point

Energy" into Google, you will be dead within a week.' (For some reason I am too scared to do this myself, so I ask my friend Rob to when I get home. It gets 67.6 million Google hits. The killer must be a very busy person.)

Simon's mobile phone goes off. It is a call from someone who reminds him that they won't be able to contact him between 15.45 and 16.00 because they have a dental appointment. He won't reveal who the call is from. 'I don't like talking about my family in case they realise I'm on to them.'

We both take a sip of coffee.

'There is a hidden civilisation underneath Antarctica,' he goes on, distracted by something he has seen through the window.

He looks back at me with a start, as if he has just remembered something really important.

'Aliens are coming next year, to Moscow.'

A few weeks later I receive an email from Simon:

Hello Lucy,
Something which may be of interest to you has cropped up.
As you may know, the Underground is part way through a programme of replacing 40+-year-old trains with newer trains. Next Monday the last of the old trains will be used on the Circle and Hammersmith & City lines, and it is possible that there will be some sort of special happening at the Hammersmith station which is used by these lines.
I plan to be at Hammersmith to see these last trains, and I expect there to be 'quite a few' other trainspotters there as well.
Below is the message about this which I received in my

email inbox. Below that are a few more links for you – not just about trains, but also one to the flying saucer which I photographed!

On the day of the event, a young security guard is playing a game on his mobile phone at the gate of the old Metropolitan line station at Hammersmith.

'Do you know anything about a "happening" here this afternoon?' I ask him, realising, for the first time, that I have no idea what I am here for.

He sighs loudly and slowly looks up at me with the same look of confusion my friends give me when I freeze leftover cabbage. 'What do you mean, happening?'

'Well, I'm not really sure. But I think it has something to do with the last of the C Stock running into this station.'

'I have no idea what you are talking about,' he says, going back to his phone.

'Well, have you seen any trainspotter types hanging around?' I get desperate. 'I'm here to meet a… friend.'

He scans me up and down, furrowing his brow.

I decide that the only way this rude prick is going to help me is if I try and get him on side. I lean into him conspiratorially, and in a shameful act of betrayal, whisper, 'I'm writing a book about trainspotters. But don't worry, I'm not actually one of them.' I give him a dramatic wink, which is both confusing and unnecessary.

He continues to stare back at me blankly, shrugging his shoulders, presumably thinking I have just escaped from somewhere.

We both stand in silence for a moment, staring at the barrier, before he finally accepts that I am not going away. 'Well, I suppose you can come in and have a look around,' he groans reluctantly, touching his card on the Oyster pad to open the barriers with an angry thud.

I wander around the platforms for the next few minutes, confused and guilt-ridden for needlessly disavowing Simon. Unable to see any sign of a 'happening' I give up and make my way back to the entrance. As I get closer to the gate, security guy beckons to me and points at the opposite platform. And there he is, his camera poised alongside two other men clutching notepads.

'Simon!' I yell and wave, walking excitedly over to him, wondering whether or not to go in for the hug. He glances up, puts a finger in the air to shush me and goes back to his filming. We stand in silence for a few minutes while I scan around uncomfortably, not having any idea what I am supposed to be looking at.

'Have you heard about the Farsight Institute?' Simon says without preamble, his eyes remaining locked on his viewfinder.

'Erm... no.'

'Remote viewing. You can see things through the eyes of another being even when you are hundreds of miles away.'

There is a distant sound of an engine and one of the notepad men suddenly looks animated. 'There she is, coming into the loading bay.'

Panic descends, and everyone runs across to the other platform. Suddenly about twenty other men appear out of the shadows to join the commotion like bats from a cave. They all scramble for the best view, pushing each other out of the way in silence.

'I'm going up to the footbridge to get a shot of it leaving,' says a tall younger chap called Geoff, who tells me he is filming for the London Transport Museum.

I relay this information to Simon. 'The footbridge!' he

exclaims, clapping his hand to his head before sprinting up the platform towards the bridge, closely followed by about fifteen men with cameras.

I follow behind and observe them all jostling to get the best position to film, still not knowing what I am supposed to be looking at. I squeeze in between Geoff and Simon and try to follow their gaze. Geoff leans behind me to talk to Simon. 'What are you filming for?'

'Citytransportinfo,' Simon chirps the name of his website and popular YouTube channel, without adjusting his gaze.

Geoff is star-struck. 'You are citytransportinfo?'

'Yes.' Simon fiddles with his camera.

'I asked you for some footage of some S Stock for a project for the Transport Museum,' Geoff says. 'Do you know who I am?'

Simon thinks for a while... 'Geoff?' The two of them share a moment of mutual respect, talking about trains for a while in a language I don't understand. Then Simon starts to stray. 'I have other interests too...' he says.

'He lost me when he started getting political,' Geoff tells me half an hour later as we sit in the Starbucks opposite. I am waiting for him to tell me a story that 'I simply have to hear'. Wearing a black beanie hat and a London Transport Museum fleece dotted with biscuit crumbs, he leans into my Dictaphone and says, 'Hello, Lucy.'

I ask him about his love for trains, and he launches into an excited monologue. 'I do a comedy gig at the Fringe Festival about my life and trains and how I don't really understand why I am interested in them,' he explains, his rubber face full of expression as he continues to talk to my Dictaphone rather than me.

'I have a mild OCD,' he continues. 'I need things to be

straight, I need lids to be on pens properly, I need them to be neat and tidy and the right way up in the pot. So maybe that is where the train thing comes from for me. The efficiency of it all, the way it just... works.'

Brimming with energy, Geoff is sociable and easy to talk to and makes a point of telling me how sociable and easy to talk to he is. Presumably a rare personality type in this circle, he seems keen on proving this to me.

'I am somewhere on "the spectrum", he says. 'I tip on and off of it... Most people on the spectrum are male. They think it must have something to do with the Y chromosome; that's why almost all train geeks are men.' He looks up at me. 'When I saw you with all of them today, I knew there was something different going on, so when you told me you were writing a book, I was like, "Aha!"'

I am still in suspense about what Geoff brought me here to tell me. 'What is the amazing thing I need to hear, Geoff?'

'OK. Are you ready for it?' He pauses for effect, leaning even closer to the Dictaphone. 'I hold the world record for travelling through all the Tube stations in the fastest time possible.'

He gives me a moment to let this soak in.

'Sixteen hours, twenty minutes and twenty-seven seconds.'

OK. This is kind of cool.

The 'Tube challenge', recognised by the Guinness World Record Association, is over 270 Tube stations, excluding the DLR and the Overground. Geoff has held the record twice now, having made twenty-five attempts in total, with his committed support team bringing him food, tracking delays and planning toilet stops, sometimes involving empty bottles.

The team spend months planning each attempt, creating a unique code within a system of painstakingly produced spreadsheets to work out the quickest possible route. 'You have to get yourself fit to run between the ends of each line,' Geoff explains. 'For example, when you get to the end of the Piccadilly line at Cockfosters, the next logical place to start is High Barnet, but it's five kilometres away, so we run it. We have to do fitness training together, and we wear proper running gear on the day.'

Ticking things off a list, challenge, community – every part of this appeals to me. Geoff may have just found a new rival. If nothing else, it would look great on my LinkedIn profile.

My time with Simon and Geoff was enjoyable, but something was missing – I hadn't yet written down a single number into a pad. I convey this to Simon, who promptly introduces me, over email, to his friend Peter Mugridge, 'a proper trainspotter'.

As I make the journey to meet Peter at Euston station, the worst happens. Despite leaving fifteen minutes' grace time for my route, a fault on the Northern line results in an evacuation and a twenty-five-minute delay. Out of breath from running up the stairs, I arrive at the station a whole seven minutes late.

'I can't believe you live in London and don't make allowances for these things,' Peter says, deadpan. He is wearing a grey waterproof jacket and carries a black shoulder bag, bursting at the seams with God knows what. His dark hair, thinning at the top, is swept back from his face and he wears thick, wire-framed glasses. I look at the floor and mutter an apology like a chastised child.

He runs to the ticketing office, beckoning to me and announcing as we run that we will be travelling to Manchester. We buy our tickets and stand in front of the departure screen – in silence so we can concentrate – waiting for the platform number to be revealed.

Platform 14.

We sprint, leaving fellow travellers in our wake to be the first ones onto the train. Apparently this is incredibly important, ensuring our access to the best possible seats. As I struggle to catch my breath, peeling off my white anorak to try and regulate my soaring body temperature, Peter happily jaunts through each carriage, inspecting each seat for... 1) being on the right-hand side; 2) being at the back part of a long window so you have as much visibility as possible; 3) lining up with the other seats so you can see out of the window on both sides.

Spotting the perfect one, he leaps into it with childish excitement. 'Bagsy the window seat,' he says, producing a napkin from his bag and wiping at the window furiously. 'I always keep one of these with me, to clean the windows,' he says, holding it up as proof. 'If I know which seat I will be sitting in, I'll clean the window on the outside too before getting on the train.'

The train starts to pull away from the station. Before we boarded the train, Peter had pointed out its unique number stencilled on the side.

Following Peter's lead, I jot down *390 134* in my pad.

Peter has worked for the same market-research company for twenty-nine years and has been trainspotting since he was a young boy. His mother told him that he reached out for a railway magazine when he was still in the pram.

'If you are wondering why I am not taking the numbers of those trains over there' – he points out of the opposite window at a cluster of trains sitting just outside Euston station – 'it's because I have seen all of them, photographed all of them and ridden on all of them already.' He grins.

'How do you know which trains you have and haven't seen?'

'They publish a book every year containing the numbers of every single train in the country – locomotives and coaching stock

– so you can tick them off as you go. It's the trainspotters' bible. The book of numbers.' He laughs. 'See, train boffins can make jokes too!'

As we travel, Peter holds a small black plastic box that hangs around his neck up to the window. It tells him the speed of the train and adds up his mileage so he can note it down.

'How far do you typically travel?'

'About eleven thousand miles a year is normal. The furthest I have travelled in a year was twenty-five thousand miles. But that was before I got married.' He points at his wedding ring.

'How did you meet your wife?'

He is visibly glad I asked this question. 'Picked her up on a train,' he says. 'The first thing I said to her was, "That's the bridge where the Great Train Robbery happened."'

As we draw near to our destination, Peter says the name of each station as we pass through it, to no one in particular: 'Stockport,' 'Macclesfield,' 'Stoke-on-Trent.' We pass a few depot yards, and he writes the numbers down.

I write 57 011, 57 018, 57 304 and 77 002 in my pad.

Peter has collected almost all of the numbers in the UK now and carries around a leather wallet containing details of the elusive few, divided across three separate 'hit lists':

1. Spotted
2. Photographed
3. Haulage (ridden on)

When he has finished, he will move on to the trains of Paris, which he has already made a dent in.

Within two hours we are standing at Manchester Piccadilly, where Peter escorts me to the information office to sign in, so we're not accused of loitering.

'I would like to sign in to take pictures of trains,' he announces to the two pretty young girls in the information office.

'Oh, we've changed our policy, you don't need to do that any more,' a petite blonde girl says. 'The staff are aware that the enthusiasts stand on the end of platform fifteen to take photos, so as long as you stand there, you will be fine.'

Peter looks surprised by this change of protocol. 'So can I sign in, please?'

'You don't need to, you'll be fine,' the girl reassures him kindly.

He gets his camera out. It looks about twenty years old. 'You can see I don't have a flash,' he shows them the place where a flash might be, 'and it doesn't have a red light.'

'That's fine,' the girl smiles back at him patiently.

'Even if it did have a red light, I would put a piece of Blu-Tack over it,' he continues.

'Thank you,' the girl says, still smiling.

'This lady is a writer,' he points at me. 'So she will be with me at all times.'

'That's fine,' the girl smiles, her patience wavering ever so slightly.

Peter smiles, waits in silence for a few seconds and decides to check just one more time.

'So, where do I need to sign?'

When we get to the viewing platform, I spot seven other men scattered around, festooned with cameras and pads. I have never even noticed these people at railway stations before. I guess they've always been here; another hidden world that was right in front of my eyes, only visible through a different lens. Peter walks up to a white-haired man wearing a flat cap.

'Anything interesting this morning?' Peter asks.

'Couple of freight trains,' he responds.

I sidle over to him. 'How long have you been into trains?'

'Since I worked as a fireman on the steam trains in the sixties,' he says, smiling. 'Wonderful job. Clouds of steam puffing up over the Yorkshire countryside.'

Finally, something I can access – the nostalgic beauty of an old steam train snaking through an emerald valley. It's a romantic image, no doubt, but the 08:14 from Liverpool Street station just doesn't have quite the same appeal for me.

Peter abandons us and gets straight to work analysing the trains pulling in and out of the platform. 'Rats,' he repeatedly says when all of the trains that go past are trains that he already has.

After half an hour on the platform, we board an electric train he has never ridden on before, a tick for the 'haulage' list.

350 407

We ride on it for half a mile, to Manchester Oxford Road, before crossing to another platform and catching another train back again.

150 113

'Why do you like trainspotting so much?' I ask on the way back.

'It's hard to say.' Peter looks pained and thinks for a while. 'But I suppose if you asked a football supporter why he has to go to all of the matches, it would be the same thing.'

Again, we're back to the idea of collecting things – bird watching, stamp collecting, drinking all the different beers in a microbrewery, communities beginning with different letters of the alphabet – all driven by that same desire to tick things off a list. I guess Peter and I aren't so different after all.

When we arrive back at Piccadilly, the men on the platform stand alone with metres between them, talking rarely, and only in transactional snippets. 'Has the 305 70 come past yet?' 'Where was the 402 506 going?'

Another train headed for the airport pulls in and Peter's eyes light up. It is two electric trains joined together, neither of which he has ridden before. He rubs his hands together and smiles, running down the platform to enter the train at the back. He walks through that train, past the cab, and into the front.

'I can count it as two separate haulages now', he says, triumphant in having found a way to game his own system.

350 402

350 404

Peter sits by the window, holding up his trusty GPS device. We travel ten miles, get off, cross the platform, and immediately get on the next train back to Piccadilly.

142 011

I catch a glimpse of my reflection in the grubby window. I look drawn and sapped of energy. Irritated, even. I am trying so hard to understand why you would put yourself through this aimless travelling back and forth. For me, trains are a means to an end, a way of getting somewhere. I look at the other people on the train with a sense of longing, jealous that they all have somewhere to go, desperate for some kind of destination. Perhaps this is another lesson.

'Enjoy the journey.' I picture Rory at Findhorn, explaining the importance of my pointless walk to restock the already restocked apartment. I can almost see his face in the window, like Simba being visited by the ghost of his dead father, his long hair billowing in the wind as his eyes crease into an enlightened smile. Have the trainspotters got it sussed? I force myself to smile and wait in vain for the serotonin to kick in.

On the way back to the airport, we whizz past a train we have been looking out for all day, the 170 303, which Peter desperately needs to photograph. He looks crestfallen as we reluctantly board the 15:15 from Piccadilly, the last train that will get us back to London in time for Peter to watch *Coronation Street*.

390 009

Just as we are about to leave, the 170 303 pulls into a platform on the other side of the station. A look of steely determination settles on Peter's face. He points in the direction of the train. 'I'll get you next time,' he says.

U is for... UFOlogists

*The only way I can explain it
is like milking a cow*

In a cross-pollination of subcultures, my first exposure to the UFO community was via Simon, the train enthusiast (conventional circular-hat guy).

'The Tall Whites and the Greys are the two alien races that come to earth most often,' he explained, seemingly elated that somebody was finally showing interest in the information he had spent years gathering. 'They use gravity waves to get to here and take nutrition through their skin. I had a visit from a Zeta Reticulan once (a "Grey"), at three in the morning. It wore an owl mask.'

This was a bit much for me. I needed to find a more pragmatic access route into this world, a slightly less paranormal phenomenon, and one experienced by more than a select few. After a few weeks of deliberation, I found my answer.

There have been roughly 6,400 crop circles recorded in over sixty countries since the mid-1980s. The circles have been a mystery since the first was sighted, with multiple theories circulating as to how and why they are made, including freak weather conditions, fairy ritual, the landing marks from alien aircraft, or messages from another planet or dimension.

In 1991 'Doug and Dave' declared that they were the hoaxers behind the UK crop-circle phenomena, creeping into fields at night and using a system of boards, ropes and tape measures to make the intricate geometric patterns. However, although most in the 'cereologist' community accept that some of the circles are man-made, they claim to be able to tell the difference between a man-made formation and an authentic one. The general consensus is that to enter a field undetected and construct a circle of enormous complexity and geometric accuracy without leaving any marks of human involvement is simply impossible.

'I have bad news,' our host tells us as we gather outside a hotel in Devizes for a crop-circle coach tour. 'There are no circles for us to visit.' He shakes his head, his huge palms turned upwards like two soup bowls.

Although there hasn't been a change in the rate the circles are appearing, we are told (there have been sixty reported already during the year of the tour), they cannot be viewed because the farmers are either not allowing access or cutting out the middle of the circles as soon as they appear.

'This is the first time in nine years of running the tour that this has happened.' The crowd breathe a sigh of collective disappointment. I share a shrug with the tall Danish man sitting next to me, none other than Sten from Findhorn, whom I've become rather fond of and had prearranged to meet for this tour.

We are briefed about what the day will entail in the absence of our quarry, and told that the first stop on the tour will be a visit to the ancient stone circles of Avebury. We arrive an hour later to find a somewhat bedraggled but friendly-looking chap with a long beard and a backpack playing with a pair of L-shaped copper rods in between the stones.

'What are they?' I ask, pointing at the thin rolls of metal in his hands.

He grins at me, holding my eyes in an intense stare. 'Dowsing rods,' he says.

'Can I try them?'

'Of course,' he says, holding out his hand. 'I'm Phil.' We shake hands and he gestures ahead of us to the meeting point of two stones. 'Just hold them in your hands loosely, point them forward and walk in between those two stones over there.'

I look up at the ten-foot stones sticking out of the ground, balance the rods facing forward and start walking. Nothing happens. Told you so, I think to myself. But then, just as I get between the two stones, the skin tightens around the left side of my hand as the rods are pulled to the right. I continue to walk, shaking my head. After a few steps, they swing back to the neutral position.

I repeat the movement three times, with the same result, handing the rods to somebody else to try without a word. What is this trickery?

After the tour of Avebury, we head to a local village hall for a talk from Michael Glickman, a world-renowned architect-turned-crop-circle-researcher, driven by his professional interest in their mathematical precision and intricate craft. Michael has published three books on the subject, including *Crop Circles: The Bones of God*, and *Cornography: The New Swirled Order*.

Michael has an open face that exudes a childish, playful spirit, his eyes deep-set and vibrant. Smart in a yellow shirt, green suit jacket and grey trousers held up with braces, he begins his talk from his wheelchair at the front of the room. 'This is a historic moment,' he says. 'Usually, the week before the crop-circle tour is spent working out which of the circles we should take you to.

There are always so many to choose from.' He looks down into his hands. 'This is a dark time for crop circles.'

He goes on, 'For fifteen years now, I have received hate mail. It gives me pleasure that the hate mail is always written terribly and full of mistakes. The moment I get a well-written piece of hate mail, I will worry about the world.' He smiles and looks around the room with avid curiosity.

'Crop circles are benign; they harm no one. They scatter toys on the floor of the nursery and say, "I am here if you want to play, children." So why do they evoke such hatred? Such venom?' He pauses for a long time, as if genuinely waiting for an answer. The room remains silent. 'Because people are scared of them,' he says, reaching out his arms. 'They don't understand them, so they are frightened. Fundamentalist crop-circle deniers all gather together on social media and feed each other's hatred. The so-called hoaxers say, "We made all of them."' He looks pained. 'But it's all horrible lies. Just an easy solution for the media. And now the farmers are siding with the hoaxers, rather than with the croppies, as they have in the past.'

He picks up his exasperated gaze from the floor and looks back at us. 'How many of you have travelled from abroad for this?' Over half of the room of sixty put their hands up. He shakes his head and sinks his gaze again. 'It's such a shame.'

Despite being new to this world, I can't help but feel genuinely devastated for this wonderful man.

'Some civilisation or federation are sending us a message,' he continues. 'They have an agenda for us, and this agenda won't change because a couple of farmers are angry. These are personal messages, for each and every one of us as individuals.' He looks around the room again, pointing at each of us with a gnarled and shaking finger, the same playful look on his face. 'I look in the bathroom mirror every morning and think, maybe I am completely mad' – he pauses to enjoy the ripple of laughter – 'and there is always that possibility. But when you consider the number of synchronicities, coincidences and intuitions, for me, there can be no doubt. I keep going back to the bathroom mirror when these things happen, to check: am I bonkers?' He grins. 'But I'm not.'

'I'll leave you with this thought,' he says, releasing the brakes from his wheelchair and moving slightly closer to the group. 'Every baby is born with an elastic band around its head, to keep its consciousness in. It is very flexible, so there is room for it to expand. Then, as the baby grows up, the powers of darkness go "chhh" with an aerosol can on the band, to freeze it. Every time the child meets a head teacher, a priest, a bank manager, they spray it a little bit more. So by the time they are an adult, they have a cast-iron band around their consciousness. What the crop circles do' – he pauses for effect – 'is soften our bands, by forcing us to question what we think we know.'

After the talk, I go over to Michael, introduce myself and launch straight into a spiel about the book to check he is happy with me quoting him. He puts his hand up to stop me.

'What's your name?'

'Lucy.'

He offers me his hand and smiles with his whole face. 'It's a real pleasure to meet you, Lucy. Let's have a cup of tea.'

At that moment Dowsing Phil walks over. He looks at Michael. 'Do you think the chemtrails have anything to do with our restricted consciousness?'

Michael shrugs, fixes a stare into the distance and rolls out his lips. 'Could be.' He nods slowly. 'Could be.'

He looks back at me and smiles again. 'But, of course, we

can't be certain. Behind every war, conflict and argument there was somebody who was "certain". You can never be certain,' he says. I wish he were my granddad.

'What are "chemtrails"?' I ask Phil.

His jaw drops. 'What?!'

'I, erm, I just don't know what they are.' I look at him blankly, drawing my lips into a long line.

'I don't believe it!' His eyes are wide. 'You know the white trails you can see in the sky?' He points at the ceiling. 'They're poisoning us. Flying over and spreading dangerous chemicals like barium to poison our crops and water.'

'What?' I pull my head back onto my neck. 'Who is they?'

'The government! They're not here to look after us. Oh no. They're trying to gain control of our food and water. Then they have us. They are already poisoning our bodies. Now they are trying to poison our minds as well, stunt our consciousness.'

I try to sit on the opposite side of the bus from Phil on the way to the next location, but he somehow finds his way over to me.

'I like what Michael said, about the baby, and the consciousness,' I say to him.

'Of course,' he says. 'Babies are born open, and as soon as they go to school, they get brainwashed. All they are taught is how to be closed.'

'Well' – I decide to be diplomatic – 'a lot of what they learn is pretty useful as well, right? Like reading and science and stuff.'

'Hardly any of it,' he says, turning away from me and staring out of the window.

The coach pulls over to the side of the road and our guide points up the hill to a huge circle that has been cut out of a crop field. 'That's the circle that was cut out by the farmer,' he says. 'But we don't have permission to enter it. You may see other people in there, and I can't stop you, but I can't recommend you go into it.'

As soon as we are off the coach, nearly everyone heads to the circle. You can clearly see where the formations within the circle would have been, the neatly laid rows of corn contrasting with those that have been cut. Somebody runs just outside of the circle and excitedly beckons us over.

'Look,' he says through a bushy brown beard. 'There is a line running around the outside of the circle.'

He is right; the line is about two foot wide, the corn immaculately laid down in one flowing direction.

Phil hands me his dowsing rods. 'Try it,' he says.

I pick up the rods, walk five steps back from the outer circle and face them forward into a neutral position. Slowly walking forward, I watch the rods closely, trying with all my might to keep a clear and open mind. As I approach the line, they start to feel as if they are being pulled by a magnet, swinging a full ninety degrees to the right.

'So the energy is going clockwise,' Phil says, leaning back, hands on hips.

Hang-on-a-freaking-minute. How can this be right? How is there an 'energy' in a crop circle that pulls two copper rods along it? This doesn't fit my model; it doesn't fit my scientific world view at all.

'So this is a genuine crop circle,' Phil nods in satisfaction. 'The energy is still here even when it has been cut out.'

The dowsing experience stays with me all day, culminating in a detour back to Avebury on my way home that evening. Was this a genuine experience? Or had I been caught up in the excitement of the group, influenced by their expectations? I had to know.

By the time I get there the field is almost pitch black, the imposing stone structures reflecting what little light there is, radiating heat like hot-water bottles for the sheep lying against them. I get out the rods I had bought for £15 from the Avebury gift shop that afternoon and stand exactly where Phil had shown me earlier.

My theory, derived over the course of the day, is as follows: when I walk past the stones my mind subconsciously wants the rods to swing, so it sends this message to my hands, bypassing my brain, and makes the rods move.

With this in mind, I walk past the stones and study my hands intently. Sure enough, my hands are leaning slightly in the direction of the pull when the rods swing. But have I moved them because I subconsciously want the rods to swing in that direction, or are they moving because the rods are pulling them? I guess I will never know. It feels like I'm not pulling them, but that doesn't fit with my paradigm. I might not have been OK with this ten months ago, but I think I am now. I don't have the same burning desire to prove things to be right or wrong, to falsify, to be reductive. Maybe it's OK to just enjoy the mystery.

For the next couple of nights, I stay at my family home in Bristol, before receiving an excited phone call from Sten on Sunday evening. 'There's a new crop circle,' he says, sounding as excited as it is possible for stoic Sten to sound. 'It appeared overnight about twenty minutes from Devizes; a group of us are taking a taxi there in the morning.'

I head straight there and find a group gathered in the circle; some doze, others meditate. There is an exciting atmosphere of curiosity. I spend some time lying in the circle, trying to feel the energy. The sun warms my body, and my dowsing rods swing as they are supposed to when I walk around the lines of the circle, but the hairs on the back of my neck don't stand up, and I don't feel the sort of 'energies' I had been promised by the numerous YouTube videos I had watched on the subject.

Despite my lack of feels in the crop circle, I am open to the idea that there are other intelligent life forms in the universe. Heck, maybe they even visit us once in a while. So I am unfazed when I attend an exopolitics conference in Leeds, aimed at those who have made up their mind that UFOs exist, and are ready to move on to the question: what next?

Let's get some definitions in here: UFOlogy is 'the array of subject matter and activities associated with an interest in unidentified flying objects'. Exopolitics is the 'militant wing of UFOlogy'. A 'contactee' is the word for anyone who has been contacted by an alien race, either psychologically or physically, and if you are then taken against your will, you are an 'abductee'.

I arrive at the venue on a Friday evening to find a surprisingly mixed audience and not a tin-foil hat in sight. There are some you would expect; awkward-looking middle-aged men wearing rain hats indoors, but also a young woman in a beautiful floral dress, a few teenagers wearing mostly black, a number of young couples who resemble my friends, and a sharp-suited character with a pocket watch and a shock of white hair.

On the first evening, we are given a talk by Stephen Bassett, a full-time political activist focused on ending the sixty-seven-year 'truth embargo' that Western governments keep around the ET phenomena. He is dressed all in black, his polo neck sitting just below his chin, with intense piercing eyes and hair cropped severely short.

'Why are we being denied the truth?' he exclaims, banging the table with his open palm.

Stephen is campaigning for 'disclosure', a formal acknowledgement from the government that they are aware of an extra-terrestrial presence engaging with the human race.

'How many people in this room believe that the UK government isn't telling us the full story about the phenomena?'

Every single person in the hundred-strong room raises their hand, including me, apparently.

'Exactly! And based on multiple polls, fifty per cent of the public in most developed countries privately accept the extra-terrestrial phenomena.' He bangs the table again. 'Fifty per cent! The BBC should be all over it! Why aren't they?'

Stephen has already petitioned the US government for 'disclosure'.

'This was their response,' he says, clearing his throat and reading from a piece of paper. '"There is no credible information to suggest that any evidence is being hidden from the public eye."'

He looks up at the audience and raises an eyebrow. The room fills with laughter.

The following morning, after a lecture on how meditation can charge gold and crystal batteries with healing energies to send to other planets, I settle for a somewhat more accessible talk on the influence of UFO subculture on Hollywood. Handsome in a nerdy way, Robbie Graham is the youngest speaker so far. He wears jeans, a grey waistcoat and black-rimmed glasses.

Towards the end of his talk, he takes a long pause and looks out at the audience. 'UFOlogists speak a great deal about the "truth",' he says, 'but rarely are UFOlogists truthful with themselves. First off, there is no such thing as UFOlogy, at least not in any meaningful sense of the word. If "ology" refers to a branch of knowledge or learning sprung from organised research – which it does – then UFOlogy is a broken twig.'

There are a few audible sucks of air from the audience.

'The UFO subject has produced thousands of dedicated researchers over the years, and thousands of books, but when it comes to understanding this phenomenon, we are all of us clueless, awash in a sea of speculation and petty ideological feuds.'

Robbie continues, his eyes scanning the audience for a reaction. 'Our obsession with UFO "truth" speaks to our insatiable yearning to grasp the essential meaning in our universe and fathom our purpose within it... UFO disclosure will, we insist... open the floodgates to our understanding of this phenomena... but this is delusional.'

This is the moment I look up at him, my eyes drawn from my elaborate doodle of an alien riding a giraffe.

'A great many people in the UFO community see the pursuit of UFO "truth" as a battle; an "us versus them". This way of thinking is not at all productive, as proven by seventy years of official silence on the UFO issue. They've not budged because they cannot...'

He switches to a slide showing a child in a supermarket, tugging on a grown-up's trousers.

'The disclosure movement looks to officialdom as an unfair parent figure. It tugs incessantly at the leg of power and says, "Dad, tell us..." Well, you know what, Dad doesn't have the answers... because, despite appearances, and the power of his ego, in a universe that is thirteen billion years old, he is just a monkey like the rest of us, flailing around for answers.'

Some of the men, particularly the ones who look like they could be trainspotters, murmur and shake their heads.

'All too often on the UFO scene, audiences are content to hear what they want to hear. To have their existing beliefs confirmed by self-proclaimed experts who know full well that their personality cult is guaranteed only by telling the crowds, and dare I say, followers, what they want to hear – that disclosure is just around the corner, and that a brighter tomorrow will follow that day.'

He flips up another slide and shifts his gaze so that he is talking up towards the image, instead of out at us. I glance over at Steve Bassett to see how he is taking this. He stares intensely at Robbie, his face unreadable.

'Disclosure has become the focus of the UFO community, marginalising the more esoteric approaches to the phenomena. In the age of disclosure and exopolitics, the pursuit of UFO truth is political rather than mystical.' He looks back out at the audience, his head lowered so he can see us over the top of his glasses. 'I'm in no doubt that some of what I say here might not sit well with the UFO community, but I wanted to share with you my own shifting perspective on this phenomenon, and the field that seeks to understand it.'

A few of the audience continue to shake their heads, but the vast majority clap loudly, some even whoop, revealing the divide between those who view the UFO question as a fight against government cover-up and scientifically quantifiable phenomena being hidden from them, and those who see it as an esoteric phenomenon, hoping it will offer us a glimpse into the nature of reality and a deeper understanding of human consciousness.

'Were you nervous?' I approach Robbie outside the venue.

'Very,' he says. 'I thought I was going to get booed off stage!'

A woman walks past and calls over to him, 'Great speech, Robbie. Very brave.'

Robbie smiles, 'It's a good indication of where people are in their thinking on the subject, actually,' he says, relieved by his own words. 'I'm pleased.'

Between the talks, people gather to discuss their alien contact and abduction experiences, many striking in their similarity. 'I was pinned down onto the bed and held there,' a short and plump fellow declares to a captivated group of listeners.

'Me too!' a passer-by joins their conversation.

Over lunch, I interview Sarah and Kevin (not their real names), both alien contactees in their forties.

'Something happened that I can't explain,' Sarah tells me, barely opening her mouth as she speaks, 'but I can't tell anyone; it would be suicide for my job.'

A chemistry teacher, with blonde hair tied into a loose ponytail, Sarah's appearance is neat and unflustered. 'Here, I can show you my evidence.' She pulls out her phone and shows me a picture of a foot with two small red marks just above the ankle bone. They look like spider bites.

'I was in agony with them. Two nights after, I had one at the top of my leg, then my arm, then my inner thigh. I tried to convince myself it was a bug, but it didn't swell up like it does with a bug. Then I stopped sleeping in my bed.'

'So you thought they were coming into your bedroom at night?' I try to understand.

'I didn't think, I knew. How else do you get marks like that?' She takes a bite of her salad. 'And I'd already seen it.'

'Where?' I ask, suddenly much more interested.

'In my bedroom,' she says, looking down at her salad. 'It woke me up. I felt this hand behind my back. I lay there and thought, shit, there's a burglar in my house. So I froze and lay there. Nothing happened, so I opened my eyes and there was a fucking Grey at the bottom of my bed.' She points at where the end of her bed would be. 'It was stood at the end messing with my feet.'

'How long was it there for?'

'Not that long. I got angry, and the light around it faded.'

Kevin – who has the look of a friendly builder, with closely cropped mousey hair and light stubble – interrupts.

'Do you ever get marks on your veins?' he shoots at Sarah, flashing us the photo he has been looking for since he sat down. The photo shows an arm covered in bruises and red marks.

Suddenly the room feels a bit colder. I shudder. 'If this is true, why is no one in the public eye writing about it?'

'It's all silenced.' Sarah looks at me, eyes wide. 'If you speak you lose all respectability, you lose your life. They will either think that you're making it up or that you've done it to yourself or something stupid like that.'

'I don't worry about it any more,' Kevin interrupts. 'The more you fight it, the more it hurts you. It's usually three in the morning. There is a loud, high-pitched noise when it starts, then you are paralysed, and a light comes up from the floor. Then a face looks at you.'

Kevin shows me another picture on his phone. It's a pencil drawing of an alien.

'This is the sort of thing that comes to see me,' he says. 'ET-looking thing but wider, about that tall' – he puts his hand out at about four foot – 'the skin is brown and wrinkly. This one time, I thought there were a lot of blonde women around me, and I could feel someone playing with me... you know... down there.' He looks at his crotch. 'Then I realised I was in pain, and that these blonde women were actually little men!'

There is an uncomfortable pause. We all look at each other, Sarah and Kevin with blank faces.

'But you only see what they want you to see.' Kevin breaks the silence.

'Yeah, they put a false memory on you.' Sarah nods in sympathy.

'Sometimes I'm so scared of going to bed, I keep all the lights on,' Kevin continues. 'They interfere in my relationships too. It's like they introduce me to people they want me to be with. For example, all my partners have had depression and gynaecological problems. All of them.'

Shit just got weird.

Sarah looks down at her feet before remembering something with a start. 'My friend's mum is getting abducted! She finds sand in her bed' – her voice gets higher – 'in the middle of bloody Wolverhampton!'

I shake my head, trying desperately to process what I am hearing, to suspend my disbelief. 'What do psychologists say about all this?' I try the same question I had posed to Kiaan the star.

'Oh, you don't go near them,' Sarah says. 'You can't. They'll put you on all sorts of pills and call you mad.'

Kevin jumps back in. 'I kicked one of them in the head once. Then I got punished. An ice-cold finger on my head. It knocked me out. Then I remember coming back down. I was dropped back onto the bed with so much force it woke my partner.'

'Did they take you onto a spaceship?'

'Oh yeah, been there loads of times.' Kevin nods. 'A room with no corners. All lit up, but no lights.'

'What did they do to you?'

'The only way I can explain it is like milking a cow.'

Sarah becomes animated. 'They are taking your bits. Your spermy things!' She screws up her face and turns to me. 'It's one of the theories of abduction; they call it the hybrid programme. They think it's something we have – perhaps emotions – that they want, so they breed with us.'

'Yeah, they're definitely taking my sperm.' Kevin nods.

V is for... Vampires

You will need some lube to get that dress on

Although they can be killed with a stake through the heart, because that would kill anybody, modern-day vampires are not averse to garlic, have a visible reflection and are not allergic to silver. But they do drink blood. Well, some of them do.

I make my debut in the community at a Gothic Boat Party, hosted by the London Vampire Meetup Group, on the River Thames. I study myself in the mirror next to my front door. Have I got the dress code right? I don't want to stick out, but I also don't want to overdo it and offend anybody. What on earth do vampires wear? I settle on a black silk shirt, purple jeans and far too much eyeliner.

After a long, self-conscious walk through east London, I arrive at the Liberty Bounds pub near Tower Bridge. My nostrils fill with a bouquet of dust and stale beer as I take in the dramatic scene. Clothing is period in style, jackets are stiff and shirts are ruffled. The men wear top hats and carry canes, and the women spill from tight corsets, their elaborate hairstyles thatched with lace hats and animal skulls. The familiar out-of-my-depth nausea brews in the pit of my stomach.

I meet my first vampire on board the ship. He is pale with long black hair that clings to his face in the heat of the evening.

Dressed in Victorian clothing, a tight suit with frilly cuffs and a lace collar, he smiles to reveal perfectly formed fangs.

'Hello.' I approach him, blushing at the idiocy of what I am about to ask. 'Are you a vampire?'

After an untrusting once-over with his eyes, he fixes his gaze on mine. 'Yeeees,' he purrs.

'How big is the community in the UK?' I seize the opportunity.

'Well, it's growing,' he says, taking a step back from me as if to regain control. 'We have a few families, and the London vampire community is pretty strong, but we're not as organised as they are in the US.'

I remember reading about this on the London Vampire Forum; it explained that unlike their American cousins, who are coming out of the coffin in their droves, many UK vamps remain hidden in today's society, a clandestine community yet to reveal their 'true nature' to their family and friends.

Happy that my vampire is now talking, I relay the memory to him. He thinks for a while, fiddling with the lace at his wrists. 'I think that's probably true,' he says. 'England is a much more cynical place than America, so people are embarrassed about coming out as a vampire. They are happy to hang out with other vampires and dress like them, but they still don't want to admit that they actually *are* vampires.'

He looks pleased with his answer and, without breaking eye contact, takes a big swig from whatever is in his wooden tankard. A thick red ribbon hangs from the handle.

'Do you drink blood?' The question falls out of me.

He furrows his brow and looks at me sideways. I worry I have pushed him too far.

'No,' he says, a smile forming as he seemingly enjoys my question. 'There aren't many sanguines left now, not since the eighties. A lot of people think it's too dangerous' – he waves his hand as if swatting something away – 'HIV and all that. So they switched to energy and became psychic vampires.' He curls his lip into a half-smile. 'Like me.'

The party continues into the early hours, ending up in the goth nightclub Slimelight, where I first meet Lee from chapter G. I spend the following afternoon nursing a throbbing head as I pore over internet forums and articles, building my vampire knowledge piece by piece.

I discover that modern-day vamps fall into two general categories: those who have a passion for vampire literature, film, folklore and fashion – known as 'life-stylers', who make up the vast majority; and those who genuinely believe they are vampires, with ancient souls that require supplementary life force. The latter group divide themselves depending on how they choose to 'feed' to remain healthy:

- Sanguine vampires believe that they need to take energy through ingesting human blood, typically from a willing donor.
- Élan vampires (not the clan's real name) live by a philosophy that enables them to take energy through living a certain type of life – more on this later.
- Psychic vampires (psy vamps) need to take energy or 'life force', typically from other human beings, to maintain a healthy, energetic balance.

I am especially interested in the idea of psychic vampirism, so I decide to follow the advice of InCarnatus, my vampire-forum friend, and read *The Psychic Vampire Codex*, a psy vamp handbook written by the famous vampire Michelle Belanger.

According to her website, Michelle, a prominent member and spokesperson of the global vampire community, had always felt different as a child, putting it down to a combination of 'genetics, environment and fate' that made her more sensitive to psychic experience. During her teens she 'identified and came to terms with' psychic vampirism – that is, the need to take energy from others in order to maintain optimum physical and mental wellbeing.

Michelle spent the next few years deepening her understanding of what it was to be a psychic vampire, framing the concept as a natural cycle of energy exchange, separating it from the negative, predatory stereotypes surrounding the traditional archetype of the vampire. She 'came to understand' the need for psy vamps to take energy as a necessary element of a universal energy cycle:

> There are many people who naturally produce too much energy than they require to sustain themselves. Many of these are called to be healers ... For every person who has a natural abundance of energy to give away, there is another person who has a natural need to take energy in, and so the energy of the Universe remains in a constant and vital flow.

For me, the idea of energy exchange is a palatable access point into this world. I accept that human beings emanate energy – you can call this 'life force' if you like, it makes no difference – and I think we all know someone who tends to sap the energy from any room they are in, just as we all know someone who seems to inject it. So it doesn't feel like a radical leap to go one step further and say that some people are energy deficient, and some have too much.

Michelle goes on to explain that most vampires live by a code of conduct called the Red Veils. This involves feeding only on partners who understand the process and are willing to be fed from, except in the case of 'surface feeding' (taking from the 'outer layers' of someone's energy field without invading their aura) or 'ambient feeding' (taking the energy collectively generated by a crowd of people). Feeding on an unwilling victim is classified as assault by the majority of the vampire community and is deeply frowned upon.

I read on. *The Psychic Vampire Codex* teaches the newly awakened psy vamp how to feed.

To 'ambient feed', you simply go to a crowded place, such as a gig or a busy city centre, and let the energy flow into you naturally. You can also visualise a net around you that catches the energy, before bringing it back into yourself.

To 'surface feed', you:

select a target from the crowd and concentrate on him or her. While focusing on the target, extend a tendril of your energy towards this person ... then focus on the person through the tendril and start pulling the energy from him or her to you.

This is typically not harmful to the target: 'at most, he or she will develop a headache or suddenly become very sleepy'.

'Deep feeding' is the most invasive feeding method and involves going into another person's chakra and taking energy at the deepest level. It is complex and 'can be very dangerous' for those who do not know what they are doing.

I mindlessly rub my throat, swallow hard and shut the book.

*

Some time passes. I am sitting on a high stool in a macabre tattoo shop on the Holloway Road.

'By the power of Bach.' A solid man with a shock of bleached-blond hair moulds my thumb and two middle fingers into the universal rock sign (or 'devil horns') and motions for me to repeat him.

'By the power of Bach,' I say.

'I will not eat with my fangs in.'

'I will not eat with my fangs in.'

'By the power of Bach.'

'By the power of Bach.'

'I will not sleep with my fangs in.'

'I will not sleep with my fangs in.'

There is a break while he tries to remember the next bit.

'Oh yeah, I like this bit.' He wriggles on his seat. 'By the power of Bach.'

'By the power of Bach.'

'I will drink far too much Jack Daniels with my fangs in,' he says with a grin.

'I will drink far too much Jack Daniels with my fangs in,' I say, smiling back.

'By the power of Bach.'

'By the power of Bach.'

'I will have crazy, amazing sex with my fangs in,' he smirks.

'By the power of Bach,' he goes on, denying me the chance to repeat the best one. 'I will not look in the mirror until Bach says it's OK.'

I figure we are done with the whole repeating thing, so I look back at him, and wait. He looks stern. 'Well?' he says.

I resist the urge to roll my eyes. 'By the power of Bach, I will not look in the mirror until Bach says it's OK.'

'That's the most important bit!' he says, motioning for me to open my mouth and hold up my lips with my devil-horn pinkies.

I am going through my 'rite of transformation', my awakening as an Élan vampire. The ceremony involves having fangs made by Bach (not his real name), a protagonist in the modern vampire movement and professional fangsmith. Apparently that's a thing.

Going through the ceremony qualifies you for entry into a global vampire community first engineered by Bach in the early nineties. It involves taking the 'Oath', as outlined above, and the 'Oracle' – picking a page you are drawn to from a book written by Bach, and reading it aloud.

A shrewd businessman, Bach's rule is that he only gives interviews to fang clients. To this end, he has made fangs for reporters from a number of the major media companies. Bach has made over 22,000 pairs of fangs in his lifetime, which, at around £100 a pair, isn't bad business. The process is a heavily guarded secret, although he did teach one other guy to make them, who then taught four more people, and was swiftly excommunicated.

The fangs are made from professional dental acrylic and moulded around the teeth so they can be slipped on and off like a loose cap. I am not allowed to close my mouth during my own fitting session, resulting in a stream of dribble that cascades down my neck and into my cleavage.

'Why do people like them so much?' I ask, attempting to dam the flood with my shirtsleeve.

He tilts his head and winks. 'They make great sex toys,' he says.

I release the dam and move my hands back to my lips, re-exposing my gums for Bach to insert the caps he has just finished sandpapering.

I don't feel very sexy.

The final stage of the ceremony is the Rite of the Mirror,

'opening your vampire eyes for the first time'. I am spun around twice and instructed to take in my reflection. I open my mouth to see perfectly shaped white fangs protruding from my canine teeth.

I run my tongue over them and open my lips into a sinister smile. Now I feel sexy.

Having read so much about him in books and on internet forums, I have to confess to being a bit star-struck when I first met Bach that morning. His piercing steel eyes drew me in as he held my gaze for longer than was comfortable. It was as if he was searching for something deep in my eyes; trying to figure me out; reading me. His size intimidated me, and his confidence had mine cowering in submission. Maybe I have been reading too many vampire books lately, but there really does seem to be something different about him, something ethereal.

'Are you going to talk to me while I have a cigarette or not?' he commands.

'Of course I am.' I trip over my words.

We stand in the London drizzle while I shiver and inhale his second-hand smoke. 'What do you call people who aren't vampires?' I ask, hoping to collect another name in exchange for my suffering.

He exhales a smoke caterpillar. 'People who hang out with vampires but aren't themselves are called black swans.'

Totally worth it.

After a Tube journey back to his apartment later that afternoon – me still wearing my fangs – we decide, or Bach decides, that we should go for a coffee.

I sip slowly at my tea as he releases a torrent of consciousness.

'Anne Rice's vampires were relevant to her era, in the same way Élan vampires are relevant to ours,' he begins. 'My clients buy my books and read my blogs, and if they vibe with me they join my clan. There have been seven hundred active members on my site in the last six months, but there are about two thousand members in reality.'

He goes on, leaning back on his chair and resting his arms as if sitting on a throne. 'The vampire is a metaphor for immortality, romance, passion, money, love, power, inspiration. These are the interpretations, and I just ritualise the experiences. I am very sensitive to psy vamps. We went on a witch hunt and kicked all of the psys out of my clan, and the sanguines. I don't mind if a couple do it as a sacred act between themselves, but it's not a scientific, psychological or medical fact that someone needs blood.'

I interrupt him. 'No, but they don't believe it's a scientifically measurable thing, do they? It's about psychic energy, which isn't measurable anyway.' I feel so defensive, I think because of the casual way he is dismissing all other forms of vampirism that aren't his. It feels a bit supremacist.

'Some do, some don't,' he says, noncommittally. 'Most blood drinkers don't even drink blood, they just say they do. All they are doing is latching onto an archetype to have a social network.' He turns over his hands. 'I drank blood. There's no freaking energy in blood, it's a sexual kink. That's all it is to me. I did it for seven years – had three donors; they were all clean. We went to the doctor's together.'

'Where did you take the blood from?'

'The back, or the lip, typically. I thought I needed it; I thought I was a sanguine. But then I stopped doing it with my girlfriend and realised I didn't need it all. It's just what you did before we all learned about hepatitis and HIV. I'm not going to put myself at risk any more. I am one of the most educated people on vampire culture in the world, and to me, drinking blood is a fetish, simple as that.'

I lean forward onto my elbows. 'How often did you do it, in the past?'

'Oh, just during sex,' he says. 'If you really think you need that to survive, that's bullshit, and I like calling people out on bullshit real fast.' His speech gathers pace as he leans forward to meet me, both hands on the table. 'Exchanging blood within a loving relationship is sacred. It is the most intimate thing you can do. People who trivialise this as food can go fuck themselves. That's not food. That's another person. It's cannibalism.'

The energy drops as he responds to the vibration of his phone. He reads a message. 'I screen people before I have sex with them,' he says, his eyes still fixed on his phone. 'I kind of have the rock-star thing going on and I get a lot of young girls who are interested in hooking up. Most of them I turn down because I lose energy during sex.'

'What about your girlfriend?' I ask, remembering him mentioning her earlier.

'Oh, Lea isn't my girlfriend,' he says, 'she's my sub [a BDSM term for the non-dominant member of a sexual relationship]. I vetted her very carefully. I don't do girlfriends.'

I sense that he wants me to ask more about this, but I'm more interested in the blood drinking.

'How do sanguines take blood?' I try.

'Oh, they use scalpels and knives and shit. There's no safe way to do it.'

We leave for the apartment he has rented across the road, me scurrying to keep up with his giant stride. Once there, we sit on the bed and wait for his French sub Lea and her friend to return from a shopping trip. 'I haven't seen Lea in six weeks,' he says. 'She's gonna come in, see me sitting on a bed with another woman and think I've picked up another sub.'

The comment hangs in the air. I choose to ignore it, hoping it's not a suggestion. I'm sure it would be an exciting and illuminating lifestyle change to become a sub, especially to a famous vampire, but I would really struggle to explain the situation to my mum.

Ten minutes later and the girls arrive. They don't speak very much English, so after a brief introduction we sit in crippling silence while Bach uses the adjoining toilet. Loudly. When he gets out we all troop outside and hail a taxi, bound for an 'industrial, fetish, gothic night' at an alternative nightclub in Vauxhall.

'You won't be allowed in wearing that,' Bach tells me as we approach the entrance.

I glance down at the all-black ensemble I had carefully selected this morning. 'It's all I have,' I say, secretly hopeful at the idea of not being let in.

He points at the sign on the door.

No street clothes, No trainers, No 'normal' suits, No denim... Naked is not an outfit, even if it's your 'thang'. Nudity is fine but you must look the part and make the effort... Our dress code is broad and we are not elitist, but we do want to ensure that everyone attending feels comfortable and safe.

'It's OK,' he says. 'I have a latex dress you can wear' – he looks me in the eyes – 'but you can't wear any underwear with it.'

Panic floods my body, but Bach holds me in an intense stare

that seems to dissipate my terror. I trust him, I realise. I'm not sure why, but I do.

'Follow me,' he says, 'we can get changed inside.' I bare my fangs at the doorman as I follow Bach into the kingdom of industrial fetish.

My mouth drops as I take in the scene: whips, latex, people wearing nothing but bridles, tassels, leather dog-masks, zipped-up gimp suits, chains, people walking from room to room carrying suitcases full of Lord knows what, cyber hair, girls kissing on the dance floor dressed in nothing but horns and cat ears. Holy shit.

Lea and her friend, whose name I still don't know, make for the toilets. I follow them.

'You will need some lube to get that dress on Lucy,' Bach shouts to Lea. 'Ask around, I think the DJ will have some.'

We walk up to the DJ, and Lea asks him confidently, and in perfect English, if he has any lube we can borrow.

'Sure,' he says, without a moment's hesitation, 'here you go.' He fishes in his pocket and hands us a few sachets of Durex Synthetic.

Once in the toilet, Lea instructs me to strip. Thankful for my recent naturist experience, I begin to undress as Lea smirks through her fangs. 'Are you shy?' she says, towering over me in a pair of huge platform boots, wearing only leather underwear framed with silver studs

'No,' I answer truthfully, marvelling at the absurdity of the situation as I strip to nothing in a toilet of a fetish club, in front of a French vampire and a complete stranger who doesn't speak English.

Lea opens the packet of lube and starts to rub it over my torso. Once satisfied, she soaks the paper-thin rubber dress in the sink and starts to pull it over my head. It is freezing cold and sticks to every part of me. She gestures for her friend to help, and both spend the next few minutes wrestling me into it. The whole thing is very undignified, as they pick and pull at my flesh, manoeuvring each part into place. Once tucked in, I am surprised by how comfortable the latex feels against my skin. I grin at my reflection to reveal my fangs as we exit the cubicle.

With only a millimetre of black latex between my naked body and the outside world, I feel surprisingly at ease as we walk through the club, the dress feeling more like a second skin than an item of clothing. I head straight to the dance floor and dance like nobody is watching, because nobody is. Nobody gives me a second glance, probably because I am actually wearing more than most of the people here.

I mimic the style I had observed at Whitby Goth Weekend: waving my hands in the air, swirling my hips, and moving my head around dramatically. I have a brief moment of euphoria before I catch a glimpse of myself in the mirror and realise that I haven't shaved under my arms for at least a week. Fuck it.

After our dance we head back to visit Bach, who is taking fang appointments in the corner from his mobile unit. He looks at me. 'You look good!' he says, before turning his attention to Lea. 'When I've finished here, we'll go have some fun in the Dark Room,' he says to her, 'before it gets too... icky.'

The Dark Room, I discover shortly after, is a chamber of comfortable couches for couples to 'explore their naughty side', guarded by a woman wearing nothing but black tape over her nipples. Only consenting parties can enter and no one is allowed in alone. A box of tissues sits on a table by the door beside a wooden chest that bursts with serrated foil packets in every colour.

Around the corner, another room, the Play Room, is

furnished with wooden stocks, cages, chains, spanking benches, gynae chairs (whatever the hell they are) and 'medical equipment'. There are experts in the rooms to offer advice on how to use the equipment, and a viewing window for passing voyeurs.

I leave the party at midnight, sad to part ways with the latex dress, wondering if my eyes will ever recover.

Running my tongue over my fangs repeatedly in the taxi home, I ponder the absurdity of my day. This is all far more real than I had expected. Vampires are a thing – an actual thing – a subculture as real as hippies and naturists. Perhaps a little less glamorous than I had expected (there is nothing alluring about awkwardly extracting spit-covered fangs to eat a packet of Monster Munch) but they do exist, and the complexity of their belief system, regardless of its validity, demonstrates an impressive commitment to understanding the phenomenon they are part of.

We are all desperate to figure out who we are, desperate for our questions to be answered, especially if we consider ourselves to feel in some way different from most people. Like the otherkin community, the vampires have pushed the question of identity to the next level, explains Joe Laycock in his book *Vampires Today*. The question they ask is 'What if I am not a human being at all? What if I am something else entirely?'

W is for... Wiccans

*Much quicker than wrapping an ox tongue
in barbed wire and burying it at midnight*

As a young teenager I spent a lot of time hanging out in a Yahoo chat room called the Graveyard. If this is where you also spent your youth (weirdo), you will remember me either as Satan_666 – embarrassingly spelt Satin_666 for the first few weeks – or Lonewolf24. You see, during this fleeting chapter of my life, I couldn't decide whether I wanted to be a witch or a werewolf and flitted non-committally between the two. This phase continued for longer than it should (a couple of months), before my obsession with werewolves came to an abrupt end when I spent a whole evening trying to evoke the transformation outlined in the young-adult fiction book *The Blooding*, and failed. I decided there and then that werewolves probably weren't a thing.

After spending our school days filling our exercise books with pentagrams and Celtic crosses, my friend Kat and I would meet to burn incense and recite internet-sourced spells through black-painted lips. We would tell our fellow chat-room members (who the hell were these people?) that we were witches and 'prove it' by saying things like 'Blessed be' and 'Harm none', responding to the creepy, yet strangely acceptable at the time 'A/S/L?' (age/sex/

location) question with, 'Our souls are thousands of years old/ genderless/nowhere and everywhere.' I think this put people off asking us for cybersex. Thank God. Maybe this is why my mum happily bought me a book of spells for my thirteenth birthday. Good job, Mum.

Equipped with this formative experience, I was excited by the prospect of re-immersing myself into the Wicca community as a (sort of) grown-up, curious to see if the aspirations of my thirteen-year-old self were still lurking somewhere, deep in the broom closet of my mind.

Wicca is largely regarded as a path of paganism, and there's a good degree of crossover between these two communities. So it would be fair for you to wonder why, despite my teenage foray, I didn't treat you to a bit of variety and choose to do something a bit different for chapter 'W'. Well, first off, and I'm not asking you to feel sorry for me here, but finding a subculture to explore beginning with W was nearly as difficult as it was for the letter J (whose idea was this bloody alphabet thing again?). But the main reason, if I'm being honest, was my desire to don my best poker face and say to my friends: 'Sorry, guys, I can't go to that gig in Hyde Park with you this weekend. Why? Oh, because I'm off to Witch Camp.'

'Of course you are,' came the disappointing response before the conversation moved on. I think my friends have officially become desensitised.

After an hour of haring around the windy roads of Oxfordshire in my floaty green pagan dress, I pull into the entrance of Witch Camp, or, more accurately, the Artemis Gathering, on a rainy summer's evening in August. Damh the Bard (remember him?) performs his pagan music on the main stage as I begin setting up my tent in a downpour. Once it's erected, I squelch over to join my fellow witches in the middle of camp and begin to explore the enchanting stalls offering robes, healing crystals, herbs, ceremonial knives and tarot readings. Mostly covered in tattoos, the women wear a contrasting mix of black gothic dresses and bright hippie colours.

Following the smell of honey around the circle of stalls, I find the bar sheltered in a large white tent, scan the numerous varieties of mead on offer and fill my battle re-enactment tankard with a measure of Lindisfarne Spiced. Taking a big swig of the sickly-sweet elixir, I make for a nearby picnic table to watch an angelic tot engrossed in waving an ivy-covered stick around in giant circles.

'Be careful!' A lady comes rushing up and bends down in front of the small girl so they are both at the same level. 'Your wand is not a toy, Ophelia; it's a very dangerous tool.' She rips it from her hand. 'I'll keep hold of it until you learn how to treat it properly!'

Common activities for the witches of today involve performing rituals and healing ceremonies, using crystal balls, tea leaves and cauldrons to perform divination, and honouring the magic of nature. And so, a bit like modern-day vampires, they are effectively reclaiming a concept from folklore, shedding the negativity previously associated with it and reinterpreting it in a new light.

I head back out to the stalls, where the smell of damp grass is infused with essential oils and herbs, to see a stream of witches emerging from their tents. Now adorned with leather masks, cloaks and pentagram necklaces, the surrounding crowd are summoned to join hands and form a circle for the opening ritual. I take the hand of a girl wearing pointy elf ears, her cotton-covered dreadlocks running down to her knees.

A female figure in a long blue dress walks around the perimeter of the circle we have formed, holding up a vast sword, as if offering it to the sky.

'Come, circle, may you be a place of power. May all goodness, happiness, positivity and knowledge be contained within you. So mote it be.'

The circle of a hundred-plus witches all repeat, 'So mote it be.'

The figure's blonde hair billows dramatically in the wind. A gold bracelet snakes down her upper arm, and a leather belt houses a ceremonial knife at her waist. Something about her draws me in, like the curious kids in *Hocus Pocus*. I visualise her warning us that the night is dark and full of terrors.

As Rollo Maughfling, the Archdruid of Glastonbury, had done at Stonehenge, she stops in the middle of the circle, opens her arms to the sky and motions for us to do the same. We all turn to face the east.

'Come, air. Great communication, great laughter and great joy be here. I call you to guard us, help us and welcome us. Hail and welcome.'

'Hail and welcome,' the circle echo.

We turn to face the south.

'Gods, goddesses, spirits of the south, grant us the gift of energy in our endeavours. Fire of passion, burning away all the negative spirits and letting only good enter here. Hail and welcome.'

'Hail and welcome.'

We turn to face the west.

'Welcome, element of water. Without you we are nothing, we can be nothing. Hail and welcome.'

'Hail and welcome.'

Finally, we turn to face the north.

'Gods of the north, the element of earth – what we stand on, what makes us, what balances us – give us wisdom. Hail and welcome.'

'Hail and welcome.'

Having successfully called down the quarters, we are instructed to sing and weave in and out of flags representing the four elements, while four children skip around the middle, each holding the end of a tied rope that wheels in the centre of the circle.

'Lady, spin your circle bright. Weave your web of dark and light. Earth, air, fire and water, bind us all as one.'

When the song is complete, we share a bowl of digestive biscuits – 'May you never hunger' – delivered to our mouths by a stout man with flowing locks of silver hair.

Later that evening, we are entertained by an energetic folk band playing before a sea of euphoric dancers who wave their whole bodies without inhibition. After the set, we follow a procession of torches to the fire pit on the other side of camp for a ritual to welcome the burning of a massive phoenix sculpture; a metaphor for us all rising together into a new era for Wicca.

The crowd sway, eyes closed as fire-breathers ignite the giant cloth and metal structure, singing repeated verses of 'Earth my body, water my blood, air my breath and fire my spirit.' Remembering the words from the song taught to me at Findhorn, I join in at the top of my voice, relieved to finally be able to blend with the group.

As the day draws to a close, I read my *Wicca* magazine by torchlight back in my tent, keen to understand the ritual I had experienced that afternoon. According to the magazine, most rituals start with the 'casting of a circle'; this involves spreading salt and walking the boundary with a ceremonial tool, like a knife or a sword, while visualising a protective barrier. Then a psychic charge is built by making an offering of some kind, culminating with calling upon whichever goddess that particular witch works with, to either ask for something or give thanks for something. A bit like saying a prayer, or making a wish, I suppose.

The evening had been as otherworldly as I had hoped for, and I was excited by the prospect of feeling like a witch again. I'm not sure I can convince my adult self to believe in natural magic, but I like the idea of it enough to give it a go. As Kiaan the star had said to me, your truth is all that matters, and a witch's model is as true to them as mine is to me. After all, I always touch wood when I say something I don't want to happen, I don't walk under ladders, I never swear on someone's life, and I sometimes toss a coin in a fountain, so what's the difference? I make a vow to myself, once again, to try and suspend my disbelief as the gentle patter of summer rain sends me off to sleep.

The keynote address the following morning is 'Meet the Witches', a Q & A session with a panel of four men and two women ('witch' applies to both sexes here) all apparently prominent figures in the Wiccan community. My hand rockets into the air.

'How has society's attitude towards Wicca changed over the last twenty-five years?'

A chap with shoulder-length hair, wearing a sharp suit and cravat, stands up and clears his throat. 'Well, it's positive and negative, really. We no longer get social services trying to take our children away. But we've sort of fallen into the same camp as the Quakers now: harmless, but not to be taken seriously. That's why you never really see any of us in public positions.'

A female witch called Tylluan stands up. 'You'd still get a brick through your window if people knew you were a pagan where I live,' she says in a strong Welsh accent. 'Mind you, in the Valleys, some people can't tell the difference between paediatricians and paedophiles.'

There is a ripple of laughter.

'Do you think they even know what it means to be a pagan?' asks a lady in the audience.

'No clue, none whatsoever. It's fear and ignorance. Utter ignorance, that's what we have to contend with.'

'I work in a Catholic school,' another lady, whose t-shirt reads 'Keep Calm and Spread Salt', joins in. 'There is no way I could tell them what I am. I want to build tolerance as much as the next witch, but the risk is too much for me.'

'How many people here would be nervous about performing a ritual in public?' Tylluan asks the audience.

There is a lot of nodding as most people raise their hands.

'But aren't we just adding fuel to the fire?' asks a man in a multicoloured jumper. 'By hiding it, we are making what we do look secretive, which keeps people thinking it's scary, or sinister in some way.'

Someone else agrees. 'I think we should be out in the open. We should be proud of what we do. Otherwise nothing will ever change.'

It seems that Wicca is at a crucial stage of its development. For most, it is safer than it has ever been to 'go public', but there is still fear and ignorance out there, and people don't want it to affect their lives. So the argument could be that all witches should talk openly about who they are and take whatever career knocks come their way to normalise witchcraft and benefit the cause, but on an individual level, people are not yet willing to do that, particularly those who work with children or in positions of public office.

This is a 'no photo' event, meaning you cannot take photos of other attendees without their express permission. As with the naturists, this rule is in place to protect those who haven't yet or may never intend to 'come out of the broom closet' as witches, and do not want to be forced into this by social media.

The room goes quiet and I decide to ask another question. 'What is the difference between a witch and a Wiccan?' I wince at the naivety of my question, but the room smiles back.

'In order to be dubbed a Wiccan,' begins a witch who had previously introduced himself as Tam, 'you need to be part of an exclusive witch family, known as a coven.' His face is red in the cold of the morning, framed by long white hair that he gathers behind his shoulder at regular intervals. 'Becoming a member involves an initiation, during which you are shown "the mysteries", which must be experienced and cannot be explained.'

How convenient.

He goes on to explain, in a broad Scottish accent, that coven members are also required to attend regular Sabbats (celebrations and festivals) and group rituals. For example, to mark Samhain (Halloween), most covens will host a 'feast of the dead', where they set twice as many places at the table; every other seat is saved for loved ones they have lost, invited to join the celebration at a time when the veil between this world and the next is at its thinnest.

'But you do not have to join a coven to be a witch,' he says. He looks out to the audience. 'How many of you here are solitary witches?' About half the room raise their hands. He gestures outward. 'These people like to practise their magic alone.'

Tam has been in a coven, also known as a lineage group, in south London for thirty-six years now and is a 'high priest', a condition for which, he tells us, is 'a soul on fire with the love of the gods and the love of humanity'. 'We worship the gods together,' he explains. 'Not by praying, but by doing, by laughing, by having fun, and by joy.'

The Q & A turns to the everyday practice of magic.

'When casting spells,' a tall male witch begins, 'we do not have to reject our rational knowledge of this realm, but simply recognise that, in doing magic, we are straying into another realm where things work differently. Our minds are connected to reality in a symbiotic manner, so that our reality affects external reality, and vice versa.'

So what we create in our minds becomes reality? I am reminded of my thought train from yesterday evening, about suspending my disbelief. But can we really *will* things into existence? There are many schools of thought that would agree with this – the act of manifesting, law of attraction, neuro-linguistic programming, the power of positive thinking, etc. – but can I truly convince myself to believe this? Just as I can feel myself tumbling back into my cynical rabbit hole, I recall the lunacy of trying to prove the fallacy of someone else's model. I picture myself, walking slowly in the pitch dark between the Avebury stones, desperately trying to work out why the metal rods in my hand were swinging, and my frustration at not being able to understand the songs during the Kabbalah 'meditations'. I'll never be able to experience these worlds fully if I keep questioning everything so literally, but it feels impossible for me to stop.

Later that afternoon we gather in a small wooden Scout hut that smells of bonfire to listen to a talk from the lead singer of last night's folk band, who looks alarmingly like Ralph Fiennes in a Robin Hood costume. With beads and feathers woven into his shoulder-length wispy hair, he wears long leather boots that curl up at the toes over black britches, a white lace-up shirt and a leather necklace. I can't take my eyes off him.

'People like me used to be known as occultists,' he begins, pensively pacing back and forward through the seated witches, radiating charisma, 'but I prefer the term... esoteric scientist. All this campaigning for paganism to become a religion stuff – I won't support that. People tell me I should be tolerant. But I will not be tolerant of religion, because it keeps people primitive. That's why I love paganism, because it isn't a system – it is a collection of individuals with their own set of spirituality.' The room is silent, hanging on his every word.

'Religion has had its day,' he says, 'it's only a matter of time before it's axed out of the world. Then we can really progress.'

He gives the example of a Yazidi girl who ran off to marry a Sunni Muslim in 2007; her family begged her to come home, and when she did, they dug a pit, put her in it and stoned her to death in front of a mob of 2,000. His point, as far as I can understand it, is that religious dogma disconnects us from our humanity.

'This is the most crucial time for paganism,' he continues. 'We are so young and so fragile, like children. We will make mistakes, naturally, but we shouldn't try and become another religion. That isn't the future.' He gestures to the woods on the other side of the window. 'If we do, we may as well go out and swing in those trees.'

At the closing of the weekend, we meet for a fire-walking workshop with Oona, a beautiful, passionate witch who dons a top hat over cascading flame-red hair.

'I love it here,' she tells us, her eyes dancing from face to face around the busy room, 'it's like coming home for me. You are all so open; you already know that we can work with the elements and that there is more than what we can see.'

She smiles, recalling a memory. 'I was up casting a circle earlier, holding a knife up in the air with my eyes closed. Then I could sense that I was being watched, so I turned around and saw two women. They asked if they could watch me. I felt so panicked, I had to explain myself. "I am a witch," I said. Then they looked at each other, smiled and said, "So are we." She laughs with the room. 'It was such a relief.'

Oona exudes radiance, an Elysian glow the like of which I haven't seen before. I don't know if it's the aesthetics – if it's because I have been conditioned to associate people who look like this with childhood tales of magic – or if it is real, but I have never before been so utterly captivated as I have with Tylluan, Tam and Oona. I spend a long time searching for a word to describe them that is accessible to me, that sits in the world of the rational and the scientific, but I have to give up. There is nothing rational and scientific about these people, and to apply that language to try to articulate the effect they have on me is redundant.

The fire that we are due to walk on in an hour (gulp) rages ten feet in the air, tended by a lady called Sheila, who wears a sparkly purple dress and no shoes. She looks at the fire and mumbles to it, conjuring up the flames with indistinguishable words, swaying from side to side in a ghostly dance.

While we wait for the fire to burn down to glowing coals, we are invited to take part in a 'cleansing ritual', using visualisation to charge an arrow with something we want to rid from our lives, before placing the arrow's head into the soft flesh at the base of our throat. The other end is propped against a board, which we are to walk towards in one quick movement, snapping the charged arrow to pieces.

'You will feel a lot of pressure, but it won't harm you,' we are promised. Oona demonstrates this, walking assertively into the arrow as it shatters and flies into the air. The arrow is made of wood, with plastic flights and a severe metal head.

'This technique is perfect for helping you to eradicate negative thinking,' she says. 'It's much quicker than wrapping an ox tongue in barbed wire and burying it at midnight. Of course, that works as well,' she adds, 'but it can get a bit messy. Who's next?'

My hand shoots up of its own accord. I walk tentatively up to the front and she hands me an arrow. Taking it, I place the head at my throat.

'Wow, that's sharp!' I say, recoiling with a start. There was no way I was going to be able to do this.

'Yeah I know,' she says sarcastically. 'I told you, they are real arrows; I got them from the real arrow shop.' Everybody laughs, lightening the weight of the room, but making me feel like a bit of a knob.

'What's in your arrow?' she asks me.

'Self-doubt and fear of failure.'

'Great,' she says. 'Now what I want you to do is flap your arms up and down three times, like wings. Then take a deep breath and walk into it.'

'OK,' I say, feeling like even more of a knob now I've heard about the wing-flapping.

'We will help you by chanting. What do you want us to say?'

'Erm... strong?' I suggest, feebly.

I lift my arms to flap them as the crowd of witches starts to chant, 'Strong, strong, strong.'

OK, I guess I have to walk into this rock-fucking-hard arrow now. Sure. I try to clear my mind of fear, try not to think about what might happen if this all goes horribly wrong. Is this a trap? Are these witches going to burn me after all? Or even worse, eat me? Is this all part of their sordid plan? Am I the human sacrifice?

Enough. I take a big step forward, and my neck sears with a split second of pain before the arrow shatters and flies across the room.

I am still buzzing from my successful ritual an hour later, my pride at the heroic act only just outweighing my embarrassment at thinking I might get eaten. But no one has to know about that.

As if that wasn't enough terror for the evening, the embers have now burned into a road for us to walk across. A road of glowing red spikes. My palms are sweaty and my breath is shallow, but I am emboldened by my triumph over the arrow. I've got this.

'It's all in the power of the mind,' Oona encourages us. 'You know you can make it, that you can master the fire, so do it. Prove it.'

I take my feet out of my red wellies onto the cold damp grass and place my foot on the glowing embers. There is a loud hissing sound as the evening moisture is wicked from my feet. I take my first tentative step and feel encouraged by the lack of pain; the road is sharp, yes, but I don't yet feel like I'm walking on fire. I carry on putting one foot in front of the other, and the coals grow hotter and hotter with each step. The pain kicks in, and I start to panic, running the last few steps and leaping into the cool grass at the other side.

I feel an overwhelming rush of relief and exhilaration as I sink my feet into the damp grass and look back over my shoulder at the embers, despite my feet being a bit hurty. Does the pain come from the panic, I wonder? Is it all in the mind? And why aren't my feet burned to smithereens? My mind grasps for a biological explanation. The skin on your feet is thick, right? And the water from the grass could have protected them? Perhaps.

The last person to cross the fire is Sheila, who dances and skips gleefully through the flames in her floaty purple dress, her eyes full of mischief. My wall of denial comes crashing down as my saddest suspicions are confirmed: there are definitely witches out there but, alas, I am not one of them.

X is for... X-treme Sports

Look at me now - I'm in fucking Star Wars

I've never been much of an adrenaline junky. I just don't get it. I don't get where the impulse to don a squirrel suit and jump from a 500-foot cliff could possibly come from. Is it a rebellion against the mundaneness of existence? A way to feel truly alive? I sign myself up for a parkour lesson with Dan Edwardes – the co-founder and director of Parkour Generations – to try and find out.

Also known as free running, parkour is essentially the art of getting from point A to point B in the fastest, most controlled and most efficient manner. It involves a lot of jumping from one high scary place to another high scary place, balancing on narrow things, swinging under things, scaling high walls, and pulling out a few flips for good measure.

The sport was originally developed in France on an estate where there was nothing else to do. After its import to the UK and exposure in documentaries such as *Jump Britain* and *Jump London*, the UK has since become the largest hub for the sport, with popularity growing at an astonishing rate, particularly in inner cities. It is now taught in schools and used as a tool to engage at-risk kids and teenagers.

Dan is a Cambridge-educated martial-arts protégé turned parkour frontman. He meets me at a train station wearing enormous baggy black trousers, a promotional t-shirt and a baseball cap covering the top of his angular face.

'It's the fastest-growing free sport in the world,' he says, as we walk together to an urban estate in south London for our lesson. 'Parkour is so much more than just exercise; it's a philosophy, a way of life. It's about being fit for purpose, and developing the confidence, both mentally and physically, to overcome any obstacle.'

I look at him walking next to me; a calm, commanding gait, his legs consuming the pavement with each perfectly executed step. I've never seen anybody be so damn good at walking.

'What is the community like?'

'Tight,' he says. 'We all share the same traits. Parkour people are pretty humble, confident and environmentally aware. There's a big element of helping others. That's why we like to be fit; we call it "fit for purpose". It gives us the confidence to help people, anything from carrying someone's suitcase up the stairs to jumping onto the tracks of the London Underground to help somebody up... which one of our guys did recently.'

I love the idea of the body being all it can – it reminds me of the circus performers, so in tune with their own physicality.

'Most adults starting out won't have moved in this way, or engaged with their environment this way since they were kids,' he says.

I decide that this probably doesn't apply to me, as I regularly pretend I'm a horse when out in the countryside, cantering down paths and jumping over ditches and stray logs.

'Oh, I behave like a kid all the time,' I say to Dan. 'So that part will be easy. It's the heights I'm worried about.'

'Well,' he says, 'the art of managing fear is like exercising a muscle: the more you practise it, the better you get at it. Parkour practitioners are exercising their ability to cope with fear every day, to face it and overcome it, so they are always shifting their comfort zones.'

I try to understand this in the context of my own experiences and realise how much easier it is for me to engage with groups of new people now than it was at the beginning of this adventure. And to be naked in front of other people; that one is a big change. Perhaps your comfort zone itself is like the elastic in an old pair of pants; the more you stretch it, the bigger it gets, and the easier it becomes to extend it even further.

We arrive at the estate where I will be doing my training, and start with a bit of jumping: from the ground up to a low wall, attempting to land perfectly balanced in a squat position.

'You have to land on the balls of your feet, as softly as possible,' Dan explains. 'If you can do it making practically no sound, then you are using your body in the most efficient way.'

I try. Jumping with two feet feels clumsy, and I am surprised by my lack of co-ordination. After a few more attempts, we move on to walking along a railing as if it were a tightrope. I can't even go one step without falling at first, but Dan makes me repeat it again and again over the course of the next twenty minutes and, by the end, I can make it nearly all of the way across. It feels good, and I really want to get better at it.

The next task is to jump from one wall to another across a sloping stairwell.

We clamber up a drainpipe to get on top of the wall. 'Really?!' I whine as I look down into the six-foot-deep abyss beneath me.

'Yeah, you can do it. You just jumped this far over there,' he says, pointing at the pathetically low wall we had been practising on.

'Yeah, but the stakes were much lower over there!'

'That doesn't matter. If you can do it, you can do it. It doesn't matter how high you are.'

I bend my knees to jump and freeze. Surely this is just stupid? I check with him, 'Two-footed?'

'Yes, you have twice the power if you jump with two feet.'

I stand there for about a minute, swinging my arms to try and coax myself into jumping. I can feel my pulse in my throat. Is this how I'm going to die? Trying to jump over a concrete stairwell? That would be a pretty stupid way to go, especially with 87,000 unspent Avios points.

I relay my thought process to Dan – anything to delay actually having to jump: 'See, all I'm thinking now is that if I don't do this, then I definitely won't fall, and I get to go home safe. But if I do, there is a chance I might fall. So it just seems irrational to me.'

This is how I felt in the battle re-enactment: I knew I should be pushing and giving it my all, but all I could think of was, 'Keep your feet, keep out of trouble and you go home safe.' I hate this about myself; it is cowardly and a direct manifestation of my inability to commit to things and be in the moment.

'True,' Dan interrupts my thought process 'but it's unlikely that you will fall, and there is an awful lot more to gain if you make it. When you land, you will be a different person to who you were when you took off. You will have more confidence. You will feel good and in control. It's transformative, like I told you.'

Of course, I am just being a wimp, trying to make excuses for myself because I am too scared to actually do it. I go to jump again and freeze at the last minute, making a bizarre growling animal noise in frustration. Then, after a few more attempts... I do it. I jump. But at the last minute, I put one foot out in front of the other and don't quite land two-footed. Whatever. It feels amazing.

'Great,' Dan says. 'Now you have broken the jump. That's what we call it when you have tried something you were nervous about and made it. Now it's just a case of perfecting it.' He gestures for me to climb back up the drainpipe and do it again.

'Out of interest, how did you force yourself to do it?' he asks me as I climb.

I beam at him, full of pride. 'I just stopped thinking about what might happen, and did it.'

'Exactly!' he becomes animated. 'Fear is either of the past – I've done this before and hurt myself – or of the future – this might happen if I fall. It is never in the moment. So if you can get your body into a state of being present in the here and now, you will be able to forget the fear, and focus on the technique.'

I try again and again, but I'm still not able to land two-footed. After another ten minutes, I am exhausted. Dan makes me measure out the distance on the ground to show that I can make it with two feet. I clear it, but only just, which doesn't give me much confidence. I climb back up and tremble on top of the wall, sweat streaming down my face, my quads burning, my pulse a loud throbbing at my temple. I try again, kneel down, and swing my arms. Then at the last minute, just as my feet have left the wall, I bail – I give up – and fall into the stairwell, where Dan lunges forward to catch me.

'See,' he says, as I climb back up onto the wall, furious with myself. 'You make your calculation before you start the jump. "Can I make it? Can I visualise myself doing it?" If the answer is yes, you commit there and then. You don't start to do it and then hesitate at the last minute, because that's when it becomes really dangerous.' He looks me square in the eye. 'That's why you fell.

Once you decide to do a jump, you do it. The focus isn't on the fear any more; it's on the technique.'

We try another four or five times, but I just can't bring myself to do it. 'Maybe we should try something else and come back to it?' I lie.

'Sure,' Dan says, knowing exactly what I am doing.

Next we learn how to vault over an eight-foot wall. He demonstrates it to me and makes it look painfully easy, moving with confidence and grace. I start by looking clumsy and pathetic, but improve over time, convincing myself to put more faith in my body as I realise how much of this is a state of mind.

After two hours of jumping, I can jump no more. My exhaustion calls for an end to our session and thankfully Dan agrees.

'Isn't all of this a bit reckless, though?' I ask him as we walk back to the station. 'That's the thrill, right?'

'Not at all,' he says. 'In fact, most parkour practitioners are risk-averse people. They carefully calculate whether or not they can make a jump, and when they know they can, their focus shifts entirely to the execution. The best way to minimise risk is to commit one hundred per cent to everything you do. It's mental discipline, not recklessness.'

With aching legs but a renewed sense of confidence, I drag my boyfriend along to Eastbourne Xtreme Festival the following weekend.

On Saturday morning we walk along the beachfront and head straight for the roller derby competition. Despite knowing nothing about this sport, I somehow thought it was a very good idea to email the organisers earlier in the week to see if I could play. My email went something like this:

Hello,
I would love to get involved in the roller derby competition.
I have never done it before but I roller skated as a kid so
I'm sure I can pick it up again.

This was the response:

Hi Lucy,
As with many extreme sports, playing roller derby takes
quite extensive training and testing prior to being able
to participate. Our rookie skaters will have completed
a minimum of a twelve-week training programme, and
passed written and physical tests, as well as competed
in some games. Unfortunately, you would not be able to
participate in this event.

Balls.

Anyway, here's how it goes: the Jammers, identified by wearing a star-emblazoned helmet cover, have to try and push through the opposing team members, before zooming off around the track to re-enter the 'pack', scoring a point for every member of the opposition they pass. The sport is extremely physical, with somebody falling over approximately every 0.00001 seconds.

We walk into the cage where it is being played, surprised to see a very alternative crowd, and take a seat next to two players from Suffolk Roller Derby.

'It's mostly women who play, but we have some men's teams and some mixed teams as well', a player covered in padding tells me. 'It's one of the fastest-growing sports in the UK.'

When the women's game finishes, it's the turn of the men. Huge burly guys with ponytails and long beards play alongside lanky, clean-shaven dads squinting through thick glasses. The sport seems to be full of people who would not have been on the sports teams at school – a sporting outlet for geeks – perhaps because they weren't cool enough, despite being really brave and physical, just like the goths playing 'maffball', and the pike unit at the battle re-enactment.

After an hour of watching people fall over, we head down the beach towards the skate park, passing a three-storey platform that people appear to be hurling themselves from.

'I have to do that!' I say, my voice heavy with inevitable dread.

Designed to replicate the experience of BASE jumping, the drop is seven metres of free fall onto a giant inflatable bag, and I am not looking forward to it.

I climb the scaffolding to try my first jump. Once at the top, my legs begin their familiar shake. The man beckons me halfway down the platform. 'Don't look over the edge,' he says. 'Just run from here, as fast as you can, and throw yourself off.'

Yeah, right.

I try this, get to the edge, and freeze. This is sooo high. The equivalent of jumping from a second-storey window down to the ground. Shit. I try three more times to run up, but stop with a jerk every time. I want to do it, I do, but it's as if my body will not physically let me. I suppose this is why human beings are so good at staying alive: an inbuilt survival instinct that prevents us from jumping from high places. Quite smart when you think about it.

I look down to see that an audience has started to gather around the platform. Great. Thirty people now stare up at me.

I tell myself to stop being so stupid, walk to the end of the platform and jump. Well, I say jump. I sort of half jump, half fall, my heart in my mouth as my limbs flail wildly during the three-second plunge. I land on the bag with a thud and the audience cheers. I do a quick calculation in my head and decide, without a doubt, that this is the bravest thing anybody has ever done, ever.

Feeling confident in our newfound ability to do extreme things, my boyfriend and I decide to head for the water-sports centre to rent wetsuits and paddleboards. 'But paddleboarding isn't an extreme sport,' I hear you say. Well, maybe not for most people, but in the roaring wind and (sort of) crashing waves, it becomes one, especially for wimps like us.

We take our boards down the beach, wince at having to walk over the pebbles in bare feet and take to the biting water. Within a few minutes we manage to stand up on our boards, looking over at each other to share a moment of mutual appreciation at how much we are nailing this, before leaning down to plunge our paddles back into the water. It is at this point that we realise the tide has been slowly sweeping us down the beach, and we are now really far from where we started.

We both panic and make for the shore on the next beach along. Once there, the surf rolls us over and over as we try and drag our boards out onto the sharp stones.

'I think I've pulled a muscle in my arm,' my boyfriend yells. I look over to see him being swept off his feet every time he tries to tug his board from the pounding surf. It looks a bit like a comedy sketch. 'It's too bloody windy!' I yell back, as I am pulled back into the sea for the fourth time.

We look at each other, wide-eyed, and share the same thought: would we die out here?

'It's too dangerous to get out this way,' I shout, battling to be heard above the wind. 'We have to go back to the beach we started from.'

331

'But it's sooo far,' he whimpers, a look of genuine fear in his eyes, 'and I've really hurt my arm.'

We manage to fight our way back into the sea and spend the next ten minutes skirmishing with the tide to get back to where we came from, panting and toiling against the continual pull to the deadly beach we had just escaped.

We finally make it, frantically pulling our boards from the swell before collapsing into a heap on our starting beach. I glance down at my watch. Since we rented the boards, only fifteen minutes had passed. I lift my arm and motion to my watch. A look of shame passes between us.

'Shall we hide from the rental guys for a while and pretend we're still in the sea?'

That evening we head to the roller disco to socialise with the derby players. The room is filled with hundreds of tattoos, facial piercings, gaping 'flesh tunnels' (holes in your earlobes that are stretched out over time by wearing progressively larger earrings), brightly coloured hair, big square baseball caps, shaved heads, leather jackets, band hoodies and snakeskin leggings. We both wear flannel shirts and jeans. Fresh-faced and groomed, I imagine us as part of a spot-the-difference competition in a puzzle mag.

'I felt really uncomfortable in there,' my boyfriend says as we leave an hour later.

'Why?'

'Because we looked really out of place. I felt like I didn't belong, like a voyeur.'

I hadn't felt at all uncomfortable. 'But they wouldn't have minded us being there at all,' I say.

He shrugs. 'Maybe not, but it would have been the same

if a guy with a face full of piercings walked into a house party with our friends. He would stand out. That's how I felt, like an outsider. It was uncomfortable.'

Of course, he is right; it does make you feel uncomfortable to be the odd one out. I have become so accustomed to being in this position that I hadn't even realised. You always feel alien in a room full of strangers who all know each other, especially if they are all dressed differently from you. But what I have learned is that the minute I engage somebody in a conversation, it humanises them, and from there it isn't difficult to find the threads that connect us – TV shows, music, a love of dogs – as human beings. We often share far more than we might think.

The following morning we head to the beach to watch a young, baseball-cap-wearing freestyle display team called Joe, Josh and Oly navigate a multi-platform obstacle course on trail and mountain bikes. They are joined by Pip, a professional parkour practitioner who moves as if gravity doesn't apply to him.

When the show is finished, I approach the boys for an interview. They agree, shyly arranging themselves around one of the platforms used during in the show.

"Technically, we are doing our hobbies for a living," Pip begins. He is young, in his early twenties, and strikingly handsome, with chiselled dark features and a muscular frame. Pip is a full-time free runner, making his money from sponsorship, demonstrations, TV commercials, and a decent role in *Star Wars: Episode VII – The Force Awakens.*

'We all started at school, and everyone was telling us we need to get a proper job, go to work every day. But now we get to do what we love. It's awesome,' Josh says, reminding me of the Border-collie-level enthusiasm of Alex the trapeze artist.

'Did you guys ever get any pressure from parents not to do this?' I ask, wondering how their lives compare to the circus performers.

'A bit,' Pip says, 'but from teachers more than family. I got suspended in school for doing parkour, so now I'm like, "Look at me now – I'm in fucking *Star Wars!*"'

They all laugh.

'My mum's a paramedic, so she hates it!' Josh says, his wild, brown curly hair caged into a baseball cap.

I decide to tell them about my parkour lesson, and my paralysis during the wall jump.

'Yeah, we have battles like that all the time,' Josh says. 'Wanting to do something but your body won't let you. Yesterday I had that' – he points above him – 'jumping up to that top platform, because I nearly fell the time before. You just start over-assessing everything. I completely froze.'

'The fear never really goes away,' Joe says. 'But you only get better if you push yourself, and you can only do that if you scare yourself.'

I am surprised by how calm and modest the boys are throughout the interview. I had expected to meet a bunch of extroverted adrenaline junkies but instead, I find them to be surprisingly thoughtful, level-headed and disciplined.

It all clicks into place, and, for a short moment, I get a bit carried away. 'Yeah, I understand that completely,' I say, as if I am a kindred spirit of these professional daredevils. 'I did this airdrop yesterday' – I point it out in the distance. It looks a lot smaller than I remember it being – 'and it was terrifying.'

They all look at me blankly. I don't think they are very impressed.

Y is for... Yogis

The universe is telling me not to put that on my back

You might think yoga is a bit too mainstream for this book, and you might be right; it has certainly been moving in that direction over the last twenty plus years. But I wasn't interested in the type of yoga done during lunch breaks in City gyms, the eye-wateringly expensive Lululemon apparel or the young platinum-haired yoga bunnies greeting each other with namaste hands. I wanted the hardcore stuff. I wanted the chanting, the spiritual growth, the vegan diet, the meditating.

An ancient Indian practice dating back to at least 2000 BC, of course this wasn't something I could expect to conquer in a lifetime, let alone during a wet weekend in Cornwall, but I at least wanted to go deeper down the rabbit hole. Were the Vinyasa flow classes I had been attending at the Fitness First gym under London Bridge just a commercialised misappropriation of the ancient spiritual practice, or were they genuinely helping me on my way to enlightenment? I vowed to improve my understanding and learn more about what it would take to become a bona fide (but, this time, clothed) yogi.

I was able to use the hilarity of our last downward-facing dog experience as bait to drag Tori along for a long weekend of yoga camp. We hit the road for the six-hour drive to an eco-community farm in the south west, passing the time by singing along to the *Mary Poppins* soundtrack in full throttle while the hammering rain did all it could to dampen our spirits.

When the GPS finally announces that we have reached our destination, we look around the waterlogged field in mild despair. As soon as our tent is erected, like, the very minute our now sopping-wet bedding is inside, the skies clear and we are able to trudge through the sticky mud to explore the site. Strewn with brightly painted signs that point out the compost toilets, solar showers and wood-burning sauna, something tugs in my chest as I am flooded with memories of Findhorn.

In the middle, next to a small earth mound with the word LOVE constructed from stones etched on its side, a bonfire flickers, hissing and spitting the rainwater from its heart. Soaking up the warmth of the fire, a lady in blue with wild wavy hair and a man with a ponytail and weathered olive skin sit at its edge, playing instruments and singing songs about Shiva. Above the bonfire is a bright yellow camper van, converted into a café and draped in colourful bunting.

We venture over to shelter from the returning rain and are immediately handed two steaming bowls of soup, lovingly prepared from ingredients grown on-site. Both emitting the same 'ahhh' sound from the old Bisto adverts, we sink into plastic chairs and bask in the sound of the drumming rain on the plastic awning, making a silent agreement that we are going to really, really like it here.

*

After a damp, sleepless night in our recklessly selected Tesco Value tent (not very 'eco' of us, I know), I manage to drag myself out of bed for the 7 a.m. meditation. The group gather in silence in a round hut overlooking the farm, wrapped in blankets in the early morning mist. We focus on our breathing for an hour, our ears full of birdsong, our noses full of incense.

When the gong sounds to mark the end of our meditation, I remain in the tent for some Bhakti (devotional) yoga, chanting and singing along to repeated verses of praise for the Hindu gods Shiva and Ganesh. A wooden flute and a shruti box, played by Buddenath and Gayatri, the fire duo from yesterday evening, accompany the chanting. When the music comes to an end, I sit with the musicians in the hut, the sun warming our bare toes as we pass around a flask of ginger tea.

Born Damon, Buddenath was given his spiritual name by a Hindu guru he lived with in the foothills of the Himalayas. He spent many years working happily as a primary-school teacher, but the more he opened up spiritually, the more difficult it became for him to stay in a mainstream job.

'I loved making music with the kids, and allowing them to be creative,' he tells me, 'but I have long hair, and I don't like to wear shoes. I just didn't really fit in, and they got fed up with me. I miss it, though. I loved teaching.'

The conversation turns to my indecisive nature, and how this has influenced my decision to write this book; trying to work out who I am and how I want to live by experiencing as much as possible of what life has to offer. I linger on the fox-hunting chapter, trying to articulate how torn I felt about taking part.

'What do you think is worse, eating meat or fox hunting?' Buddenath asks. He doesn't wait for an answer. 'Eating meat is worse,' he declares. 'The fox is wild and grows up in its natural habitat. It is free. And to be hunted is a natural way for it to die. Animals in the meat industry are born slaves. They are imprisoned for as long as they exist and are not allowed to live their own lives. Then they die young in an unnatural, sterile environment where they are part of a mechanised process. They are never treated as individuals.'

Before giving me time to pick up on this outburst, he wanders off barefooted across the sharp stones as I frantically scribble his words in my notebook.

I turn my attention to my other companion.

'I am truly wonderful at manifesting, at asking the universe for something,' Gayatri tells me as we sit outside the camper van for breakfast together. 'You just have to have complete faith, and it will come. For example, I want a harmonium at the moment, so I have asked the universe for one.'

'Can't you just go and buy one?'

She looks at me as if I have just said something utterly stupid. 'No, I don't have the money.'

'Of course.' I recoil at my ignorance.

After the second flask of ginger tea, which Gayatri waves her hand over and mumbles something before we are allowed to drink, I wander over to the Apple Barn at the other side of camp for my first physical yoga class of the weekend: Ashtanga. Our teacher, John, has been practising for twenty-eight years. With a long, twisted beard and sharp Dionysian eyes, his magnetism silences the room as he walks purposefully into the class. John is undoubtedly a real, bona fide yogi.

Without a word of introduction, he leaps into an extended sun salutation, floating from one position to another like a ballet dancer.

'Some of you may just want to learn to do a handstand,' he

says, perfectly balancing his entire body weight on one hand, like the clown's daughter at the circus, but with a fluidity that makes him seem superhuman, 'but yoga isn't just exercise. First and foremost, it is a spiritual practice. Get this right, and the body will follow.'

He motions for us to begin our own salutations and we settle ourselves into a downward-facing dog.

'Step or float your feet to the front of the mat.'

There is a mass 'thud' as we all follow the instructions, followed swiftly by a flamboyant fart that reverberates from the front of the class. My head shoots up, alert as a meerkat, as I let out an involuntary, 'Pah!' No one joins in the laughter, and I spend the next five minutes wishing Tori wasn't having a lie-in.

'When you are doing yoga you are drawing the energy up from the ground, through your body,' he says. 'You have to help the energy flow through your chakras and release any blockages.'

Next we are guided through a series of balancing poses, including headstands, handstands and windmills. I manage a few, but cannot hold them for long and repeatedly end up in a tangled heap on the ground.

Perfectly toned with long blonde hair and flawless bronzed skin, the girl in front of me is able to do everything.

'Hi, can I sit next to you?' I approach her after the class as she warms herself next to the wood burner.

'Sure. I'm Helen,' she says.

Helen is a children's yoga teacher, and one of the most beautiful things I have ever seen. I can't help but hate her a little bit.

'The kids love yoga,' she says. 'They change so much as they learn, becoming much more focused and relaxed. It teaches the kids to be more aware of their minds and bodies and to think independently. They spend more and more time hunched over computers these days, so their bodies don't develop properly, and they carry tension from a very young age.' She smiles with her whole body. I think she might be an angel, or at least a very, very pretty yogi.

Helen used to be a professional swimmer, finding yoga as a means to loosen her tightened muscles.

'Do you hang out with other yogis?'

'Oh yeah,' she says. 'We are all on the same spiritual path, and it's comforting to share in that. We all understand why we make the sacrifices we do in life.'

There is a pause while she thinks and makes the long 'hhhmmm' noise I have become accustomed to hearing in these New Age circles.

'I broke up with my boyfriend last year,' she continues. 'We were together for a long time, and although he was tolerant of my practice, he never really *got* it. He didn't really know *why* I did it. There were other reasons, of course, but the more yoga became part of my life, the further apart we drifted.'

Leaning towards the fire to soak up its warmth, I look at her perfectly toned body with envy, curious about what I would have to give up in order to look like her. 'Have you had to make a lot of sacrifices to get to your level of... (*don't say hotness, don't say hotness*) ... hotness?'

Dammit.

She laughs. 'Well, I don't drink any more,' she says, her cheeks now a dark shade of pink. 'And I get up at five a.m. every day to fit in my two-hour practice before work. I switched to a vegan diet too; I want to put the best things I can into my body.'

I take solace in the fact that she probably wouldn't be much fun at the office Christmas party.

But there is a bigger question here, isn't there? Why am I so obsessed with the way Helen's body looks? Is this what yoga is really about? As John had told us at the beginning of class, yoga is supposed to be concerned with self-realisation – spiritual, emotional and mental – and a physical body in optimum health is not the end itself, but simply a vehicle for meditation. Even though I know this is true, it's hard for me to disentangle the physical aspects of yoga from the spiritual roots of the practice. It's as if my mind has been hijacked by the body-beautiful industry to assume that, if you are thin, muscular and bendy, you must have got all of that spiritual stuff right as well. Of course, this isn't necessarily true, and in fact it can be the opposite if you allow your fixation with the physical body to get in the way of your spiritual practice. The tightrope between mental and physical health is a difficult one to balance on.

After a vegan lunch of lentil bake and salad – which was all you could ask for in a meal, so long as flavour, texture and general enjoyment were not part of your criteria – Tori joins me for the first class of the afternoon, Rolfing – a combination of movement education and tissue manipulation. Although not an actual yoga practice, Rolfing is a complementary exercise that sits somewhere under the New Age umbrella of alternative therapy and can often be found in similar circles.

'Why do we practise yoga?' our teacher, Andrea, asks us.

'To get me out the house on a Tuesday night,' a chap from the back of the class quips.

'It gives us a reason to be attentive to our minds and bodies,' I say, feeling smug.

'For strength and flexibility,' another chap to my right says.

'You are all right,' she says, which annoys me because I was feeling competitive. 'It is good for all of us in different ways. The body wants to be healthy all the time, but it isn't always. Why is that?' She throws the question out to us.

The 'it gets me out the house' chap shouts from the back again, 'Because we drive ourselves mad in our head and we fill our bodies full of shit.'

'That's true,' Andrea says. 'Now, I presume none of you eat meat' – Tori and I trade looks, feeling both irritated and guilty – 'but the white film you see over the top of meat is what's called connective tissue. We have it too, and when our connective tissue isn't used, it stiffens and sticks together; that's why you often hear those clicking and fizzing noises when you stretch. It's the sound of the fibres in our connective tissue ripping apart.'

We are then instructed to study each other's walks. Tori and I discover that ours are completely different: mine more forward-leaning and determined, rolling from heel to toe; and Tori's more backward-leaning, toes pointed and legs out in front like a dressage pony. We are asked to reflect on how our walk compares to our personality, and it is obvious to me that I lean into life, consuming it like Pac-Man consumes yellow dots; driving forward and never waiting for life to come to me. Tori is more relaxed and at ease with herself and is much better than me at living in the moment.

'Your walk is who you are,' Andrea tells us. 'I'm not telling you to change it, just to observe it and use it to help you understand how movement and intention are linked.'

After the class we take a solar-powered shower, using organic products so as 'not to harm the wildlife in the grey-water pond.' Tori had left her towel at the other side of the room, so she got out of the shower and walked across the room stark naked in front of one of our fellow, male, yogi wannabees. I was so impressed. There is no way she would have done this before our naturist experience. Later that evening I get the urge to prove my own liberation by plunging into the ice-cold water bath next to the sauna in only my pants.

Sleepy and warm, we leave the sauna for the evening's entertainment in the Apple Barn. An open log fire roars in the corner, and the floor is a sea of yoga mats, cushions and sleeping bags. It sounds as if someone is playing the drums on the plastic roof as the rain continues to hammer down. We are here for a 'sound bath': an hour of listening to didgeridoos, singing bowls, vocalisations, drumming, chimes and rainmakers. The musicians walk around the room, playing their instruments over our heads as we lie on the floor with our eyes shut. At the end of the session, we all 'Om' together. A Sanskrit word (*Aum*) that translates as 'source', the Om chant is often used to mark the beginning and end of a yoga practice, the vibrations rising from the bottom to the top through your chakras, to create a state of calm and wellbeing that prepares you for meditation.

The Om continues, vibrating through the group as we experiment with our tone to create a rich harmony.

This is more like it. I go to bed feeling peaceful, warm and relaxed.

On our final afternoon, I hug Tori a reluctant goodbye as she makes an early escape back to London and scramble up the meandering path that leads to the meditation hut for the class I have been looking forward to all weekend, 'Tantra with Fiona'. Although not strictly a branch of yoga, what Western culture has come to know as 'tantra' – a form of self-realisation through weaving together and expanding our internal energies – does use various yogic and meditative practices along its path. As with most of Eastern spirituality, it has been appropriated and often misinterpreted by the West, moving from a principle of what was essentially self-negation (enlightenment) to the material promise of 'spiritual orgasms' and 'deeply connected' tantric sex. And so what in reality is a complex and at times conflicting collection of spiritual texts that span the Hindu and Buddhist traditions has been reduced in Western culture to a practice that is easier to digest, and, no doubt, easier to sell. Tantra embraces opposites, asserting that there is nothing that is not Divine, bringing into this Divine sphere everything that the Judeo-Christian tradition would classify as impure, ecstatic and decadent. So perhaps it's not surprising that the West has embraced this particular aspect of tantric tradition, the belief that has converted sex, in all of its salacious glory, from sinful to spiritual.

'Don't worry,' Fiona opens with, 'I am not going to couple you off and tell you to get down to business.' The hut fizzes with relieved giggles.

Fiona has a master's in sexology, the scientific study of human sexuality. Also a trained massage therapist, she has a shock of short, bleached-blonde hair and a strong Aussie accent.

'I go into schools and talk to kids about sex,' she tells us, 'but I am only allowed to teach them what not to do. Sex education in this country is just about warning kids about the dangers of STIs. It's such a shame. They don't get to hear about the positive things. There is still this big taboo around sex.'

She stands up. 'OK, on your feet, you lot. It's time to wake up our bodies.' Fiona looks all of us in the eyes, scanning the room before settling her gaze on Gayatri. 'Aha,' she says, 'you look like the right person to lead this.'

She couldn't have been more right. Gayatri leaps into action, shaking her whole body and making a loud shivering noise – 'brrrrrr' – we all copy. She jumps up and down and makes a guttural growling noise that crescendoes into a shrill scream. We look around at each other and attempt to copy, all with slightly less enthusiasm.

'Come on, guys!' she yells, leaping up and making tribal noises as she gyrates her body. 'Let's be animals!' She drops to all fours and stalks around the hut, roaring, hissing and pretending to scratch at my heels as she passes me. Oh God. 'Just let yourself go,' I tell myself, as I collapse to the floor and do my best impression of a tiger. A few others join us as we turn into snakes and drag ourselves across the floor on our bellies, battling with crippling discomfort and trying desperately hard to pretend that this is all completely normal.

After five minutes the torture ends. We go back to our places and are directed to squat down, rotate our hips back and forth in a huge circle, and make caveman grunting noises – 'Ugh, ugh,' we all say, humping the air with eyes jammed shut. What we are doing here is connecting our masculine base energies with our higher feminine energies to resolve the conflict of our dualistic nature. Of course we are.

Finally, we are taught the Ashwini Mudra technique, or 'horse gesture'. We kneel down, fill our lungs, and are told to tense and release our anal sphincter muscles rhythmically. We repeat the process for ten minutes, adding in other breathing techniques and visualisations to draw the energy from our root chakra to our crown.

I leave the hut feeling a little violated, and not much wiser about what tantra actually is. What I have learned is that there isn't a lot I won't just go along with to fit in. I hope I never find my way into a human-sacrificing circle.

The weekend is closed with a kirtan. Don't be fooled, though; interesting as it may sound, kirtan turns out to be another chanting session with the same line of a song being repeated over and over again by Gayatri and Buddenath.

I had promised one of the ladies in the group a lift home earlier that afternoon, not realising that she wanted to stay for the entire kirtan, so I am forced to wait until the end before I can make my exit. After three hours of chanting, I can't take any more.

'We really have to get going,' I say, noticeably irritated. 'My drive home is over four hours, and it's already nine p.m.'

'You could start lugging my stuff up to the car?' she suggests.

I am not up for this at all. The car is parked at the top of a long muddy hill, and I feel the least she could do, having already delayed me so much, is to help me to carry her stuff up to the car.

'If I do that, I'm not coming back for more stuff,' I say. 'I'll just have to meet you up there.'

She finally finishes chanting with the group and starts to load me up like a packhorse: two rucksacks on my back, two bags in my hands and her tent across my elbows. She looks down at the one remaining item, her camping backpack.

'The universe is telling me not to put that on my back,' she says. 'I put too much of myself into the chanting; I don't have any energy left.'

She looks at me. My mouth is open and I don't know what to say. I am loaded up to breaking point with all her stuff, and she is too lazy to carry her own fucking backpack.

'Can you help, Peter?' She turns to Peter, who must be in his seventies.

'Unfortunately, I have a bit of a bad back,' he says in a really cute old-man way.

'Oh, it's fine once you get it on,' she says, lifting it onto his back without giving him a chance to protest. With that she disappears to the toilet, carrying absolutely nothing, leaving Peter and me to slog up the hill to the car.

'The universe is telling me not to give you a bloody lift,' I scream after her.

Well, I don't, actually. I'm British, remember? Instead, I punish her by being a tiny bit off with her during the two-hour drive to Bideford.

Z is for... The Zeitgeist Movement

Everything money touches turns to shit

The propensity for humans to be tribal — to look for different ways to build community based on shared interests, values, or fashion — is, for me, a given. But is our propensity towards tribalism damaging, unavoidably fostering prejudice and intolerance? What if the community we built was to include every member of the human race, rejecting any differences between us as trivial theatre? Could we use our desire to socialise and form community to create a better world? If your answer to all of the above is 'yes', you might want to consider looking into the Zeitgeist Movement (TZM).

That's how easy it is to get lulled into the movement, but something you should also be aware of is that if you do decide to pledge your allegiance to TZM, you will also have to accept a whole lot more... erm... fringe beliefs, for example, that 9/11 was an inside job, that a cabal of bankers controls the global financial system, and that a cure for cancer actually exists but is being covered up by big pharma.

Two months after googling 'subcultures beginning with Z', I find myself sitting on a broken plastic chair in a tiny room full to bursting point, surrounded by an unusual combination of pierced flesh and suits. Some look like lifelong squatters, others like bankers on their lunch break. I nervously wait for the meeting to start, trying to blend into the crowd around me, as always, wearing my New Look leather jacket, a baseball cap and ripped jeans ('Hey, Siri, what do activists wear?').

'Change will come, don't be in any doubt about that.' Ross stares at us intently as if we are a group of pupils he has just scolded.

This is the first meeting of the year of the London Zeitgeist Movement, set up to prepare for 'Z Day', an internationally co-ordinated day of presentations, films, exhibitions and the coming together of social change activists to raise awareness. The event will take place in a 400-seater auditorium, and there is no doubt in this room that it will sell out.

TZM calls for radical social change based on the belief that our current modus operandi – i.e. constantly consuming and striving for growth within a planet of finite resources (aka capitalism, or what they term 'the market system') – is the result of a distorted value system that is immoral and should be replaced by a technologically advanced system that scientifically plans the social sphere 'in the interest of all'. If you are lost already, don't worry, so was I, until I spent an entire day watching all three of the *Zeitgeist* movies on YouTube. To be honest, even after watching them, I was still very confused.

The movement was the brainchild of Peter Joseph, creator of the *Zeitgeist* movie series, a documentary-style art project that went viral, reaching millions of viewers. The first movie, released in 2007, focused on the learned human tendency to obey authority through the proliferation of some fundamentally dangerous conspiracy theories, and what happens when this is taken to extremes. It also poses the question of 'Who is really in control?' (hint: the banks – 'a century-long pyramid scheme'). The follow-up, *Zeitgeist Addendum*, introduced the foundational idea that sustainability and science – not money – should be the guiding forces of the 'system' we live in, and the most recent movie, *Zeitgeist: Moving Forward*, questions the need for private property and money, highlighting the current worldwide situation as 'disastrous' and calling for a global revolution.

According to TZM, there is a lot more that science and technology can do for humanity than it is currently able to because the shackles of capitalism limit its potential. The movement firmly believes that we have the resources to feed the entire planet, provide everyone with clean drinking water, build cutting-edge hospitals all over the world, and create clean energy for all, but money invariably gets in the way of these things because scarcity is 'built into the system' to keep prices high, only serving to encourage corruption and greed.

'What's the point of voting in the system as it is?' Ross asks, his face reddening. 'It's like saying, "Would you like to vote for me smacking you in the face or poking you in the eye?" Yes, it's democratic, because I get to vote on it, but I don't like any of the options, so it is irrational for me to vote for either.'

Zeitgeist, literally translated, means 'time ghost', or 'spirit of the age', the foundational paradigm of a given society. TZM advocates moving from our current model – a monetary-based economy – to a resource-based economy (RBE), in which the resources are controlled by society as a whole, rather than governments. Hmm. Sounds like communism, I hear you say. Well, yes and no. TZM would argue that while the idealised end state of utopian communism and an RBE are very similar, a key difference is a focus on utilising technology and science (for example, through automation, using technologies like FarmBot, aquaponics and permaculture) to increase the quality of living for all, removing the monotonous physical labour that characterises the dystopic communist states of China and North Korea.

'It's all this bloody "everyone is entitled to their own opinion" bullshit,' Ross says, now the colour of a London bus. 'No, they're fucking not! The doctor doesn't need your opinion on how to treat your child. The engineer doesn't need your opinion on how to build a bridge. That is why we have experts. Science is not subjective.'

A hand goes into the air. 'Why don't we turn this into a bit of a business? We can all put money in and fundraise. Then we can really go somewhere, sell out arenas, make sure everybody knows about the movement?'

'Hmmm' – Ross screws up his face – 'we have talked about this a lot, and I think the consensus is that it feels a bit hypocritical. Everything money touches turns to shit.'

Like Findhorn, although the techno-utopian world of TZM feels a million miles away from that gentle, otherworldly place, the movement seems to be in a bit of a catch-22 when it comes to money. After the meeting, I pick this issue up with Alex, a restaurant manager and long-term member of the London TZM community.

'We have this problem with money,' he explains. 'We need it, but we don't trust each other. As a movement, we tend to attract fringe members of society, which is OK, but these people inevitably have no real power. It's nice to think that revolution can happen from the bottom up, but, in reality, it never works like that. We need to attract people with power in this system if we are going to make a difference. We can't just ask people nicely to change. People will read our leaflets and they might think it's a good idea, but then they have bills to pay and kids to feed, so they forget.'

Alex was right. During each of the TZM talks, meetings and film screenings I attend, I can't help but notice a lot of supporters of the movement are towards the bottom end of the financial system.

Take Adam, for example. In his thirties, with an orange beard and long dreadlocks, Adam spends much of his free time holding up a 'free hugs' sign and shouting through a megaphone at pedestrians in the shopping district of Maidstone. I agree to accompany him to a performance he is due to give in Brighton, shortly after Z Day. We meet in the pouring rain under the awning of Boots the chemist and huddle under my umbrella for the walk to the venue.

'That's the good thing about you women,' he says. 'You always remember stuff like umbrellas.'

Arriving just in time for the soundcheck, we are greeted by a chap wearing a floppy flower hat with a beard flowing down into his lap, a woman with a shaved head, a man dressed as a pirate with a corset, and two Staffie dogs running laps of the performance space. I sit on one of the wooden chairs positioned in front of the stage while Adam prepares for his performance and the audience settle on to various wooden chairs and scattered floor cushions. After twenty minutes arranging an on-set chair and table, taping his megaphone to a microphone stand and obsessing about the camera angles, the audience is in place and Adam is asked to begin.

But he has disappeared.

'Is he ready?' a bald-headed man with a camera asks me five minutes later.

'I don't know,' I say, leaning my head around the stage flats to look for him. Adam is standing in the wings wearing a straitjacket.

'Are you ready?'

'Yes, should I start?' He looks confused.

'Should he start?' I turn back to the man.

'Of course he should,' he says. 'I don't know what he's waiting for... erm... action?'

Adam fumbles out in his straitjacket, looking panicked, and begins his skit by talking to an onstage camera about how he is being chased by agents of 'the system', but has managed to hide from them by having himself sectioned.

'This might be the last thing you ever hear from me,' he says dramatically, before exiting stage right.

So far, so good.

He returns moments later, sans straitjacket, and wanders over to the megaphone to begin the next stage of his performance – a rally speech.

'How can you bring kids into a world like this?' he asks the audience. 'It's so selfish. The system is based on infinite resources. And do we have infinite resources?'

'Yeah, the sun!' someone shouts out from the audience.

Adam looks annoyed. 'This is a performance!' he says. 'It's not an interactive presentation. You're being like someone who goes and shouts at the actors while they're filming *Coronation Street*.'

'Free Deirdre Rachid,' someone else shouts from the audience.

Adam puts his serious face on. 'OK,' he says, 'back into character now. No more interruptions.'

A member of the audience lights up a spliff.

'We go on consuming our host planet, taking all of its resources and suffocating it... and what else behaves like that?' He leaves a silence. 'CANCER.' The word cuts through the hall like a knife as Adam is given a signal by the cameraman to wind up his performance.

He continues talking for the next few minutes with admirable passion about how screwed up our system is, before leaving the stage to a ripple of applause.

As I juggle with my conflicting emotions of respect for his tenacity and offence that he thinks I am an awful person for wanting to have kids, Adam suddenly realises he has to run for his bus, 'So we won't have time for that drink.' The bus, he tells me, takes three hours to make a one-hour train journey, but he can't afford the train. He explained during an earlier interview with me that he works two hours a day moving horse muck from one place to another and spends his spare time making podcasts. He lives in a boarded-off part of his mum and dad's living room; they call it the 'rabbit hutch.'

I know I am painting a bit of a depressing picture of Adam, but I should probably note here that I didn't find him a depressing person at all. I think the 'you women' comment about remembering the umbrella was probably a misjudged compliment, and he was largely very kind to me and welcoming of my foray into his world. Earlier this year I had watched him give a speech at the Pagan Pride festival and spent a few hours with him at a Nottingham pub afterwards, where we discussed far-ranging philosophical questions over a beer. I am genuinely inspired by the dedication he has to his activism and admire his level of certainty and commitment to what he genuinely believes would create a better world, whether this certainty is misplaced or not. I suppose all I am trying to convey in describing his living situation is that it's not difficult to wonder why Adam might want to change the status quo.

It made convenient sense to me that most people I had met in this community had done badly out of the system and were unhappy with their lot, so I am glad to be proved wrong when I meet Barney Fleming (not his real name) on a summer's evening in Blackheath. I was introduced to Barney after offering to write an article about the TZM London chapter meeting for them to publish on their website, as a way of trying to build rapport with the group. They weren't interested in my article, but Barney did agree to meet with me on the proviso that I change his name and share his story as one of the early and integral members of the UK TZM community. We meet at an organic food shop promising 'healthy, delicious smoothies', and for some reason I decide to pretend I'm really trendy by ordering the 'Green Cleanser'. Don't ever be fooled into doing this. It was a mistake of gargantuan proportion. I think it was mainly algae. Nevertheless, I gulp it down with masked horror as Barney tells me his story on the benches outside.

'My wife and I do great out of the system,' he begins, his face and general downbeat demeanour reminding me of Badger from *The Wind in the Willows*. 'We own our house in London outright, and we have no debt whatsoever. But you can't be truly happy, not when you see what is going on around you. Ultimately, the question is where are we going on this planet? How are we gonna manage it properly? It all begins when we realise we are going to have to work together as a species.'

He takes a sip of his health drink, leaving me with my thoughts for a moment. Is it true that no one can be happy so long as there is suffering in the world? The thought makes me feel suddenly guilty, and lacking.

I tune back in to Barney. 'When you break it down to people, it's amazing how much they say, "Ah, but they are different from us." So, I say, let's find the common ground and work up. We all eat, drink, go to the toilet, need shelter. That's the important stuff. Everything else is just made up by humans.'

I lean back and forward in a full body nod, remembering how intimidated I was by the High King of Albion, and my realisation that the real world is just as made up by humans as my weekend of LARPing in Teutonia.

'I don't wanna hear about the countries, the nations... It's all gang culture gone mad. The Jews and the Muslims are no different than the Crips and the Bloods in LA. Everybody is just fighting for self-preservation. Kids don't care about culture, about race, about "pride of a nation" – they just want to be warm, fed and loved. All of that other stuff is just conditioning.'

Although I can see the logic of what Barney is saying – of course kids want to be warm, fed and loved – the thought that going to the toilet and eating food is the major thing that binds us as a species is utterly depressing. I think about the romance of the battle re-enactment, the pagan rituals at Stonehenge, the joy at being part of such an ancient tradition.

'But surely we lose something when we do away with tradition?' I protest. 'What about our culture? I mean...' – I raise my eyebrows and gesticulate wildly – 'where does that leave Morris dancing?'

He laughs, and I can't help but join him, surprising myself with my own suddenly expressed passion for Morris dancing.

'Well,' he says, 'to me that's just theatre. It's acting out a romanticised idea of the past. We forget that things were fucking hard back then. I used to sit and talk to my grandma as a kid, and she would say, "Never let anyone tell you about how great the past was. It was really, really hard, especially for working people." She would have loved a washing machine, but instead she had an ice-cold tub and a stone. For me, all tradition is theatre – it's harmless, but we need to accept it for what it is. When it comes to making the important decisions about how we should organise ourselves as human beings, in the real world, we have to base them on the here and now; on science, not tradition.'

I like the idea of one nation, of humanity coming together as one enormous tribe. It's a beautiful image. But is this realistic? How can everybody in the world be part of my tribe when I haven't even met them all? How can I connect with them and build relationships with them? And if I can't, then how else will I fulfil my human desire to build community, and to surround myself with a warm and supportive group of people I love and trust? How will my tribe build its identity if there aren't any other tribes? How can there be like-mindedness if there is no one who has a different perspective, no one who has a different personal taste? The questions flash before me like a stock-market ticker.

'Don't speak to me about nationalism,' Barney goes on, impassioned by his train of thought. 'We were originally immigrants from Ireland, yet my mum still says things like, "It's these bleedin' Eastern Europeans," and I'm like, "Mum, *we're* immigrants!" And she's like, "Well, it was different then." No, it wasn't! How do you have the right to tell anyone else on this planet where they can and cannot live? You are becoming the very people who spat on you when you opened your mouth back in the seventies, because we were the "terrorists" then. People forget these things so quickly.'

Both energised by where our conversation is headed, we decide that it's time to progress onto the hard stuff and wander through Blackheath village towards the common in search of a pub. As we walk and make small talk, I explain my thoughts on the movement so far. Summarised as follows.

I agree that the negative effect our current 'system' of consumption is having on our planet, and on our fellow human beings, is unsustainable, and that here we should take a lesson from the pagans and recognise that we are symbiotically related to this planet. I also agree that we need to do more to address the horrendous gap between this planet's haves and have-nots; that some starve while others pay to have their stomachs stapled is simply absurd. But I'm not sure that addressing either of these requires a *complete* overhaul of our system. For example, although their business models may need some work, the popularity of businesses like Getaround, Freecycle and Airbnb suggest that the public sentiment supports a movement that makes better use of what we have, as opposed to the constant loop of making, consuming and discarding that keeps the economy chugging along to the detriment of our planet. A drive for sustainability has also firmly implanted itself into our national conscience, as we begin to hold our fashion industry and the companies that produce our energy and food to an increasingly higher standard when it comes to environmental issues. So perhaps the evolution has already started, and perhaps evolution is better than revolution.

We find our quarry, order two pints, and carry them out onto the grass to continue our discussion.

'The deaths of Morrison and Hendrix weren't accidents,' Barney says. I have no memory of how we got onto this subject, as my Dictaphone was switched off during the wander. 'They wanted control, so they arranged the deaths.'

'Who's they?' I ask.

'Oh, the CIA, the government, the people who run the show.'

I am frustrated that we have ended up back here after such an interesting conversation. 'But they are just human beings like you and me,' I say, exasperated.

'No, but they're not. They work for a system with sociopathic tendencies. I'm not paranoid. It happens. Now "conspiracy theory" is a dismissive term for those who question the official line. But we have to! I mean, look at what's come out about the paedophile rings and the Catholic Church. Things get covered up all the time. You can't just blindly accept and obey.'

'But how do you know Hendrix and Morrison were assassinated by "them"? I don't understand where you get your information from.'

'It's all on files in—'

'But have you seen these files?'

'Me personally? I've seen copies of them, yeah. But there are interviews with people who work for the FBI, the CIA. All legit, traceable guys, telling us that these were set-ups.'

'But they could be lying to you, and manipulating you just as much as you presume the government are.'

'They could well be, and then you have to follow the story. Where does it fit? Who benefited? Follow the money, all the time. That's the secret of this system: if you follow the money, you'll get the answer.'

I wonder if Barney sees himself as a Morpheus character, trying to explain to me that we are all in *The Matrix*. But who is Agent Smith? Who is 'the system'? I can't help but think that some people just need to invent an enemy, an outside actor to blame it all on, because that would be much easier, wouldn't it, to abstract a villain, a 'cabal' to pin it all on rather than wrestle with the complexities and nuance of the way the real world operates. Money has become the new dirty word, but I don't buy into the idea that human beings are all entirely good until corrupted by the evil, malevolent system of capitalism.

'OK, we've talked about tribalism,' I say, trying to stifle my frustration, 'and how we need to move on from this. But a lot of the people I've met from TZM still use this concept of "them" as being separate; of "the system" as if it is this external malevolent force.'

Barney looks at me and shrugs. 'Well, a lot of people have gone crackers through this. People on the edge emotionally. They are looking for something, and they think they've found it, the answer to everything. But it's not. You have to draw back from that and realise that it's just a way of thinking about something.'

Ouch. That feels like a real betrayal of those who follow this movement as a prospective saviour of all humankind, the people who devote their lives to it, dismissing them as being 'crackers' and 'on the edge emotionally'. Is Barney just saying that TZM is effectively a thought experiment that challenges our assumptions? It is easier to buy into this way of looking at it, I suppose, far easier than to believe that, as the *Zeitgeist* movies suggest, the US will eventually merge with Canada and Mexico (the currency will be the 'Amero') and later with all of Europe, Africa and Asia, microchipping citizens along the way to suppress dissent against this new One World Government. Can you really unravel the mission of TZM from the conspiracy theories that underpin its very creation as a movement? I don't think so.

I decide it's time to wrap up the interview and sit with my thoughts on the train ride home. Human beings have preference, personality, and yes, maybe this is merely the result of social conditioning, but does anyone want to live in a world of biological drones with no culture, no differentiators? For me, this is what makes life so rich, so dynamic, so interesting. It would feel like an act of betrayal for me to trivialise all I've experienced this year as theatre. There is more heart to it than that. If I were to have written this book backwards, I might have had a different experience with TZM – I may have been drawn into it more, been less cynical – but the reignited occultist/hippie/geek in me can't help but rail against it.

God, I've changed. Someone bring me my bespoke suit. Quickly.

Afterword

... instead of watching the telly

After six flights, eleven B & Bs, six hotels, 8,500 road miles, 200 pints (probably more), seven letters to royal family members, thirteen carefully crafted costumes, one quadruple vodka shot, twenty-nine nights under canvas, at least a hundred hours of YouTube 'research', nine newly acquired membership cards, twenty-four polished apples, three naked photos in the BN magazine, 1,079 speculative emails, and countless pleading Facebook statuses 'Does anyone have any contacts in the ___ world?', I now have twenty-six ceremonious ticks on my whiteboard, been twenty-six different versions of myself, and spent a year in the life of twenty-six different subcultures. I have let my FOMO run amok, which has been exhausting, but so worth it, and the journey is finally over.

It has been an absolute privilege to spend a year among this charming island's most fascinating people. The collectors, the escapers, the nostalgics, the spiritualists, the geeks; they have welcomed me, a complete stranger, into their worlds and educated me, looked after me, even converted me.

As well as the thrill of finding myself in some utterly bizarre situations – from the latex lubing session at the vampire fetish night to my naked rendition of 'Ernie (The Fastest Milkman in the West)' – writing this book has taught me about the importance of community in an increasingly isolating society, about the unquenchable human thirst for a sense of belonging, and about the misguided trust we put in our own world view. It has offered me a whole new perspective on the world, the kind you only really find in the downward-facing dog of a naked yoga class.

I learned that human beings are excellent at finding increasingly inventive ways to socialise. For many battle re-enactors, naturists, goths, Morris dancers and SF fans, the social side of the community is far more important than their respective activities (trainspotting was the only real exception to this). You might join a choir because you like to sing, join a Morris side because you like to dance, or join a naturist society because you like to get your boobs out, but what keeps you there? The knowledge that someone has your back; that they will look out for you; that you are part of something. The fuzzy stuff.

'It is safe here, everybody looks out for the kids and you don't have to lock your things away.' I lost track of the number of times I have heard people say that over the last year. It's as if subcultures are recreating the concept of village life – your door is never locked and the kids can play safely after dark – where we know our neighbours not only well enough to borrow a cup of sugar from them, but to socialise with, to build community with, to share the upbringing of our children with. I don't have a clue who my neighbours are in London, and I have lived in the same area for the last five years. So perhaps it's obvious why, in an increasingly urbanised society, we seek community in other guises – in re-enactment regiments, by how we dress, or what we choose to collect.

But then there was the interesting question posed by the TZM community: is it dangerous to be tribal? Does it simply serve to instigate and maintain separation – the 'us' versus 'them', the birth of 'other' – leading to prejudice, discrimination, and in the worst cases, war? I think our human tendency to be solipsistic about our tribe, to harbour a sense of superiority that what we do is best, right and true, is the root cause of fanaticism. You can find fanatical pagans and cereologists, just as you can find fanatical atheists and hoaxers, but when you become obsessive about your tribe – when you become rigid and consumed by the idea of being 'right' – you flip the concept of community on its head.

My experiences this year have forced me to conclude that the desire to build a tribe is too deeply ingrained in humanity to reject it in favour of one homogenous 'tribe of man'. I think the answer to this question, of whether or not it is dangerous to be tribal, depends on our capacity to be open, flexible and curious regarding what is outside of our communities. What I do know is that there is more that makes us similar than different, more that connects us than separates us, despite our all too often obsessive focus on the latter.

A good indication for me as to the openness of a community was the degree of censorship I needed to apply during my conversations with them. Some people, perhaps unsurprisingly, did not like the fact that they were sharing these pages with circus performers, naturists and vampires. But when my LARPing adventure was over, and I told my Lions of Albion family I was off to immerse myself in a week of UFOlogy, they all laughed and said, 'Eeewww weirdos!' They were joking, of course. In fact, they were probably the least judgemental group I could have hoped to meet. Perhaps because they know that what they do is also seen as 'weird' by outsiders, or perhaps because they simply know the truth: that we are all a bit odd really.

It's all connected, you see. All of it. A tapestry of humanity made from different threads that weave and dance around each other. The Kabbalists are connected to the vampires via their appeal to energy manipulation, the extreme sports fanatics to the yogis via the concept of transformative practice and the drag queens to the LARPers via their celebration of the mask. And so on, ad infinitum.

Anyway, enough of my ramblings, let's address the important question: did I succeed in my quest? Have I cured my FOMO? Decided which version of myself I want to be, which world I want to live in, and committed to living in it?

Absolutely not.

In fact, I think it's got worse. I enjoyed my year in the life so much that I think I'm addicted. I remained a member of Dacre Morris for months longer than I needed to, returned to TitanCon the following year, will definitely go LARPing again, plan to do another course at Findhorn, camp at the yoga eco farm again, go to Pagan Pride, attend another London Vampire Social and probably do another battle re-enactment. Heck, I might even venture onto a nudist beach one day (after a few glasses of wine, obviously). But you know what? I don't care. I love all of it. And I think my biggest achievement this year is coming to the realisation that this is just who I am; that I will never settle; never be content living in just one world; never commit to being a predefined version of myself. I just can't wrestle myself into that box. And why should anyone have to?

I am a black swan, a private, a warrior priestess, a 'have-a-go' Rawdon, a mundane, a 'red welly bagger' and a textile. I am whatever I wake up as in the morning, and not always the same person who goes to bed that night. But so long as I get to live all of these bizarre and bonkers versions of myself, and embrace the variety of the human experience, that's just fine with me.

Acknowledgements

A profound thank you to all those contained within the pages of this story. Special mentions to Auriol Mackeson-Sandbach and all at Bryngwyn Hall, Chris Burfitt, Vic James and the Rawdons Regiment, the Flying Aces, Sue Appleby, the Squirrels, Lee Armstrong, Zarah Leoni, Charles Everett, Alan Dawson, Rob Woodall and the RHoB crew, the Findhorn Foundation, Terry and the wonderful and, very sadly, late Jane Williams, Svetlana, Gill Jones, Jimmy McPaul, Mark Chevallier, Dave Munro and the Knights of the North, all at Dacre Morris, Andrew Welch and Clive Edwards, Kim, Shaft, King Arthur and Damh the Bard, Jason Sutton and Dave Sparkle, Barry O'Sullivan, TitanCon ('HODOR'), Peter Mugridge and Simon, Sten Bus, Dan Edwardes and Adam Zeitgeist. Thank you for welcoming me into your worlds without hesitation or judgement.

Thank you to my patient, fun and insanely knowledgeable editor Rachael Kerr and to all at Unbound for making my dream a reality.

The biggest thanks of all must also go to my wonderful friends for their unwavering companionship, support and guidance, especially Gary Landes, Lynsey Eames, Tori Bischoff, Rosi Croom, Rob and Jo Whiddett, Clive Woodward, Hatdog Appleby, Sian Hawkins, Moira Quinn, Zoe Stanley, Kasia Muszynska and Tom Smith. And to my loving and supportive family, Mathieu, Fox and Archer Leonelli, Amy, Dan, Jasper, Harvey and Fern Allison, and Caroline and Bob Feltham. Sorry for being such a weirdo. I love you guys.

A Note on the Author

Featured in *Stylist* magazine's '25 Most Ambitious, Strong and Adventurous Women under 30', Lucy Leonelli is a self-proclaimed social tourist with an unquenchable thirst for exploring, experiencing and understanding the world's most colourful subcultures and communities. Born in Bristol, she now runs executive recruitment for a technology firm in Silicon Valley and lives in Berkeley, California, with her husband Mathieu, their sons Fox and Archer and T-Rex the corgi.

Unbound is the world's first crowdfunding publisher, established in 2011.

We believe that wonderful things can happen when you clear a path for people who share a passion. That's why we've built a platform that brings together readers and authors to crowdfund books they believe in – and give fresh ideas that don't fit the traditional mould the chance they deserve.

This book is in your hands because readers made it possible. Everyone who pledged their support is listed below. Join them by visiting unbound.com and supporting a book today.

Anna Adams
Ines Alexander
Shelby Alexander
Sally Alexanders
Julia Allen
Rachel Allen
Amy Allison
Jeremie Alquier
Michael Alvarez
Stacey Archbell
Bastien Asencio
Katy Atchison
Lady Auriol Marchioness
    of Linlithgow
Kevin Aylward
Janine Baker
Jennifer Baker
Kurt Bannister

Krystal Barghelame
Adam Barnett
Lorna Barnett
Nick Barnett
Laila Barratt
Priyanka Basnyat
Claire Beaumont-Wraith
Pippa Bell
Bill Benoist
Paula Bewley
Victoria Bischoff
Jeroen Blaas
Crimson Black
Chris Booton
Liz Boston
Dan Bradley
Gemma Bradshaw
Martin Branham

Adrian Bray
Lisa Brice
Brian Browne
Jonathan Bryant
Brett Burris
Yohan Busidan
Sten Buss
Oliver Cameron
Justin Campbell
Peter Carlisle
Edd Cavanna
Mark Chevallier
Samantha Chidley
April Ciaccio
Jackie Clews
Charles Cockerton
Jaycee Cole
Zarina Contractor
Robert Cox
John Crawford
Chris Crocker
Rosi Croom
Julia Croyden
Andrew Curry
CVG Solutions
Stephanie Da Silva
Laura Dale
Jack Danger
Alice Davis
Alan Dawson
Bill DeLacy
Dan Dermy
Yoann Desgrange
Liz Dexter
Louise Dixon
Daniel Doulton

Kelly Ducourty
Jane Dunster
Lynsey Eames
Clive Edwards
Chris Ellis
Jez Ellis-Gray
Erin English
Audrey Espey
Harry Evans
Charles Everett
French Face
Caroline Feltham
Robert Feltham
Derek Fidler
Belinda Finch
Katharina Fischer
Robert Fisher
J+K Flank
Lizzie Fox
Liz Francis
Jim Gaudette
Jessica Geach
Sharon Gibson
David Gilchrist
Hazel Gill
Sue Gill
Casey Goldman
Justine Gomes
Adshead Gordon
Edward Grenville
Peter Gumbrecht
Gary Guo
Richard Halton
Rob Hardy
Jinny Harman
Maria Harrington

Neil Hart
Sian Hawkins
Iain Haywood
Jo Healey
Joseph Heber-Suffrin
Jennifer Heller
Lucy Henzell-Thomas
David Heron
Graham Heydon
Kathryn Hill
Loren Hiser
Trevor J Hitch
Kate Hockenhull
Mike Hong
Andrew Howarth
Sarah Howarth
Bryn Hughes
Charlotte Hughes
Emma Hulmes
Nick Hungerford
Claire Hurrell
Leanne Hutchison
Tracy Isacke
Stephanie Jackson
Mr Jakobek
Heidi James
Victor James
Natasha Jarvis
Tony Jenkins
Gill Jones
Kaiser Foundation
    Rehabilitation Center
Alexander Karberg Smith
Andy Keen
Stuart Keirle
Neil Kelley

Helen Kempster
Emily Kennedy
Karen Kent-Webster
Edward Kevis
Michael Khor
Dan Kieran
Caitlin Kight
Antonia Kimbell
Ami Komoda
Katie Kostiuk
Mike Krosin
Gary Landes
Mike & Janet Landes
Felicity Lane
Angela Lanier
Ben Latreuille
Patrick Lau
Padraig Laverty
Antoine Leonelli
Dash Leonelli
Dimitri Leonelli
Fox Leonelli
Mathieu Leonelli
Pierre Leonelli
T-Rex Leonelli
Yann Leonelli
Kon Leong
Sylvie Leroy
Stephen Livingston
Simon Lowes
Layla M
Stephen MacKinnon
Ashish Mahadwar
Emily Malin
Charlotte Malliff
Maya Mancuso

Rebecca Mangan
Neal Mann
Leo Marchand
Lindsey Margen
Freya Marie Lawton
Piers Marmion
William Marnoch
Vicks Marshall
Max Maufe
Emilie Mazzacurati
Niki McCann
Daniel McFawn
Tom McGibbon
Kerry McGovern
Sean McKenna
Jimmy McPaul
Nicole McWilliams
Simon McWilliams
Emma Mee
Bridget Mitchell
John Mitchinson
Jeremy Mobbs
Lee Moore
Aaron Moss
Peter Mugridge
Alexandra Muller
Dave Munro
Meghana Muppidi
Kasia Muszynska
Carlo Navato
David Neill
Majeed Neky
Hannah Nicholson
Hazel Nicholson
Niels Aagaard Nielsen
Tim O'Connell

Troy OBrien
Harriet Parsons
Lauren Parsons
Thomas Paterson
Nudie Paul
Lisa Peacock-Edwards
Roko Pedisic
Mackenzie Pedroza
Jayne Pellatt
Karen F. Pierce
Graham Pile
Mark Pinto
Holly Pither
Peter Pluim
Justin Pollard
Jeff Polsky
Hedley Potts
Lawrence Pretty
Bill Pritchard
Moira Quinn
Neil Raja
Richard Ramos
Loïc Raynal
Kevin Rayner
Alice Reetham
Mark Richardson
Martin Richardson
Martin Risau
Michael Ritchie
George Rivera
Emily-Jane Robinson
Anna Rogers
Emily Rowley
Lloyd Russell
Leia Sabir
Meurig Sage

Naomi Said
Karin Sakwanda
Nicola Salha
Rick Salter
Duncan Sandes
Kevin Seidel
Hahns Shin
Chris Simmonds
Belis Sly
Jonathan Sly
Mike "Cuz" Sly
Simon Smiler
Karen Smith
Thomas Smith
Eric Spengler
Margaret Squires
Wendy Staden
Jenny Staples
Emily Starling
David Stelling
Dawn Stephens
Graham Stephens
Shelli Strand
Selina Sun
Gerry Taylor
Lynne & Matt Taylor
Richard Taylor
Sarah Taylor
Christopher Tholstrup
Wenley Tong
Isla, Jago and Marley Torn
Doug Tracy
Beverley van der Sluis
Alessandro Vigilante
Eliza W
Ivan Wainewright

Pippa Walker
Sam Wallace
Sam Walters
Stephen Wares
Sarah Webster
Mark Weisbaum
Benoit Wells
Alison Wenz
Zak West
Josephine Whiddett
Judy Whiddett
Rob Whiddett
Michael White
Julie Wicklund
Steve Wilks
Helen Williams
Karen Williams
Terry & Jane Williams
Kerry Wiltshire
Megan Wood
Kate Woodward
Jade Wright
Yaroslav Writtle
Anna Yay
David Zolet